Oxford & Asquith

MEMORIES
AND REFLECTIONS
1852 ~ 1927

BY

THE EARL OF OXFORD
AND ASQUITH, K. G.

VOLUME TWO

LITTLE, BROWN, AND COMPANY

BOSTON 1928

CONTENTS

ILLUSTRATIONS

MEMORIES AND REFLECTIONS
1852 – 1927

CHAPTER I

THE SHADOW OF WAR

THERE is no more debatable problem in the minor ethics of Literature than the relations between what is called the professional or political diarist and the world of his actual or potential readers. The question is constantly coming to the front, not only in such familiar and leading cases as those of the " Greville Memoirs," and it raises issues which are by no means easy to determine. We may, I think, take it for granted that such a record as was diligently kept for years by Charles Greville was not intended by the writer to die with its author, whatever may have been the manner or vehicle by which he ultimately contemplated that it would be disclosed. Greville was a literary artist with a keen eye, a facile pen, the instincts and foibles of a gossip, and with unusual and in some ways unique opportunities for obtaining first-hand knowledge of contemporary persons and events.

There seems to me to be no occasion why, after a decent interval, such a journal should not, with all possible verification of details, be published with the same freedom and fullness as the correspondence of the dead. There is no more ground for a permanent embargo of secrecy in the one case than in the other.

Heavy obligations, dictated by good taste and good feeling, are, of course, imposed upon those in whose discretion it lies how much to publish and whether to publish at all, but these are the sort of risks that every man who leaves any interesting writing behind him, and is free to choose an executor, must be ready to face. He can escape them by the simple process of destruction.

I have not myself, except for a brief period, kept what is technically called a " Diary ", but I have been in the habit of jotting down irregularly my impressions of noteworthy persons and incidents while they were still fresh in my memory. I believe this to be an innocent and even a useful practice, for though I have on the whole a serviceable working memory, experience has shown me that no faculty is more subject to lapses, particularly when it is a question of preserving the *ipsissima verba* of a conversation. For the period I now approach I have drawn freely upon such of these contemporary notes as were accessible, and also upon letters to a few intimate friends, which they have been good enough to place at my disposal.

Immediately before the War, the question of the Amendment Bill in connection with the Home Rule Bill, which had passed the House of Commons in three successive sessions, went through a number of phases. The Amending Bill, introduced by the Government on June 23, 1914, embodied the proposal that any Ulster county should be entitled to vote itself out of Home Rule for six years. The Lords transformed it into a shape which the Nationalists and the majority of the House of Commons could not accept, by definitely excluding the whole of Ulster. Before and after that proceeding, efforts were made to attain an agreement. There were comings and goings of negotiators, and long discussions of Ministers.

Without prejudice to the decision of other matters, such as the time limit, which, from Sir Edward Carson's point of view, was at the moment the real difficulty, conversation turned on the geographical delimitation of the area that might be excluded temporarily or permanently. There was debatable territory, particularly in the two counties of Fermanagh and Tyrone, where the racial and religious intermixture presented exceptionally intricate difficulties. I had talks with the protagonists on both sides. Each of them had his difficulties. I had hoped to the last that an agreement might be reached, but the question of Tyrone, on which neither side would give way, was an intractable problem. The following are extracts from contemporary notes.

June 24. Lord Rothermere and Lord Murray of Elibank are to open negotiations with Sir E. Carson and Mr. Bonar Law. *June 25.* I see no harm in them going ahead. *June 27.* Law will support any reasonable settlement with Carson. *June 29.* Redmond says he must have Tyrone and Fermanagh.

July 1. Lansdowne's speech last night gives us the impression that he is in an expectant attitude. At any rate there is nothing truculent in it.

July 4. Ll. G. came to see me: he had made little or no progress with Redmond for the moment. Montagu suggests that I should have a talk with B. Law with the object of each of us putting pressure on the Irish in regard to Tyrone.

July 6. On reflection I thought it better not to open out to-day to Law on Ireland. I felt that we might both have been tempted to say things which we should

afterwards wish unsaid. But I may very likely have
a secret talk with Carson.

July 8. I had an interesting talk yesterday with
Carson. It showed how little progress the negotiations
had made. Carson is quite anxious to settle, but makes
much—honestly, I am sure—of his difficulties with
his own friends. We had a long and rather dreary
Cabinet this morning trying to solve the old problem
of how to get a quart into a pint pot.

July 9. I had a long call from Stamfordham, who
wanted to report to the King about Ulster prospects,
etc. I pointed out to him that the Lords by omitting
the plebiscite, etc., and cutting up Ireland as if it was
a butcher's joint to suit their own palate, were not help-
ing towards peace.

July 13. I have had two interviews. The first with
Lord Northcliffe at "The Master's"[1] flat. He has
been "doing Ulster" and is much struck with the
Covenanters, whom he regards as a formidable, though
most unattractive crew. I talked over the question of
areas, etc., with him and tried to impress on him the
importance of making *The Times* a responsible newspaper. After I got back to the House I had half an
hour with Redmond and Dillon, also mainly about
areas. I found them in a decidedly impracticable
mood, and I foresee great difficulties in the coming
week which will practically decide whether we can
come to an agreement.

July 15. I had a short talk with B. Law. I pointed
out to him that a failure to settle would mean a general
election with a very difficult situation at the end of it

[1] Lord Murray of Elibank.

for whoever was victorious. An arrangement between the Irish parties is possible and practicable in the case of Fermanagh, but neither party is prepared to give way, in the sense of partition, on Tyrone.

July 16. It has been decided that I should advise the King to intervene with the object of securing a pacific accommodation, through a Conference of the representatives of all parties concerned — both British and Irish.

July 17. I found the King in a tent in the garden. He was full of interest about the Conference,[1] and he made the really good suggestion that the Speaker should preside. It was arranged that I should write a memorandum stating the reasons why I advised a Conference, and that he would send a most cordial reply amounting to an invitation.

July 18. (H.M. Yacht *Victoria and Albert.*) Stamfordham came to see me, just before I started, to settle the form of "invitation" which will go out to-morrow for the earliest possible date.

July 24. The Conference (which held four meetings at Buckingham Palace) has broken down,[2] and I announced to the House the terms of the Speaker's report. Nothing could have been more amicable in tone or more desperately fruitless in result. Later we had a

---

[1] The Buckingham Palace Conference.

[2] Lord Ullswater in "A Speaker's Commentaries" describes the difficulty of separating the Protestant and Roman Catholic populations, particularly in Tyrone and Fermanagh, and says: "When we found that we were not in sight of achieving any result, Mr. Asquith turned to me and asked if I had any solution to offer. I made a suggestion that the two counties should be included either in the North or the South, and should, after an interval of say three or five years, be called upon by a plebiscite to decide whether they wished to remain where they were or to be transferred. . . . My proposal was not approved by either party and the Conference broke down."

meeting at Downing Street — Redmond, Dillon, Ll.G., Birrell and I. I told them that I must go on with the Amending Bill, without the time limit: to which, after a good deal of demur, the Irishmen reluctantly agreed.

At 3.15 we had a Cabinet, where there was a lot of talk about Ulster, but the real interest was Grey's statement of the European situation, which is about as bad as it can possibly be. Austria has sent a bullying and humiliating ultimatum to Servia, who cannot possibly comply with it, and demands an answer in 48 hours — failing which she will march. This means almost inevitably that Russia will come on the scene in defence of Servia, and if so it is difficult both for Germany and France to refrain from lending a hand. So that we are within measurable distance of a real Armageddon.

July 26. No one can say what is going to happen in the east of Europe. The news this morning is that Servia has capitulated on the main point, but it is very doubtful if any reservation will be accepted by Austria, who is resolved upon a complete and final humiliation. The curious thing is that on many, if not most, of the points Austria has a good and Servia a very bad case, but the Austrians are quite the stupidest people in Europe. There is a brutality about their mode of procedure which will make most people think that this is a case of a big Power wantonly bullying a little one. Anyhow, it is the most dangerous situation of the last forty years. It may incidentally have the effect of throwing into the background the lurid pictures of civil war in Ulster.

July 29. The Amending Bill and the whole Irish business are, of course, put into the shade by the coming war, for it now seems as if nothing but a miracle could avert it. After dinner I went across to E. Grey and sat with him and Haldane till 1 A.M., talking over the situation and trying to discover bridges and outlets. It is one of the ironies of the case that we, being the only Power who has made so much as a constructive suggestion in the direction of peace, are blamed by both Russia and Germany for causing the outbreak of war.

July 30. We had another turn of the kaleidoscope to-day. I was sitting in the Cabinet room with a map of Ulster and a lot of statistics about populations and religions, endeavouring to get into something like shape my speech on the Amending Bill, when a telephone message came from Bonar Law to ask me to go and see him and Carson at his Kensington abode. He had sent his motor, which I boarded, and in due time arrived at my destination. I found the two gentlemen there, and Bonar Law proceeded to propose in the interests of the international situation that we should postpone for the time being the second reading of the Amending Bill. He thought that to advertise our domestic dissensions at this moment would weaken our influence in the world for peace. Carson said that at first he had thought it impossible to agree, as it would strain still further the well-known and much tried patience of his Ulstermen, but he had come to see that it was now a patriotic duty. I, of course, welcomed their attitude, but said I would consult my colleagues before giving a definite answer. When I got back I saw Lloyd George and Grey and we agreed that it was right to close with the offer. Redmond, whom I saw afterwards, thought it an excellent chance of putting off the Amending Bill. The City, which is in a terrible state of depression and paralysis, is for the time being all against English intervention. The prospect is very black.

July 31. We had a Cabinet at eleven and a very interesting discussion, especially about the neutrality of Belgium and the point upon which everything will ultimately turn — are we to go in or stand aside? Of course everybody longs to stand aside, but I need not say that France, through Cambon, is pressing strongly for a reassuring declaration. Edward Grey had an interview with him this afternoon which he told me was rather painful. He had, of course, to tell Cambon, for we are under no obligation, that we could give no pledges and that our actions must depend upon the course of events, including the Belgian question and the direction of public opinion here.

August 1. When most of them had left, Sir W. Tyrrell arrived with a long message from Berlin to the effect that the German Ambassador's efforts for peace had been suddenly arrested and frustrated by the Tsar's decree for a complete Russian mobilization. We all set to work, Tyrrell, Bongie,[1] Drummond and myself, to draft a direct personal appeal from the King to the Tsar. When we had settled it I called a taxi, and, in company with Tyrrell, drove to Buckingham Palace at about 1.30 A.M. The King was hauled out of his bed, and one of my strangest experiences was sitting with him, clad in a dressing-gown, while I read the message and the proposed answer.

There was really no fresh news this morning. Lloyd

---

[1] Sir Maurice Bonham Carter, Lord Oxford's private secretary.

George, all for peace, is more sensible and statesman-like for keeping the position still open. Grey declares that if an out-and-out and uncompromising policy of non-intervention at all costs is adopted he will go. Winston very bellicose and demanding immediate mobilization. The main controversy pivots upon Belgium and its neutrality. We parted in fairly amicable mood and are to sit again at eleven to-morrow, Sunday. I am still not quite hopeless about peace, though far from hopeful, but if it comes to war I feel sure that we shall have a split in the Cabinet. Of course if Grey went I should go and the whole thing would break up. On the other hand, we may have to contemplate, with such equanimity as we can command, the loss of Morley and possibly, though I do not think it, of Simon.

August 2. Things are pretty black. Germany is now in active war with both Russia and France and the Germans have violated the neutrality of Luxembourg. We are waiting to know whether they are going to do the same with Belgium. I had a visit at breakfast from Lichnowsky, who was very *émotionné* and implored me not to side with France. He said that Germany, with her army cut in two between France and Russia, was far more likely to be crushed than France. He was very agitated, poor man, and wept. I told him that we had no desire to intervene, and that it rested largely with Germany to make intervention impossible if she would (1) not invade Belgium and (2) not send her fleet into the Channel to attack the unprotected north coast of France. He was bitter about the policy of his Government in not restraining Austria and seemed quite heart-broken.

Then we had a long Cabinet from 11 till nearly 2, which very soon revealed that we are on the brink of a split. We agreed at last with some difficulty that Grey should be authorized to tell Cambon that our fleet would not allow the German fleet to make the Channel a base of hostile operations. John Burns at once resigned, but was persuaded to hold on at any rate till the evening when we meet again. There is a strong party against any kind of intervention in any event. Grey, of course, will never consent to this and I shall not separate myself from him. Crewe, McKenna and Samuel are a moderating intermediate body. Bonar Law writes that the Opposition will back us up in any measure we may take for the support of France and Russia. I suppose a good number of our own party in the House of Commons are for absolute non-interference. It will be a shocking thing if at such a moment we break up.

Happily I am quite clear in my mind as to what is right and wrong. (1) We have no obligation of any kind either to France or Russia to give them military or naval help. (2) The dispatch of the Expeditionary Force to help France at this moment is out of the question and would serve no object. (3) We must not forget the ties created by our long-standing and intimate friendship with France. (4) It is against British interests that France should be wiped out as a Great Power. (5) We cannot allow Germany to use the Channel as a hostile base. (6) We have obligations to Belgium to prevent it being utilized and absorbed by Germany.

CHAPTER II

AUGUST, 1914: CABINET CHANGES

ON Monday, August 3, it was decided to dispatch a telegram to Germany requesting her to give us an assurance that the neutrality of Belgium would be respected. The whole situation and its antecedents were explained by Sir Edward Grey in his historic speech in the House of Commons on the afternoon of the 3rd. In my Cabinet letter to the King of that day I had to report that four of my colleagues had tendered their resignation, adding an expression of my hope that some of them might be induced to reconsider their position.

Two of them, Lord Beauchamp and Sir John Simon, yielded to my counsels and consented to retain their offices. The other two, Lord Morley and Mr. Burns, did not see their way to alter their resolution.

In a previous book[1] I have published their letters of resignation. I will add here Lord Morley's reply to my final appeal.

PRIVY COUNCIL OFFICE,
WHITEHALL, S.W.
August 4, 1914.

MY DEAR ASQUITH, —

Your letter shakes me terribly. It goes to my very core. In spite of temporary moments of difference, my feelings for you have been cordial, deep, and close, from your earliest public days. The idea of severing these affectionate

[1] "The Genesis of the War," pp. 220-1.

associations has been far the most poignant element in the stress of the last four days. But I cannot conceal from myself that we — I and the leading men of the Cabinet — do not mean the same thing in the foreign policy of the moment. To bind ourselves to France is at the same time to bind ourselves to Russia, and to whatever demands may be made by Russia on France. With this cardinal difference between us, how could I either honourably or usefully sit in a Cabinet day after day discussing military and diplomatic details in carrying forward a policy that I think a mistake? Again I say, divided counsels are a mistake.

I am more distressed in making this reply to your generous and most moving appeal than I have ever been in writing any letter of all my life.

Ever,

M.

To fill up the vacancies, Mr. Runciman was transferred to the Board of Trade, and Lord Beauchamp succeeded Lord Morley as President of the Council. The two new members who were for the first time introduced into the Cabinet were Lord Emmott (Office of Works) and Lord Lucas (Board of Agriculture). Both are now dead, and as they were exceptionally fine representatives of two absolutely diverse types of public men, I will endeavour to give a brief appreciation of each.

LORD EMMOTT

Alfred Emmott came of a stock of Yorkshire Quakers, but as his grandfather and father settled and prospered in Oldham, where he himself was born and bred, Lancashire can claim him as one of her sons. He was educated at a Friends' school, and took a degree at London University, before entering his father's firm of cotton spinners in 1881 at the age of twenty-three. He

August 4. 1914.

My dear Asquith,

Your letter shakes me
terribly It goes to my
very core. In spite of
temporary moments of
difference, my feelings for
you have been constant, deep,
and close, from your earliest
public days The idea of
severing these affectionate
ties & associations, has been far
the most *poignant* element, in the

stress of the last four days.
But I cannot conceal
from myself that we —
I and the leading men of
the cabinet—do not mean
the same thing in the
foreign policy of the moment.
To bind ourselves to France
is at the same time to
bind ourselves to Russia, and
to whatever demands may

be made on by Russia or
France. With this essential
difference between us, how
could I either honorably or
usefully sit in a cabinet
day after day discussing
unlikely and diplomatic
details in carrying forward
a policy that I think a
mistake? Again I say,
divided counsels are a
mistake.

I am more distressed

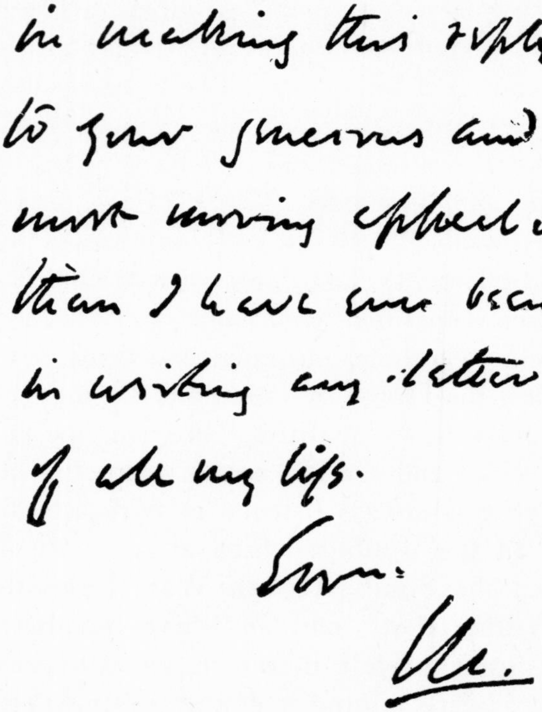
in making this reply
to your generous and
most moving speech
than I have ever been
in writing any letter
of all my life.
Yours
W.

showed from the first a natural aptitude for business, and soon became a conspicuous figure in the cotton trade. He was a good citizen, took an active interest in the government of the town, and was elected Mayor of Oldham in 1891. Like Chamberlain and Fowler he graduated in the school of municipal administration before he attempted to enter the House of Commons. Oldham was a two-membered constituency, and by a rare coincidence both seats became vacant at once in 1899, during the lifetime of Parliament. The by-election which ensued was remarkable for the personnel of the candidates on both sides. The Conservatives, who had been in possession of both the seats, selected as their champions an outsider and debutant, Mr. Winston Churchill, and a veteran Trade Union leader, Mr. Mawdsley, who fought as a " Conservative working man." The Liberal candidates were Mr. Emmott and Mr. Walter Runciman, who came out first and second on the poll. Emmott continued to represent Oldham until he left the House of Commons for the Lords.

He had no showy qualities. His was the genius of common sense, and though not an inspiring or lively speaker, he was always listened to with attention and respect. In the troubles which arose in the Liberal party over the South African War, Emmott was a strong " Imperialist," and an active member of the Liberal League. I felt, therefore, some surprise when C.-B. and I were talking over the composition of the new Government in December, 1905, and we came to the important post of Chairman of Committees, that he at once suggested Emmott. It was an excellent appointment, as was proved by a most exacting test — the Committee stage of the Finance Bill of 1909, when the Chair was beset, both on the right and the left, by impatient Radicals and obstructive Tories. There have been nimbler minds among the many Chairmen whom I have known, but none of them possessed a sounder judgment, more unfailing dignity, and a keener and stronger sense of fair-play.

After six sessions of exceptional severity, a change of scene and work was not unwelcome to him, and he accepted in 1911 my offer of the Under-Secretaryship of the Colonies with a seat in the House of Lords. His new post, for which, by his early experience and interests he was admirably equipped, was altogether congenial to him. He sat in the Cabinet from August, 1914, to May, 1915, when on the formation of the Coalition he patriotically agreed to accept an outside and unremunerated office—that of Director of the War Trade Department—where he did invaluable work up to the end of the War.

The political cause to which Emmott held most tenaciously was Free Trade, and his last appearance in the House of Lords, only three days before his death (December, 1926), was in the Committee stage of a Merchandise Marks Bill. He and I both agreed that it was a puerile and shamefaced, and so far as it went a mischievous, instalment of thinly veiled Protection, and he took an active part in the discussion and the divisions. There was in him that day not the slightest sign of physical or mental decadence, and it was without any presage of weakness or infirmity that his laborious and well-spent life came to a sudden end.

LORD LUCAS

Auberon Herbert, Lord Lucas (always known to his friends as "Bron"), was the son of Auberon Herbert, brother of the Lord Carnarvon who was Disraeli's colleague, and afterwards Viceroy of Ireland in the Gov-

ernment of the "Caretakers." No two brothers could
have been less alike. The younger of them started public life as a philosophical Radical, and during a short
parliamentary life was Dilke's associate in his crude
campaign against the monarchy. He was a cultivated
man and an agreeable and accomplished writer, in
character chivalrous to the point of quixotry,[1] with a
certain angularity of vision which made it difficult for
him to work with others. He lived in an unconven-
tional way amid simple and almost austere surroundings, and sent " Bron," his only son (born in 1876), to
Bedford Grammar School, whence he went on to Balliol in 1895. For the story of his life I cannot do better
than quote, with one or two omissions, the admirable
sketch, by one who knew him well, in the " Balliol War
Memorial Book," privately printed for the College in
1924:

He had never rowed at school, but he was a fine natural
athlete, and found a place in his last two years in the University boat, as well as in the famous Balliol Eight of 1899
which contained five Blues. He had very little of the ordinary sportsman about him; his tastes were rather those of
the gipsy, and he had an astounding knowledge of birds and
beasts and every wild thing. Far better than the ritual of
games, he loved his private adventures in the by-ways of the
country-side. He didn't do much in the Schools, taking a
Third Class in Modern History, but his most intimate
friends were scholars like Cuthbert Medd and Raymond
Asquith, and he developed a great love of poetry and music.
For politics he at that time cared not at all. With his petu-
lant mouth and great wondering eyes he had the air of one
who was amused and a little puzzled by life.

At the outbreak of war in 1899 he was off at once to
South Africa, taking the first chance he got, which was that

[1] He once risked his life to save from death a drowning pig.

of a *Times* correspondent.[1]   There he was abundantly happy.   He was not specially interested in military affairs, but he loved the spacious land and the adventurous life. . . . Advancing too far forward in an action, he got a rifle bullet in his foot.   The wound was mismanaged, and when he came back to England his leg had to be amputated below the knee.   To most men of his type such a loss might well have been crippling.   To him it simply did not matter at all. He rode and played tennis and stalked just as before.

Presumably under Raymond Asquith's guidance he, who had been at Oxford a member of the Canning Club, became a Liberal candidate for Parliament.[2]   His uncle (on the mother's side) died in the summer of 1905, and he succeeded to the baronies of Lucas and Dingwall, and became the owner of several great houses.   He was neither oppressed by, nor unappreciative of, his new possessions, but he always preferred his home at Picket Post in the New Forest.   Then there befell him the most fantastic fate. When the Liberal Government came into power, as one of the few Liberal peers he was marked down for preferment. He became Mr. Haldane's private secretary in 1908, and later Under-Secretary for War, and in 1911 for a short time Under-Secretary for the Colonies.   He was never a

---

[1] In the Sudanese and South Africa Wars, some of the most promising of our young men volunteered as newspaper correspondents, and in that capacity made familiar acquaintance with the realities and hazards of war. Among them, in addition to "Bron" Herbert, were Winston Churchill, and Hubert Howard, who was killed at Omdurman.

[2] He was no doubt also influenced by his close friend, Edwin Montagu, afterwards to become Secretary of State for India. "Bron's" constituency was one of the divisions of Hunts. I remember going to speak for him at St. Neots. Just before the meeting we were told that an American gentleman wished to see us, and when his card was brought up he turned out to be Mr. William Jennings Bryan of Nebraska, the famous Democratic politician and candidate for the Presidency. He was spending a few days in England on his way to the Continent, and, the fiscal controversy being in full blast, he occupied his evenings in going to hear the principal combatants. He told us that the night before he had heard Mr. Chamberlain, and the following night he intended to catch up the Duke of Devonshire. He sat in the front seats at our meeting, and gave vigilant attention to all that went on. As he had the reputation of having spoken more words in public than any orator, living or dead, I asked him, on our way back in the train, what struck him as the main difference between an English and an American audience. "Sir," he replied, "your people have a totally different sense of humour from ours." I thought it best to leave it at that.

good speaker, but his honesty and natural courtesy pleased even his opponents. In 1911 he went as Parliamentary Secretary to the Board of Agriculture, where he was a real success, for he was a true countryman, knowing at first hand what most politicians are only told. In 1914 he entered the Cabinet as President of the Board of Agriculture, and held the post till the formation of the Coalition in May, 1915. It was an odd destiny for a gipsy — to be a Cabinet Minister in spite of himself at thirty-eight.

When he left the Cabinet he found what he had always been seeking. Though he was many years over age, he managed to join the Royal Flying Corps, where his wonderful eye and nerve stood him in good stead. Soon he became a most competent pilot. He was for a short time in Egypt, and was back in England in the spring of 1916, engaged in instructing recruits. He was offered the command of a squadron, but refused till he had gained experience on the Western front. He went out to France in October of that year, and in a flight in strong weather over the German lines was reported missing.[1] Early in December news came from the German side that he was dead. When our troops advanced to victory in the autumn of 1918, they found his grave.

There can have been few careers with such abundant fulfilment. . . . He had found the secret of happy living in which the fires of youth never burn low, and the ardour and adventure of life are never dimmed.

The sketch is fitly concluded with some beautiful lines from the Elegy written by one of " Bron's " most intimate and dearest friends.

IN MEMORIAM. A. H.

O liberal heart fast-rooted to the soil,
O lover of ancient freedom and proud toil,
Friend of the gipsies and all wandering song,
The forest's nursling and the favoured child
Of woodlands wild —

[1] Just a month after his friend, Raymond Asquith, had fallen in action.

O brother to the birds and all things free,
Captain of liberty!
Deep in your heart the restless seed was sown;
The vagrant spirit fretted in your feet;
We wondered could you tarry long,
And brook for long the cramping street
Or would you one day sail for shores unknown,
And shake from you the dust of towns, and spurn
The crowded market-place — and not return?
You found a sterner guide;
You heard the guns.   Then, to their distant fire,
Your dreams were laid aside;
And on that day, you cast your heart's desire
Upon a burning pyre;
You gave your service to the exalted need,
Until at last from bondage freed,
At liberty to serve as you loved best,
You chose the noblest way.   God did the rest.

                              MAURICE BARING.

I resume here my extracts:

August 3. This morning two letters arrived for me, one from John Morley, the other from Simon, announcing that they must follow John Burns's example. They are both characteristic productions. At the Cabinet later in the morning Beauchamp declared that he must do likewise. That is four gone. We had a rather moving scene in which every one all round said something, Lloyd George making a strong appeal to them not to go, or at least to delay it. Anyhow, they all agreed to say nothing to-day and to sit in their accustomed places in the House.

Bonar Law and Landsdowne came to see me early this morning. They were in general agreement, but laid great stress upon Belgian neutrality. The Germans have delivered an ultimatum to Belgium and forced themselves on their territory, and the Belgian King has made an appeal to ours. After lunch we all went to the House of Commons. Grey made a most remarkable speech almost an hour long, for the most part almost conversational in tone and with some of his usual ragged ends, but extraordinarily well reasoned and tactful and really cogent, so much so that our extreme peace lovers were for the moment reduced to silence, though they will soon find their tongues again.

August 4. I think the effect produced by Grey's speech has not died down. It is curious how going to and from the House we are now always escorted and surrounded by cheering crowds of loafers and holiday-makers. In the evening I had a call from Bonar Law, who is afraid that we shall make use of the truce to spring a trick on his party by suddenly proroguing and putting the Home Rule and Welsh Church Bills on the Statute Book as a *fait accompli* before they can say "knife." I assured him that there would be no thimble-rigging, but it is not easy at the moment to decide exactly how to deal with the Bills. The best thing of course would be a deal between Carson and Redmond, which is far from impossible. J. M. remains obdurate and I fear must go. He wrote me a particularly nice letter (quoted on pages 15–18). We had an interesting Cabinet, as we got the news that the Germans had entered Belgium and had announced that if necessary they would push their way through by force of arms. This simplifies matters. So we sent the Germans an ultimatum to expire at midnight requesting them to give a like assurance with the French that they would respect Belgian neutrality. They have invented a story that the French were meditating an invasion of Belgium and that they were only acting in self-defence, a manifest and transparent lie. Winston, who has got on all his war-paint, is longing for a sea fight in the early hours of the morning to result in the sinking of the *Goeben*. The whole thing fills me with sadness. The House took the fresh news to-day very calmly and with a good deal of dignity, and we got through all the business by half-past four.

Photo: Russell, London

VISCOUNT GREY OF FALLODON

CHAPTER III

THE FIRST TWO MONTHS OF WAR

IT is no part of my purpose to enter into competition with the historians of the War, either in its strategical or its political aspects. All the salient facts material to the formation of a judgment are not only by this time public property, but have been canvassed and appraised by writers in all the countries concerned from every possible point of view, and with a bewildering diversity of conclusions, both as to persons and policies, and as to the things done and — a more fertile and fascinating theme — the things that might have been done but were left undone.

Even before the reconstruction of the Government by the formation of the first Coalition in May, 1915, it had been found expedient from time to time to enter into confidential communication with the leaders of the Opposition on matters upon which in normal conditions the Cabinet would have acted entirely upon its own judgment. I may give two illustrations of very different degrees of importance. The first concerned the negotiations for the potential transfer of Constantinople to Russia, in the event of Turkey persisting in active belligerent alliance with the Central Powers. This would involve such a material departure from traditional British policy that I thought we ought not to commit the country to it without the knowledge, and so far as might be the concurrence, of the Conservative leaders.   Accordingly, with the consent of my colleagues, I invited Lord Lansdowne and Mr. Bonar Law to take part in the Cabinet deliberations on the matter.

Another question upon which it seemed to us that the necessary legislation should be agreed upon in advance was the duration of the existing Parliament.   The House of Commons had been elected in December, 1910, and as its term was limited by the Parliament Act to five years, it would, if its life were prolonged to the last legal moment, expire in December, 1915.   It was obviously in the general interest highly undesirable that the country, which was straining every nerve to ensure an effective prosecution of the War, should be distracted by being called upon in such conditions to prepare for and in a few months to confront the turmoil of a general election.   Accordingly it was determined by the Cabinet early in April, 1915, to communicate with the leaders of the Opposition as to the expediency of postponing registration and the dissolution for another year.

The root difficulty in the early conduct of the War on our part—a difficulty experienced in nearly the same degree in France—was how to combine rapid and effective executive action in the various theatres with the maintenance of Cabinet responsibility and control.   This was the case quite as much after as before the formation of the Coalition in May, 1915.[1] Various expedients in the way of delegation were tried, and on September 22 I proposed to the Cabinet the

---

[1] The drawbacks and delays which resulted are described — not unfairly, but in somewhat over-sombre traits — by Sir W. Robertson, who (as he says), being occupied at the Front, had no personal experience of this phase of the War at home. ("Soldiers and Statesmen," Vol. I, c. 4, *passim*.)

creation of two Committees — one to deal with the actual conduct of the War and its problems: the other to concern itself with the financial outlook. I recorded at the time that "after a good deal of discussion" the proposal was "approved in principle." When the details came to be worked out, there was for a time a fusillade of cross-criticism, but by the end of October I was able to make the following announcement on the subject of the War Committee to my colleagues:

The proposal, as I understand it, is that there should be a small Committee of the Cabinet, not fewer than three or more than five in number, to deal executively with the conduct of the War.

It is understood that the Committee will from time to time call to their aid, for the purposes both of discussion and decision, other members of the Cabinet, either because their departments are concerned in the particular matter which is being dealt with or for other special reasons.

The Cabinet to remain as it is, in numbers and composition.

The *plenum* of the Cabinet to be kept constantly informed of the decisions and actions of the Committee, and in all questions which involve a change or new departure in policy to be consulted before decisive action is taken.

Almost concurrently with the formation of the newly constituted War Committee two other important steps were taken for the efficient prosecution of the War: the substitution of Sir Douglas Haig for Sir John French as Commander-in-Chief on the Western Front; and the appointment of Sir William Robertson to be Chief of the Imperial General Staff at the War Office, with greatly enlarged powers.

Here I may continue the use of my *aides-mémoires:*

August 5. I have taken an important decision to-day: to give up the War Office[1] and install Kitchener there as an emergency man until the War comes to an end. It was quite impossible for me to go on now that war is actually in being. It requires the undivided time and thought of any man to do the job properly, and I hate scamped work. K. was, to do him justice, not at all anxious to come in, but when it was presented to him as a duty he agreed. It is clearly understood that he has no politics and that his place at Cairo is kept open so that he can return to it when peace comes back. It is a hazardous experiment, but the best in the circumstances, I think. We had a longish Cabinet, at which we decided to ask to-morrow for a stiff vote of credit, 100 millions, which will carry us on for a long time and produce a good immediate impression.

Oddly enough, there is no authentic war news either by land or sea. All that appears in the papers is invention. Winston's mouth waters for the *Goeben,* but so far she is still at large. I am truly sorry for the poor Lichnowskys. They are broken-hearted, and she spends her days in tears. After the House I had a War Council, a rather motley gathering: Lord Roberts, Kitchener, Ian Hamilton, French, Douglas Haig, etc., with Haldane, Grey, Winston, and myself. We discussed the strategic situation and what to do with the Expeditionary Force, and adjourned till to-morrow, when we shall have over a representative of the French General Staff.

[1] I had assumed the Secretaryship of State for War after the Curragh affair.

August 6. We had our usual Cabinet this morning, and decided with much less demur than I expected to sanction the dispatch of the Expeditionary Force of four divisions. We also discussed a number of smaller schemes for attacking German ports and wireless stations in East and West Africa and the China Seas. Indeed, I had to remark that we looked more like a gang of Elizabethan buccaneers than a meek collection of black-coated Liberal Ministers. After the Cabinet I went to the Palace and had a talk with the King before the Privy Council at which Kitchener was sworn in and I handed over my seals to him. It will be amusing to see how he gets on in the Cabinet. I had to introduce the Vote of Credit, and though I had not had more than about five minutes to prepare I think I made a fairly successful speech.

August 10. We had a long and rather critical Cabinet this morning, the main question being what I was to say on the adjournment about the Home Rule and Welsh Church Bills. Redmond was pressing for prorogation and immediate placing on the Statute Book. Carson sent a rather threatening letter in the opposite sense. We had a very animated debate, and for a time it seemed as though we should come to a deadlock. Happily not for the first, or perhaps the last, time I was able to devise a form of saving words which pleased everybody, and which I have just (5.15) read to the House with the benediction of Bonar Law and not a single question from any quarter. The Expeditionary Force is moving on oiled castors. A considerable part of it is in France. There is not a whisper of this in the newspapers.

August 11. Sir John French came to pay me a farewell visit this morning. We had a long Cabinet, in which a large part of the talking was done by Winston and Kitchener, the former posing as an expert on strategy and the latter as an expert on Irish politics. At lunch we had Cassel and Sir Edward Goschen just returned from Berlin. Goschen gave a lot of interesting particulars about his last days there. At the end his German footmen took off their liveries and spat on them and refused even to carry down his boxes.

August 12. The only interesting thing is the arrival of the *Goeben* in the Dardanelles and her sale to Turkey. The Turks are very angry at Winston's seizure of their battleships here. As we shall insist that the *Goeben* shall be manned by a Turkish instead of a German crew it does not much matter, as the Turkish sailors cannot navigate her except on to rocks or mines. Meanwhile the embarkation of the Expeditionary Force goes smoothly and steadily on.

August 17. Turkey has come into the foreground, threatens vaguely enterprises against Egypt, and seems disposed to play a double game about the *Goeben* and the *Breslau*. Winston, in his most bellicose mood, is all for sending a torpedo flotilla through the Dardanelles to threaten and if necessary to sink the *Goeben* and her consort. Crewe and Kitchener very much against it. In the interests of the Mussulmans in India and Egypt they are against our doing anything at all which could be interpreted as meaning that we are taking the initiative against Turkey. She ought to be compelled to strike the first blow. I agreed to this, but the Turks must be obliged to come out and tell us whether they are going at once to dismiss the German crews.

August 18. Redmond I hope is coming over to-night and I have told Birrell to see him first thing to-morrow and to impress upon him that some *modus vivendi* is in the existing circumstances absolutely necessary. The choice is between three courses: (1) Agreement upon the basis of provisional exclusion from the operation of the Home Bill of six counties or there-abouts. (2) Passing the Bill as it stands with a suspensory clause, say for a year, capable of renewal. (3) Holding up the Bill till next session, with a provision that it should then be in precisely the same position as it is now, and entitled to the full benefit of the Parliament Act.

Everyone is very pleased with the smoothness and secrecy of the Expeditionary Force. Winston is engaged in chasing a German cruiser about the North Sea with two of his flotillas and hopes to run her down before nightfall.

August 20. The poor Belgians have been having a bad hammering and are now driven back to Antwerp, and Brussels is in the hands of the Germans. For the real purposes and fortunes of the campaign this is all to the good, for it means that the Germans have to spend two, or possibly even three, days more to the dis-arrangement of their time-table, before the real fighting on the great scale begins. It looks as if our troops may be in the thick of it before long. We are now sending off another division, the Fifth. We had a rather long Cabinet this morning, all sorts of odds and ends about coal and contraband.

August 21. The old bother about Tyrone and those

infernal snippets of Fermanagh and Derry, etc.,
popped up again, and Redmond does not see how he
and Carson can be brought nearer than they were at
Buckingham Palace three weeks ago. I have since seen
Bonar Law, who won't have course No. 2 [mentioned
under date the 18th] at any price, and says that his
party would regard itself in that case as being jockeyed
and treated shabbily. He could agree to No. 1 provided we could give him the six counties, and would
then concede a three years' time limit.

We had a long Cabinet this morning, mostly about
details connected with the War. The real centre of
interest, political, not military, at the moment is Turkey
and the two darkest horses in the European stable, Italy
and Rumania. The different points of view of different
people are rather amusing—Winston violently anti-
Turk; Kitchener strong that Rumania is the real pivot
of the situation; Masterman eagerly pro-Bulgarian, but
very much against any aggressive action *vis-à-vis*
Turkey which would excite our Mussulmans in India
and Egypt; Lloyd George keen for Balkan confedera-
tion; Grey judicious and critical all round; Haldane
instructive; and the "Beagles" and "Bobtails" silent
and bewildered.

August 24. Early this morning I was aroused by
Kitchener bringing French's telegram announcing the
fall of Namur. Very bad news, for we all assumed
that Namur was safe if not for a fortnight at least for
two or three days, and, though our soldiers seem to have
held their own, its fall of course takes out the pivot
from the movement which was in contemplation. The
general effect is that the French Fifth Army has had to

fall back and take a new line, and our own men in consequence have had to fall back also from the forward positions at and about Mons. It is a bad check, to say the least.

August 26. When I came back from the House I had a long visit from Winston and Kitchener and we summoned Edward Grey into our councils. They were bitten by an idea of Hankey's to dispatch a brigade of Marines, about 3,000, conveyed and escorted in battleships to Ostend, to land there and take possession of the town and scout about in the neighbourhood. This would please the Belgians and annoy and harass the Germans, who would certainly take it to be the pioneer of a larger force, and it would further be quite a safe operation as the Marines could at any moment re-embark. Grey and I consented, and the little force is probably at this moment disembarking at Ostend. Winston, I need not say, was full of ardour about his Marines and takes the whole adventure, of which the Cabinet only heard for the first time an hour ago, very seriously.

At about eleven P.M. I got French's telegram announcing that, much against his will, he was falling back on Péronne, which is between St. Quentin and Amiens. His men were in excellent condition and most anxious to take the offensive, but the French commanders were persisting in further retirement. Happily the telegram this morning is more reassuring. They seem to be regaining confidence and are even taking the aggressive in Belgium and Luxembourg. French's situation is not a very pleasant one, in command of an unbeaten army, full of fight, yet compelled always to go back. I hope it is only a passing phase.

I am very anxious now to get all the party machinery on both sides to work, first to stir people up about the War, for there is, I fear, in some places a growing apathy, and next, to bring the multitude of idle, able-bodied loafers into the recruiting net. I have just had a visit here [House of Commons] from Lord Roberts. He is particularly keen for the moment about two things, the bringing over of the Indian troops, and the enlistment and training of both sets of Irish volunteers.

August 27. Winston has been scoring some small, but not unimportant points. His 3,000 Marines have "taken" Ostend, and are scouting about the country in the region, and the *Kaiser Wilhelm,* a huge armed German liner, has been sunk by the *Highflyer.*

August 31. The Irish on both sides are giving me a lot of trouble just at a difficult moment. I sometimes wish we could submerge the whole lot of them and their island for, say, ten years, under the waves of the Atlantic. I have had interviews to-day, in the intervals of more urgent things, with Redmond and with Bonar Law, inspired by Carson, and they almost fill me with despair.

September 1. We are a good deal mystified and perturbed by the war news, and particularly by French's determination to retire beyond the Seine, which would mean that for at least a week to come he would be of no effective use to the French in withstanding the further German advance. A telegram in this sense, in reply to our remonstrance earlier in the day, came in just before midnight and I had a conference after twelve P.M. downstairs with Kitchener and Winston, McKenna and Jack Pease, and later Lloyd George. We came to the decided conclusion that the only thing to be done was for Kitchener to go there without delay and unravel the situation. He is a real sportsman when an emergency offers, and went straight home to change his clothes and started by special train from Charing Cross about 1.30 this morning. Winston provided him with a fast cruiser at Dover, whence he would make his way from Havre to Paris. Hardly a dozen people realize that he is not at the War Office to-day.

September 2. After dinner a telegram came in from Bertie[1] and Kitchener. K. had straightened out French's position and thought he had better return at once, and as Grey and I concurred, he left Paris at six this morning rather to my relief, for you never know how far the German cavalry may have penetrated and he would be the best bag they could secure.

We had our regular Cabinet in his absence this morning, and the kind of thing that comes up day by day can easily be judged by this short synopsis of topics: naval air reconnoitring at Dunkirk; protection of London against bomb-throwing from Zeppelins; Greece and Turkey on the verge of war; proposed offer of financial help to Rumania and Serbia; Japan: Can she help with her fleet or army, or both? Scheme for pledging State credit to deal with the discounting of post-moratorium bills, etc., etc., etc.

September 3. K. successfully accomplished his return journey and repaired here soon after seven last evening, when we had a second Cabinet. He went to Paris, saw French and his staff there and the French

---

[1] Ambassador at Paris.

Minister for War, Millerand. I asked K. if Millerand
was at all optimistic about the situation. He said,
"No," but, on the other hand, they are not at all de-
jected, indeed quite composed. They were on the eve
of moving, bag and baggage, out of Paris. It is plain,
from K.'s account, that there has been a good deal of
misunderstanding and something approaching friction
between French and Joffre, each, I suppose, thinking
that the other was not giving him full measure of the
right kind of support. Moreover, although we have
sent French all, and more than all, he needed to renew his army and replenish his supplies and equipment, there has been a lot of disorganization on the
lines of communication and he has not received his
proper reinforcements either of men or material. K.
did his best to put all this right, and we are going
as soon as possible to send French the 6th Division,
fresh men who have seen no fighting, so far, and are
intact and unfatigued. The two Indian divisions, the
first of which is well on this side of Aden, will be
halted for a few days in Egypt before proceeding to
Marseilles.

There is no doubt from what K. reports that
French's troops, always fighting and always retiring,
have been a good deal battered and they need a few
days' rest. He estimated his casualties up to yesterday
at about 8,000, of whom a large proportion are missing.
He thinks that in a few days some 2,000 of these will
have returned to the colours. When it comes, if it does,
to anything like an investment of Paris, I am disposed
to believe that the Germans, with their immense line
of communications and the heavy losses they have suf-

fered, may yet have a very bad time. Recruiting is now going on at such a tremendous rate — 30,000 men a day — that it will soon become impossible to digest the new material and provide it with clothing and arms. The mines sown by the Germans in the North Sea continue to give a lot of trouble, mostly to our own and neutral trawlers.

September 8. I have just been reading a telegram from Bucharest to the effect that the Kaiser has written to the King of Rumania, whom he is most anxious to enlist on his side, that the German troops in France will have crushed the Franco-British forces in twenty days. He says he will then leave 500,000 German troops in occupation of France and turn his attention to Russia. Meanwhile Kitchener calculates that in six months' time he will have fifty divisions of trained troops, which means a little more than one million men. I told him that the new recruits were badly overcrowded. He did not deny it, but smiled grimly and said the damned fools of doctors were always insisting on ridiculous allowances of cubic space. They would not allow in this room (the Cabinet room) more than eight men, while we know it can easily accommodate sixteen or more. He added that there was an ample supply of tents, which in this weather one would think preferable to barracks.

September 9. The adventurous Winston is just off to Dunkirk to superintend his new flying base. He will be back by lunch-time to-morrow. He has shown me a very private letter to himself from French, who keenly resented K.'s visit. French seems in quite good spirits and very pleased with his army. If they were multiplied by six, he says he would get to Berlin in six weeks without French help.

September 14. We had a longish Cabinet, mostly occupied with odds and ends. It is rather interesting to know, as Kitchener told us, that we have by now sent to French 213,000 men and 57,000 horses.

September 14. I have just been dragging together some disjointed notes about what I am to say on the Irish Bill. I do not think it will be very serious, for the Tories, at their party meeting, resolved to have only a single speech, a snarl from Bonar Law; and the Cecils, who wanted to roam and range at large, seem to have been silenced. It will be a really big thing if before the end of the week we get Home Rule on the Statute Book after three years of ceaseless conflict and worry. If this comes off I might almost begin to intone the *Nunc Dimittis.*

Later. House of Commons, 5.45. This afternoon has been quite dramatic. I made a quiet, rather humdrum speech, pitched purposely in a low key, which was well listened to by the Tories as a whole. Then Bonar Law followed with his usual indictment of us, and me in particular, for lying and breaking faith, treachery, etc. He was so offensive that both Illingworth and McKenna, who were sitting by me, left the House, lest they should be unable to overcome their impulse to throw books, paper-knives and other handy missiles at his head. He did not really make out much of a case, and watching his people carefully I do not think they were at all united or enthusiastic. At the end of his speech the whole Tory party walked out of the House by way of washing their hands of responsibility for our wicked ways. It was not really a very impressive spectacle, a lot of prosaic and for the most part middle-aged gentlemen trying to look like early French revolutionists in the Tennis Court. Still, it was unique in my, or anybody's, experience. Several of the Irish and of our Radicals went and sat on the Opposition benches above the gangway.

September 15. I feel as if a great weight were off my chest. The Suspensory Bill went through all its stages on oiled castors in about seven minutes. The result is that before the week is over the Home Rule Bill will be law. No one who has not gone through the whole business for the last three years can realize fully what that means.

September 19. Joffre is very anxious that we should make a diversion on the north coast of France to frighten the Germans as to their lines of communication, so Winston has sent there, to reinforce his aeroplanes and armed motor-cars, his Marine brigade of about 3,000 men. As he mentioned cavalry, I, thinking of the old joke about horse marines, began to chaff him as to the composition of his force, only to discover that he had, with K.'s consent, dispatched the Oxfordshire Yeomanry, his own corps, with "Brother Jack." I fear we shall see very few of them back again.

September 22. Kitchener presented himself to-day in what he called frankly a white sheet, admitting that the recruits had been and were being badly treated in the way of clothing, boots, and other necessaries. He says that his orders have not been carried out and he is furious with the War Office. We agreed to dismiss the Chief Director of Contracts. and to set on foot a better and more business-like system. I thought this had been done. It was certainly ordered at least three weeks ago.

September 29. Winston turned up this morning and gave me a full and vivid narrative of his journey to the Front. He left here on Saturday morning and spent Sunday with French and his troops, returning after a visit to his own little army at Dunkirk, on Monday night. He went all along the English line, about fifteen miles, and saw everything that was to be seen. The army was in the best possible condition, and in a perfectly impregnable position, for the most part lining the north bank of the Aisne. French intends, if he can get Joffre's assent and if Joffre can spare enough men to fill the gap, to disengage, as they call it, and to make with his whole force a great outflanking march via Amiens, Arras, Douai, Tournay, to the line across Belgium from Brussels to Cologne. He thinks he could do it in a week or nine days, and the long march will be good for his troops. It would relieve Antwerp, which is going to be sorely pressed, take the Germans in their flank and rear, break up their communications, and if successful put an end to the invasion of France. It is a great scheme, heartily approved by Kitchener, and I hope that Joffre won't put spokes in the wheel.

The Americans are raising difficulties about the seizure and detention of cargoes sent in their ships ostensibly to Holland, but for German consumption. We naturally do not want to have a row with them, but we cannot allow the Germans to be provided for. Rufus has agreed to go to America for a fortnight to try and settle up both our financial and diplomatic difficulties. He has been a tower of strength.

CHAPTER IV

TWO VISITS TO DUBLIN

DURING my tenure of the office of Prime Minister I paid two public visits to Dublin: the first in July, 1912, during the progress of the Home Rule Bill after the way had been cleared by the passing of the Parliament Act; the second in September, 1914, the period which I have now reached in my narrative, a month after the outbreak of the Great War.

On the first occasion, when I described my mission as that of an "Ambassador of Peace," nothing could have exceeded the enthusiasm of the population. Our torchlight drive in an open carriage, which we shared with Mr. John Redmond, had all the accompaniments of a triumphal procession. The only jarring note came from a handful of Suffragettes, one of whom, as I have mentioned in an earlier chapter, threw a hatchet at us, which grazed Mr. Redmond's cheek. The meeting held the next night was one of the most remarkable that I have ever addressed. It was calculated that when I rose to speak the cheering continued for seven minutes. I dwelt mainly on two topics: the Ulster threat of civil war, and the future relation between the two islands. I will select from what I said two salient passages:

Great Britain has a majority of chosen representatives in favour of Home Rule. In Ireland there is a majority of four-fifths of the representatives of the people in favour of Home Rule. But because one-half of the representatives of the Province of Ulster is opposed to it, the thing cannot be carried through except at the cost of civil war. And there are English statesmen occupying positions of trust and responsibility who do not hesitate to come to Ulster and encourage the minority in that Province to take that view.

I am not in the least embarrassed when asked, as I constantly am, What are you going to do in the event of a civil war? I tell you quite frankly I do not believe in the prospect of a civil war. Minorities have their rights; they have not only their rights, but their susceptibilities, which ought to be considered and provided for. But to say that a minority, before any actual wrong has been or can be done to them, are, in defiance of the terms of an Act of Parliament and of the supreme authority of the Imperial Parliament, upon a suspicion or apprehension that they may peradventure at some future date be injured— to say that a minority are entitled on such grounds as that to thwart and defeat the constitutional demand of a vast majority of their fellow-countrymen, and to frustrate a great international settlement, is a proposition which, in my opinion, does not and never will commend itself to the conscience or to the judgment of the British people.

THE FUTURE

Why is it that alone in the whole British Empire this island of yours, nearest to us in space, most closely related to us by the ties of kindred and of social and business intercourse, why does it alone continue to be a source, not of strength, but of weakness? "I am convinced," wrote one of the greatest, perhaps the greatest, of Irish thinkers and writers, Edmund Burke, "that no reluctant tie can be a strong one." We wish to make that tie no longer reluctant and compulsory, but spontaneous, voluntary, affectionate, real. There is nothing incompatible between the vision of Ireland as a nation and loyalty to a United Kingdom in which Ireland is an integral and an enfranchised and self-governing part. Let us join, let us unite the two streams that they may flow together to the common enrichment of Ireland and of the Empire.

The next time I visited Dublin — September 25, 1914 — and addressed an Irish audience, the conditions were very different. The extent of the transformation can only be realized by recalling the language used in the House of Commons by Mr. Redmond immediately after Sir Edward Grey's historic speech on August 3:

In past times when this Empire has been engaged in these terrible enterprises, the sympathy of the Nationalists of Ireland, for reasons to be found deep down in the centuries of history, have been estranged from this country. What has occurred in recent years has altered the situation completely. A wider knowledge of the real facts of Irish history have, I think, altered the views of the democracy of this country towards the Irish question, and to-day I honestly believe that the democracy of Ireland will turn with the utmost anxiety and sympathy to this country in every trial and every danger that may overtake it.

To-day there are in Ireland two large bodies of Volunteers. One of them sprang into existence in the North. Another has sprung into existence in the South. *I say to the Government that they may to-morrow withdraw every one of their troops from Ireland. I say that the coast of Ireland will be defended from foreign invasion by her armed sons, and for this purpose armed Nationalist Catholics in the South will be only too glad to join arms with the armed Protestant Ulstermen in the North.*

A week before the meeting in Dublin (September 18) Parliament had been prorogued, and the Official Report records what happened before the House of Commons dispersed.

"MR. CROOKS: Would it be in order to sing God save the King?

"In response all the members present joined in singing the National Anthem, the occupants of the Press and other galleries standing.

"AN HON. MEMBER: God save Ireland.

"MR. JOHN REDMOND: And God save England, too."

Before the end of August I had invited the chief magistrates of the four principal cities in the different parts of the United Kingdom — London, Edinburgh, Dublin, and Cardiff — to summon a town's meeting which I would myself address. I had already spoken in London and Edinburgh when I came to Dublin. The meeting was held in the Rotunda under the presidency of the Lord Mayor, a Nationalist, and on the platform were the Lord-Lieutenant (Lord Aberdeen) and a number of leading Unionists and Nationalists. The speakers included, besides Mr. Birrell, the Chief Secretary, and myself, Mr. Redmond and Lord Meath. The huge audience was unanimous and enthusiastic.

I will only quote one passage from my speech:

I should like, beyond this inquiry into causes and motives, to ask your attention and that of my fellow-countrymen to the end which, in this war, we ought to keep in view. Forty-four years ago, at the time of the war of 1870, Mr. Gladstone used these words. He said: "The greatest triumph of our time will be the enthronement of the idea of public right as the governing idea of European politics." In the interval little progress, it seems, has as yet been made towards that good and beneficent change, but it seems to be now at this moment as good a definition as we can have of our European policy — the idea of public right. What does it mean when translated into concrete terms? It means, first and foremost, the clearing of the ground by the definite repudiation of militarism as the governing factor in the relation of states and of the future moulding of the European world. It means next, that room must be found and kept for the independent existence and the free development of the smaller nationalities, each with a corporate consciousness of its own. Belgium, Holland, and Switzerland and Scandinavian countries, Greece and the Balkan States — they must be recognized as having exactly as good a title as their powerful neighbours, more powerful in strength and in wealth, to a place in the sun. And it means finally, or it ought to mean, perhaps, by a slow and gradual process the substitution for force, for the clash of competing ambition, for groupings and alliances and a precarious equipoise, of a real European partnership based on the recognition of equal right, and established and enforced by a common will. A year ago that would have sounded like a Utopian idea. It is probably one that may not, or will not, be realized either to-day or to-morrow. If and when this war is decided in favour of the Allies it will at once come within the range, and before long within the grasp, of European statesmanship.

Herein lay the germ of the League of Nations.

CHAPTER V

CONTEMPORARY NOTES:
OCTOBER–DECEMBER, 1914

OCTOBER 1. The Germans are pounding away with their big guns at Antwerp, and though the Belgians are in a large numerical superiority they seem for the moment to have lost morale. One cannot be surprised at this, or blame them, for the Germans have been unusually active the last few days in burning their villages and shooting the inhabitants. The fall of Antwerp would be a great moral blow to the Allies, for it would leave the whole of Belgium for the moment at the mercy of the Germans. The commander telegraphs that he does not think they can hold out for more than another three days. Of course it would be idle butchery to send a force like Winston's little army there. If anything is to be done it must be by Regulars in sufficient numbers. We had a conference here last night, and sent over three good officers to report and to urge upon the Belgians to disregard their forts and to entrench themselves. The French telegraph that they are willing to send a division and to put it under a British general.

We resolved to-day that if the French co-operation is satisfactory we would divert our 7th Division which was going to join Sir John French and not throw it into Antwerp, but endeavour to raise the siege and capture the German big guns. In the meanwhile Winston is going in for a big mining operation in the North

Sea. I cannot help feeling anxious about Antwerp and the course of events in the next few days.

October 3. I found on my return from Cardiff that strange things had been going on here. The Belgian Government, notwithstanding that we are sending them heavy guns and trying hard to get in troops to raise the siege of Antwerp, resolved yesterday to throw up the sponge and leave to-day for Ostend, the King with his field army withdrawing in the direction of Ghent. They calculated that after their departure Antwerp might hold out for five or six days, which seems very doubtful. This is a decision quite unwarranted by the situation, for the German besieging army is only a scratch force and in one way or another a diversion is certain in the course of a few days. So we at once replied urging them to hold out and promising Winston's Marines to-morrow, with the hope of help from the main army and reinforcements from here.

I was away, but Grey, Kitchener and Winston held a late meeting and, I fancy with Grey's rather reluctant consent, the intrepid Winston set off at midnight and ought to have reached Antwerp at about nine this morning. He will go straightaway and see the Belgian Ministers. Sir John French is making preparations to send assistance by way of Lille. I have had a talk with K. this morning and we are both rather anxiously awaiting Winston's report. I do not know how fluent he is in French, but, if he was able to do himself justice in a foreign tongue, the Belges will have listened to a discourse the like of which they have never heard before. I cannot but think that he will stiffen them up.

October 5. Far more interesting than anything else

for the moment is Antwerp. Winston succeeded in bucking up the Belgians, who gave up their idea of retreat to Ostend and are now going to hold Antwerp for as long as they can, trusting upon our coming to their final assistance. Winston had already moved up his Marines from Dunkirk, and they are now in the Antwerp trenches. We hear to-day that they are doing well, but have already had 70 casualties. He had also sent for the rest of his Naval Brigade. We are doing our best for the Belgians, though we are dangerously short of Regulars in this country. K. is sending over to-day to their help a force consisting of the 7th Division, 18,000 of our best infantry, and a Cavalry Division. They ought all to be in Belgium by Wednesday or Thursday at the latest, and it is to be hoped that Antwerp can last as long as that. K. has appointed one of the best of our younger generals, Sir Henry Rawlinson, to command the whole.

Then comes a real bit of tragi-comedy. I found when I arrived here this morning a telegram from Winston, who proposes to resign his office in order to take the command in the field of this great military force. Of course, without consulting anybody, I at once telegraphed to him warm appreciation of his mission and his offer, with a most decided negative, saying we could not spare him at the Admiralty. I had not meant to read it at the Cabinet, but as everybody, including K., began to ask how soon he was going to return, I was at last obliged to do so. Winston is an ex-lieutenant of Hussars, and would, if his proposal had been accepted, have been in command of two distinguished major-generals, not to mention brigadiers, colonels, etc., while the Navy were only contributing their little brigades.

October 6. Winston persists in remaining there, which leaves the Admiralty here without a head, and I have had to tell them to submit all decisions to me. I think that Winston ought to return now that a capable general is arriving. He has done good service.

October 7. The Court and Ministers have retreated to Ostend and the Belgian army appears to be completely worn out. The trenches are good and strongly protected and our men could, I believe, hold them against any assault that the second or third German besiegers would deliver, certainly until relief comes. But when the bombardment of the open town once begins, the inhabitants, some 300,000 or 400,000, are sure to get into a panic and to demand capitulation. Our forces will in no case surrender, but if the worst comes will retire on the road to Bruges and Ghent, where they will find Rawlinson's corps entrenched and waiting for reinforcements. Much of this I got from Winston, who returned from the Front early this morning. I had a talk with him and Kitchener over the situation, and we telegraphed to French asking him to spare some troops for the relief of the siege, if Joffre and he think it possible.

Winston is in great form and I think has thoroughly enjoyed his adventure. He was quite ready to take over in Belgium, and did so, in fact, for a couple of days, the army, the navy, and the civil government. The King remains at Antwerp. Winston says he is curiously cool and detached.

We spent the rest of the morning at the Committee of Imperial Defence, where there were amongst others:

Balfour, Fisher, Sir Arthur Wilson, Esher, Lord Nicholson, besides the regular team. We had a very interesting discussion on the possibilities of a German invasion or raid, the conditions being, of course, totally different from any we had ever imagined in our long hypothetical inquiries. Everybody agreed that nothing of the kind was likely to occur at present, which is just as well, as during the next fortnight we shall have fewer Regular troops in the country than has happened for years. Much our weakest point is deficiency in guns and ammunition. This will not be thoroughly put right until the beginning of January, though everybody concerned is working night and day.

October 8. The news this morning from Antwerp was distinctly bad. The Germans had been bombarding away all night, and General Paris, who commands Winston's Naval Division, talked of evacuating the trenches, while General Rawlinson, who is still at Bruges, sent a report that the Germans had advanced through Termond and were threatening to cut through the line of retirement on Ghent both of the Belgian field army and of our naval force. The French have diverted the relief force which they had promised to send Winston from Paris, and Rawlinson with his 7th Division, unsupported by the French, is not quite strong enough to keep the road of retirement open.

Kitchener has just been with us and is coming again to confer with me and Winston. I have still some hope that things may come out right, but both at Antwerp and on the extreme left in France the next forty-eight hours are a critical time. Sir John French ought to-day to be at Abbeville.

Later. Just had a conference with K. and Winston about Belgium. There is, I fear, nothing to be done but to order our naval men to evacuate the trenches to-night, and Rawlinson will meet them and the remains of the Belgians at Ghent, after which point they are safe. Antwerp is, I am afraid, now in flames, but if the naval men get safely away, Sir John French's army will be well reinforced and ought to be able to make what Winston called a punch of an effective kind on the German right. Poor Winston is very depressed, as he feels that his mission has been in vain.

October 9. The news of the retirement is good. Rawlinson telegraphed this morning that 2,000 of the Naval Division passed through Selzaete, close to the Dutch frontier, this morning, making their way via Bruges to Ostend, and that the remainder were expected to go through before dark this evening. Once they get to Ostend they will embark in transports for home, having had their baptism of fire.

Edward Grey and Winston dined here last night. It is impossible to imagine a greater contrast.

October 10. Winston has just been in to talk over the situation. We both agree with Hankey — who is a good influence — that this last week, which has delayed the fall of Antwerp by at least seven days and has prevented the Germans from linking up their forces, has not been thrown away.

October 12. Oc[1] came to lunch yesterday and I had a long talk with him after midnight, in the course of which he gave me a full and vivid account of the expedition to Antwerp and the retirement. Marines of

[1] Brigadier-General Arthur Asquith.

course are splendid troops and can go anywhere and can do anything, but Winston ought never to have sent the two Naval Brigades. I was assured that all the recruits were being left behind, and that the main body at any rate consisted of seasoned Naval Reserve men. As a matter of fact only about one quarter were Reservists and the rest were a callow crowd of the rawest recruits, most of whom had never fired off a rifle, while none of them had even handled an entrenching tool.

October 15. The news to-day is neither very good nor very bad. French has got all his troops round and has linked up with Rawlinson. He lost one of his generals yesterday: Hubert Hamilton was killed by a shell.

I went to see the King this morning before the Cabinet at 11, and he agrees to open Parliament on November 11. He is much exercised about the Prince of Wales, who is eating his heart out to go to the Front, his battalion of Grenadiers being already gone without him. It is proposed that French should take him on his staff.

October (undated). Since I came back I have had a long call from Winston, who, after dilating in great detail on the actual situation, became suddenly very confidential and implored me not to take a conventional view of his future. Having, as he says, tasted blood these last few days, he is beginning, like a tiger, to raven for more, and begs that sooner or later — and the sooner the better — he may be relieved of his present office and put in some kind of military command. I told him that he could not be spared from the Admiralty, but he scoffs at that, alleging that the naval part of the business is practically over, as our superiority will grow greater and greater every month. His mouth waters at the sight and thought of K.'s new armies. Are these "glittering commands" to be entrusted to "dug-out trash" bred on the obsolete tactics of twenty-five years ago, "mediocrities who have led a sheltered life mouldering in military routine," etc., etc.? For about a quarter of an hour he poured forth a ceaseless cataract of invective and appeal, and I much regretted that there was no shorthand writer within hearing, as some of his unpremeditated phrases were quite priceless. He was, however, three parts serious and declared that a political career was nothing to him in comparison with military glory.

October 21. We had a rather interesting discussion on Home Defence and the possibility of a German invasion, which preoccupies and alarms the mind of Kitchener. His view is that the Army is doing all it can both at home and abroad, and that some of the big ships ought to be brought into the home ports. Winston made a very good defence of his policy, which is in a word, or at least in a very few words, that the function of the Fleet is not to prevent the landing of an invading force, but to strike at and destroy the enemy's covering fleet. All the same, it is agreed to be desirable to have a lot of sheltered or protected harbours into which no submarine can penetrate and in which some battleships and cruisers can lie in safety.

Lloyd George, who generally has a point of view of his own, is very down on the Russians for not taking us more into their confidence, both as to the actual and potential strength of their armies and as to their real plan of campaign. He says, quite truly, that for aught we know the Germans may be holding them back by a mere screen of troops while they are massing their real attack upon the Allies in Belgium and France. We must try to get them to be less secretive and to throw more of their designs into the common stock. Another urgent matter about which there threatens to be an acute difference of opinion amongst us is whether we should not supply the starving civil population in Belgium with food. Edward Grey and I are rather *pro;* Lloyd George, McKenna, Kitchener and the others strongly *contra.* We shall have to decide to-day.

October 28. The sinking of the *Audacious* — one of the best and newest of the super-dreadnoughts, with a crew of about a thousand — is cruel luck for Winston, who has just been here pouring out his woes. After a rather heated discussion in the Cabinet we resolved not to make public the loss at this moment. I was very reluctant, because I think it is bad policy on the whole not to take the public into your confidence in reverses as well as in successes, and I only assented to immediate reticence on the grounds that (1) no lives were lost, and (2) that the military and political situation is such that to advertise at this moment a great calamity might have very bad results.

Winston's real trouble, however, is about Prince Louis and the succession to his post. He must go, and Winston has had a most delicate and painful interview with him. Louis behaved with great dignity and public spirit, and will resign at once. Winston proposes to appoint Fisher to succeed him and to get Wilson to come on also as Chief of the Staff, which I think will be very popular.

We have had a royal row between Kitchener and Lloyd George about Welsh recruiting and the Welsh Army Corps. They came to very high words and it looked as if either or both of them would resign. The whole thing could be settled in ten minutes by the exercise of a modicum of common sense and imagination.

November 3. We have got down to three Cabinets a week and to-day is a day off, which is a great relief. I had a long visit from K., who is far from happy about what is going on at the Front. French is still quite confident, but his losses day by day are so great that he calls urgently for more men. K. has already sent him nineteen battalions of Territorials and he is prepared to send another division, I think, but French, perhaps not unnaturally, clamours for Regulars, and the 8th Division, which is the only one we have in hand here at present, is still very soft and, in K.'s opinion, unfit for really severe fighting. He may have to send them, for it is difficult to refuse French, but it is not an agreeable prospect. The 7th Division, which was sent only three or four weeks ago, is now reduced to about 5,000 out of 18,000, and the possibility, of course, is that less good and less trained troops would suffer in even greater proportions.

K. is quite easy now about invasion. Winston and Fisher are bringing a lot of big battleships with Jellicoe's consent, down to reinforce Burney's fleet in the Channel. My own opinion of K.'s capacity increases daily. I think he is a really fine soldier and he keeps his head and temper wonderfully considering how he is tried. Lloyd George, who has just been here about another matter, is now an enthusiastic Kitchenerite. Speaking of their reconciliation and of the way in which Kitchener met him over his little Welshmen, he said: "He is a big man, and what is more does things in a big way."

November 6. We had a longish Cabinet this morning with bad news from East Africa, where our Indian troops have had an unsuccessful brush with the Germans. After lunch I found, on descending to the Cabinet room, Winston and Freddy Guest, the latter over for a day on a secret mission from Sir John French, a most disagreeable affair. It has been reported to French, by some poisonous mischief-maker, that when K. was at Dunkirk last Sunday he asked the French generals whether they were satisfied with Sir John, and even suggested, as a possible successor, Ian Hamilton. I do not believe there is a word of truth or even a shadow of foundation for the story, but it appears to have given great distress to Sir John French, and led him to think that he had lost, or was losing, the confidence of the Government. Hence Freddy Guest's mission, which was to me and not to K. These noxious weeds only grow in prepared soil, and in this case, apparently, an estrangement, or at any rate a coldness, of long standing existed between French and K. I have written French what I think is a very nice and reassuring letter, and Winston is going to do the same.

November 28. Desperate efforts are being made to find some territorial formula which will bring Bulgaria and Rumania into the fighting line alongside of Serbia and Greece. It is not an easy job. Meanwhile Edward Grey is taking Sunday off. He left on Friday and Haldane is in charge for a couple of days of the Foreign Office.

Poor old H. has been violently attacked, apropos of spies and such nonsense, by the *Morning Post,* as a thinly veiled friend of Germany, who having recklessly reduced our infantry and artillery had palmed off on us the Territorial Army.

December 19. Walmer Castle, Kent. Sir John French is due to arrive at Folkestone to-morrow, Sunday morning, about 10.45, where he will be met by K., who will motor him here. We are then to put our heads together.

December 20. Walmer Castle, 3.30 p.m. The great men have come and gone and were really most interesting. They arrived, each with his own familiar, from Folkestone about noon, and I turned them into a room to talk together for about half an hour and then joined them. I found K., with his chart of Russian and German divisions, emphasizing the pessimistic point of view. French, on the other hand, would have none of it. He is quite convinced that the Germans have lost their best troops and officers, and is satisfied that even if they were able to polish off the Russians and push them beyond the Vistula, which he believes to be impossible, no troops that they could bring from the East to the West could ever go through the English and French lines. He says that the troops they now bring to the Front are of the worst quality and are only forced into action by battle police. On the other hand, he thinks our army better than it has ever been, and the French well led and generalled.

The two Field-Marshals are an extraordinarily disparate couple and not born or moulded to work easily together.

A private matter that was exercising French was an idea he had got to replace General Murray, who has been Chief of his Staff since the beginning of the War, by Henry Wilson. However, he has now quite dropped it and Murray will go on.

December 22. Winston and Kitchener had a meeting of reconciliation and fell on one another's necks yesterday. To-day at the Cabinet they were on the friendliest terms. It was rather interesting, I mean the Cabinet, as K. produced his scheme for the old and new armies. Of these there will be, in the first instance, six each of three Army Corps. The first of them will be ready in March, and the others will follow in quick succession.

We discussed at length the Russian situation in Poland and French's proposed movement to the extreme left flank of the coast. K. presented the most gloomy view of the Russian position. Winston said to me yesterday, apropos of Sir John French, "What a good thing it is to have an optimist at the front," to which I rejoined: "Excellent, provided you have also, as we have in K., a pessimist in the rear." According to K.'s estimate, if the Russians lost Warsaw the Germans might bring back forty divisions to reinforce the attack on the front. We are agreed that with all these facts and estimates on the table Joffre and French should have an immediate conference as to the best strategy for us in the West during the next two or three weeks while the Polish situation is still undecided.

Christmas Day. I received this morning a telegram from Spring Rice at Washington. He is convinced that both the German and Austrian Ambassadors there are working for peace. The only person they communicate with is the President. I gather that he thinks that the Germans would gladly agree to evacuate Belgium and give full compensation and securities against future attack. This, of course, would not be good enough either for France or Russia, but it is significant as showing how the wind is blowing.

December 28. K. has just been to see me to talk about the position of our troops in France. We have been urging the French to let us go to the extreme left and take the offensive along the coast. Cambon is now over there and has been pressing our view on Millerand. The reply is that Joffre has no objection in principle, but feels that some time ago he did not receive the support he expected from British troops in carrying out an enveloping movement, and he attributes it to want of energy on the part of our Chief of the Staff, Sir A. Murray. This both K. and I believe to be another proof of the constant intriguing in certain quarters. We are quite determined that it shall not succeed, and K. has suggested, with my entire approval, that Murray, if displaced, shall be succeeded by Sir William Robertson.

December 29. I have had two very interesting memoranda to-day on the War, one from Winston and the other from Hankey, written quite independently but coming by different roads to very similar conclusions. Both think that the existing deadlock in West and East is likely to continue, and W. points out that the flanking movement we urged on the French a month ago is much more difficult now that the Germans have fortified, line by line, almost the whole of Belgium. The losses involved in the trench-jumping operations now going on on both sides are enormous and out of proportion to the ground gained. When our New Armies are ready, as they will be soon, it seems folly to send them to positions where they are not wanted and where, in Winston's phrase, they will "chew barbed wire" or be wasted in futile frontal attacks.

Hankey suggests the development of a lot of new mechanical devices, such as armed rollers to crush down barbed wire, bullet-proof shields and armour, smoke balls, etc. But apart from this both he and W. are for finding a new theatre for our New Armies. Hankey would like them to go to Turkey and in conjunction with the Balkan States clear the Turk out of Europe. Germany and what is left of Austria, would be almost bound to take a hand. Winston, on the other hand, wants, primarily of course by means of his Navy, to close the Elbe and dominate the Baltic. He would first seize a German island, Borkum for choice, then invade Schleswig-Holstein, obtain naval command of the Baltic and thus enable Russia to land her troops within 90 miles of Berlin. This plan, apart from other difficulties, implies either the accession of Denmark to the Allies or the violation of her neutrality. There is here a good deal of food for thought. I am profoundly dissatisfied with the immediate prospect — an enormous waste of life and money day after day with no appreciable progress, and it is quite true that the whole country between Ypres and the German frontier is being transformed into a succession of lines of fortified entrenchments.

December 31. I got a lot of figures this morning. One is Winston's estimate of the men, including wounded, prisoners, and refugees, horses and stores, which he has transported across the sea since the War began, with, as he complacently and accurately notes, no fatal accident nor any loss. The total in men is 809,000, horses 203,000, stores 250,000 tons. Kitchener estimates the numbers of effective French troops at not more than 1,250,000 with the same number in reserve to make good losses and wastage.

Delcassé is still extremely anxious to bring the Japanese into the European theatre. The Japanese Government is very adverse to any such plan and says that public opinion there would not stand it, nor is it easy to see what inducement in the way of material gain could be offered them, except the certainty of retaining Kiauchau. I confess I am not very much enamoured of the idea, but Winston derides any scruples as born of perverted sentiment, and remarks with truth, "The great thing is to win the war." We have lost 5,000 men in this desultory trench fighting in the last fortnight.

As to Sir A. Murray, the French are very keen to get rid of him as Chief of the Staff. They do not seem to have any specific charge against him, except that he speaks poor French and is not sympathetic. Both K. and I think that Robertson is the right man to succeed him. Winston is for Haig, but it would be almost impossible to replace him where he is.

CHAPTER VI

THE EARLY MONTHS OF 1915

JANUARY 1. I received to-day two long memoranda, one from Winston, the other from Lloyd George — the latter is quite good — as to the future conduct of the War. They are both keen on a new objective and theatre as soon as our new troops are ready, Winston of course for Borkum and the Baltic, Lloyd George for Salonika, to join in with the Serbians, and for Syria.

January 5. Old Fisher seriously proposed, by way of reprisals for the Zeppelin raids, to shoot all the German prisoners here, and when Winston refused to embrace this statesmanlike suggestion sent in a formal resignation of his office. I imagine that by this time he has reconsidered it.

January 6. At the Cabinet K. read us French's long memorandum proposing a movement on Ostend and Zeebrugge, for the success of which he computes that he needs fifty battalions from home and an enormous supply of artillery and ammunition. He also proposes to break up K.'s New Armies and use them battalion by battalion for strengthening and enlarging his force. This is repugnant in the highest degree to K., also to Haldane, and, though it has some arguable merits, can, I am sure, never be assented to. There is, alas, constant friction between K. and F., which is part of the price one has to pay for having a military instead of a civilian Secretary of State. Winston is sure that F. and his staff

believe that when the New Armies are ready to take the
field, say about the beginning of April, K. means to
supersede French and himself take command and finish
the War.

January 7. We had a sitting of our War Council
to-day, quite a good body — self, A. J. B., K., Winston,
with his two septuagenarian sea-dogs, Fisher and Wilson, Grey, Haldane, Crewe, and Hankey. We agreed
that we now back up Sir John French in his projected
Ostend-Zeebrugge operation. W. pressed his scheme
for acquiring a base at Borkum, a big business, as it is
heavily fortified and the necessary preparations will
take till near the end of March. By May or June there
ought to be over one million men either at the Front
or available to go there, a special reserve here for making good wastage in the overseas force of nearly 400,-
000, and a Home Defence Army of about 500,000. This
is, I think, a good record. There remains for discussion the larger question of theatres and objectives, in
regard to the choice of which one must always keep
in view the chances of bringing in Italy, Rumania, and
such minor but not negligible quantities as Greece and
Bulgaria. We shall have another meeting to-morrow.

January 10. Winston writes that he has been colloguing with K. For the moment they are on the most
sugary terms, and I think both agree to advise French
to take Haig in place of Murray.

January 11. Walmer Castle. General Murray has
just been here with Winston for over an hour. We
talked over the whole situation and prospects at the
Front. He is a very attractive type of soldier, highly
cultivated and, as we both thought, extremely intelli-

gent. The real difficulty of the position is this. Joffre wants French to reoccupy what is called the Ypres Salient and Sir John is under some kind of promise to him to do so when called upon. But French cannot do this and also undertake the flank coast operation with the objective of Ostend and Zeebrugge, unless he is given at least fifty battalions more troops. If Joffre releases him from his promise he would be quite ready to go in without reinforcements for the other job, which he greatly prefers, provided he can be equipped with three or four weeks' supply of ammunition for his heavy guns. Murray told us that an English chemist, Robert Mond, brother of Sir Alfred, has a plan for undermining and causing the collapse of great works like those of La Basse by water power.

January 12. I was interrupted by a visit from Kitchener, who came, I think, principally to ventilate his indignation over Curzon's speech in the Lords the other day. He says that he has now here and in France about one and three-quarter millions of men under arms, an absolutely unexampled feat when you consider that we have only been five months at war and have lost on net balance some 80,000 men. French comes over this afternoon and is dining with K. to-night, so we shall have our War Council to-morrow.

January 13. Our War Council began at twelve, adjourned at two, and sat again. A most interesting discussion. French sat next to me on one side, A. J. B. on the other; next to French, K., then old Jackie Fisher, Winston and Sir Arthur Wilson, the naval trinity, and beyond them Crewe, Grey, and Lloyd George. French and K. were polite and almost mealy-mouthed to one another. Happily the great question upon which they are nearly at daggers-drawn—how the new K. armies are to be organized, as separate entities, or intermingled with old units—though broached, was tacitly postponed to a later and more convenient date. Winston showed a good deal of rugged fluency, if such a phrase is possible.

January 14. I had the better part of an hour with the King. He is extremely indignant about the German treatment of our prisoners, which seems to be very bad. French had been to see him and was as optimistic as ever. I told him that my view is that neither the French nor the Germans can add anything really substantial to their present forces, that the most they can do is to replace wastage, and that by the end of the summer this process will be coming to an end and they will continue to diminish. The exact reverse is the case with ourselves, and if you add the chance, or more than chance, of Italy and Rumania coming in, the odds in the long run are largely on our side.

January 20. Hankey came to see me to-day to say that Fisher, who is an old friend of his, had come to him in a very unhappy frame of mind. He likes Winston personally, but complains that on purely technical naval matters he is frequently overruled ("he out-argues me"), and he is not by any means at ease about either the present disposition of the fleets or their future movements. Though I think the old man is rather difficult, I fear there is some truth in what he says.

January 21. The main point at the moment is to do something really effective for Serbia, which is threatened by an overwhelming inrush from the Austrians,

reinforced by some 80,000 Germans. If she is allowed
to go down things will look very black for us, and the
prestige of the Allies with the wavering and hesitating
States will be seriously impaired. I have urged Grey
to put the strongest possible pressure upon Rumania
and Greece to come in without delay, and to promise
that if they will form a real Balkan *bloc* we will send
some of our troops to join them and save the situation.
I am sure that this is right and that all our side-shows,
Zeebrugge, Alexandretta, even Gallipoli, must be postponed for this. The troops must come either from
those that we already have in France, or from those
which we were going to send there. There is a report
that General Castelnau, who is one of the best French
generals, is strongly of opinion that things there have
reached a condition of stalemate, that neither side can
do more than push a little here and retreat a little there.
If so, it seems a criminal waste at such a critical time
to put in new and good troops into that theatre.

There are two fatal things in war. One is to push
blindly against a stone wall; the other is to scatter and
divide forces in a number of separate and disconnected
operations. We are in great danger of committing
both blunders. Happily K. has a good judgment in
these matters — never impulsive, sometimes inclined
to be over-cautious, but with a wide general outlook
which is of the highest value.

January 22. I have just come back from K.'s dinner
to meet Millerand. The other colleagues there were
Haldane, Grey, Lloyd George, and Winston. The
French War Minister was, of course, the principal
guest. I sat next to him at dinner. We had quite an

interesting conversation.   He cannot speak a word of
English, but was apparently able to follow my French.
He is all against Sir John French's plan, and says that
Joffre is anxious that we should pour all our troops
during the next month into his theatre, in order that
we may be organized and carry out a really effective
coup.   Of course I put to him strongly the Balkan situation and the irreparable disaster which would be involved in the crushing of Serbia.   He professed to be
quite alive to this.   Lloyd George, with the aid of an
interpreter, and E. Grey after dinner pressed our point.

I do not know what the actual upshot will be, but I
am sure it is all to the good that we should often have
these personal interchanges.   Millerand talks well,
with the inimitable French *netteté*, and is not at all
rhetorical or phrase-making.   He left on me quite a
good impression of solidity and good sense.

January 26.   Freddy Guest appeared, and brought
me some rather interesting messages from Sir John.
Firstly, the doctor reports that Sir A. Murray is so
seriously run down and bad in one lung that he must go
home for at any rate a month or two.   French would
like him to come out again when he has recovered and
command the Third Army.   He knows every inch of
the ground, and though he had not been a complete
success as Chief of the Staff, Sir J. has a very high
opinion of his general ability and I think a considerable
dread lest —— should be sent out. K. and I telegraphed
yesterday evening that we approved of Robertson as
Murray's successor, and R. has assumed his new functions to-day.   Secondly, an agreement has been come
to between Joffre and Sir John for such rearrangement

of troops as will give us the whole of the extreme left flank and put us in direct touch with the Belgians.

The Balkan situation is still very cloudy, Greece looking for the moment the most promising of the lot. The Rumanians are becoming alarmed at the concentration in Transylvania of Austrian and German troops, and a lot of Germans whom we thought were destined for Serbia have apparently been diverted into this quarter.

January 27. Beatty is satisfied that he did immense damage to at least three of the German battle cruisers.[1]

January 28. A personal matter which rather worries me is the growing friction between Winston and Fisher. They both came to see me this morning before the War Council and gave tongue to their mutual grievances. I tried to compose these differences by a compromise, under which Winston was to give up for the present his bombardment of Zeebrugge, Fisher withdrawing his opposition to the operation against the Dardanelles. When at the Council we came to discuss the latter, which is warmly supported by Kitchener and Grey and enthusiastically by A. J. B., old Jackie maintained an obstinate and ominous silence. He is always threatening to resign and writes an almost daily letter to Winston expressing his desire to return to the cultivation of his roses at Richmond. K. has now taken up the rôle of conciliator, for which one might think that he was not naturally cut out.

I have just received from Herbert Samuel a memorandum headed "The Future of Palestine." He goes

---

[1] Battle-cruiser action of January 24 in which the *Blücher* was sunk.

on to argue, at considerable length and with some vehemence, in favour of the British annexation of Palestine, a country the size of Wales, much of it barren mountain and part of it waterless. He thinks we might plant in this not very promising territory about three or four million European Jews, and that this would have a good effect upon those who are left behind. It reads almost like a new edition of "Tancred" brought up to date. I confess I am not attracted by this proposed addition to our responsibilities, but it is a curious illustration of Dizzy's favourite maxim that " race is everything " to find this almost lyrical outburst proceeding from the well-ordered and methodical brain of H. S.

January 30. We had a second meeting of the War Council before dinner on Thursday, and dispatched Winston to go and see French in order that both he and Joffre may realize the importance we attach to being able to send at any rate two divisions to help the Serbians. Winston and Fisher have, for the time at any rate, patched up their differences, though Fisher is still a little uneasy about the Dardanelles.

January 31. Walmer. Winston arrived soon after breakfast this morning, travelling, in his usual regal fashion, across the Channel in a Scout and then in a special train which was kept waiting while he spent the morning here. He was away for two whole days and, as generally happens with him, managed to see everything that was to be seen. He was recognized by the soldiers wherever he went, and was cheered by the Welsh regiments and saluted as " Good old Winston," which gave him much innocent and natural pleasure.

He had four interviews with Sir John French and a pretty hard tussle. In the end they came to a sensible compromise which both K. and I had rather urged last week, viz. that for the purpose of taking over the French lines on the left between us and the sea, which will set free a lot of Joffre's men, we should send the divisions he needs on the understanding that he will let us have two of them back to send to the Balkans some time towards the end of March, if the situation there makes it in our opinion politic.

Of course he thinks, as does Bridges, who was with the Belgians — and neither I nor Winston differ from them here — that from a purely strategic point of view it is a pity to divide your forces instead of concentrating them. But this is one of the cases where policy overrides mere strategy, and if the effect of our stepping in to the active assistance of Serbia is to bring in Rumania and Greece it would mean in material terms an addition of perhaps 800,000 men to the Allies. Winston is for the moment as keen as mustard about his Dardanelles adventure.

February 8. I had a rather interesting luncheon at Edward Grey's — Delcassé, Cambon, Kitchener, and Winston. Winston was very eloquent in the worst French anyone ever heard. *"S'ils savent que nous sommes gens qu'ils peuvent conter sur"* was one of his flowers of speech. We all agreed that the Serbian case is urgent and that we must promise to send them two divisions, one English and one French, as soon as may be to Salonika and force in the Greeks and the Rumanians. We must try to get the Russians to join if possible with a corps. Lloyd George told us he has got

Sir John French's assent to this, but I have told K. to send for him and he is coming over to-night in one of Winston's destroyers.

February 9. We have a War Council at No. 10, which Sir John French has come over to attend. The main question, of course, will be how soon, and in what form, we are to come to the aid of Serbia and whether and how far the French and Russians will join in. French will no doubt kick even at a single division being abstracted from his force, but he must be made to acquiesce in this. The two danger points at this moment are Serbia and Mesopotamia, where we have a rather weak Indian force at the confluence of the Tigris and the Euphrates threatened by what is reported to be a heavy Turkish advance. The whole situation in the Near East may be vitally transformed if the bombardment of the Dardanelles by our ships next week goes well. It is a great experiment.

Lloyd George and Montagu have just come back from Paris, where they saw all the people who count, and are much impressed by the weakness of the present French Ministry. It is a kind of Coalition Government of all the talents, its members hating and distrusting one another, afraid of the Chamber, afraid of the Press, and afraid of everything. It is, except perhaps for the poor, fugitive, exiled Belgians, by far the most unstable Government among all the belligerent Powers. Throughout the financial negotiations the Russians have shown far more backbone, and I am not sure that it is not going to be the same in the sphere of diplomacy.

We had a longish War Council which lasted from

five to seven. French was there, as always, optimistic, quite convinced that the Germans could not ever break through in France or Flanders, certain that the Russians were doing well in the Eastern theatre, and altogether sceptical as to a German-Austrian attack on Serbia. He told us amongst other things that Joffre was equipping himself with a full apparatus for bridging the Rhine. With some difficulty we brought him to the point of agreeing to send one division to Salonika, if he got a good Territorial Division in exchange.

February 10. I have been sitting the last two hours with our Committee on Food Prices, its last meeting, as we have the debate to-morrow when I must let loose such information as I have acquired. Runciman has been our best member, although the others have all contributed something, and we have a clever young Cambridge Don called Keynes as secretary. We agreed to join with France and Russia in lending the Belgians 20 millions. They are in a very bad way. A destination and use have at last been found for Winston's squadron of armoured motors which has been lying practically derelict at Wormwood Scrubs for the last two or three months. They are to be sent out to take part in the war in German South-West Africa.

A telegram came this morning from Carden, the admiral, that the operation at the Dardanelles, which was to have been begun next Monday, has had to be postponed for a few days as the requisite mine-sweepers could not be got together sooner. I hope it won't be delayed any longer, as it is all important as a preliminary to our *démarche* in the Balkans. So far it has been a well-kept secret.

February 13. I have just been having a talk with Hankey, whose views are always worth hearing. He thinks very strongly that the naval operations should be supported by the landing of a fairly strong military force, and I think we ought to be able to do this without denuding French. If only these heart-breaking Balkan States could be brought into action the trick would be done with the greatest of ease. It is of much importance that in the course of the next month we should carry through a decisive operation somewhere, and this one would do admirably for the purpose.

February 17. I have just had L. G. here for half an hour talking at large on the situation. Our Serbian *démarche* is off for the moment, as the Greeks shy at it, so our eyes are now fixed on the Dardanelles. The Dardanelles affair will begin, we hope, on Friday morning. I am very anxious to see how it develops.

February 18. Winston has been tactless enough to offer Sir John French, without K.'s knowledge, a brigade of his Naval Division and two squadrons of his famous armoured cars which are being hawked about from pillar to post. K. came to me and complained very strongly both of the folly of the offer itself, and of its being made without any previous consultation with him. French was evidently very puzzled at what to do with these unwelcome gifts, the Naval Battalions still being raw and ragged, and the only use he could suggest for the cars being to remove from them their maxim guns for the use of his troops.

Kitchener takes rather a gloomy view of the Russian situation. The Germans have undoubtedly given them a bad knock and have taken a large number of prisoners. Happily the weather there is still very wet, and the country being sodden as well as naturally swampy and wooded, the German pursuit will be hampered and the Russians may be able to get back into cover.

February 23. I had a busy and rather tiresome morning. The gale is at last abating in the region of the Dardanelles, and the ships were going to resume this morning their pounding of the forts. Winston is sending off his Naval Division on Saturday to be at hand when the military part of the operation becomes riper.

February 26. Our War Council lasted nearly two and a half hours. Winston was not at his best. K., I think on the whole rightly, insisted on keeping his 29th Division at home, free to go either to the Dardanelles or to France, until we know, as we must in the course of the next week, where the necessity is greatest. The Russians are for the moment retiring and out-manœuvred, though one knows they have a curious knack of making a good recovery. Lloyd George is anxious to go out as a kind of extra ambassador and emissary to visit Russia and all the Balkan States and try and bring them in. Grey is dead opposed to anything of the kind. We accepted K.'s view as right for the immediate situation, to Winston's unconcealed dudgeon.

February 27. Our two rhetoricians, Lloyd George and Winston, as it happens, have good brains of different types. But they can only think talking: just as some people can only think writing. Only the salt of the earth can think inside, and the bulk of mankind cannot think at all.

March 1. Winston is breast-high about the Dardanelles, particularly as to-night we have a telegram from
Venizelos announcing that the Greeks are prepared to
send three divisions of troops to Gallipoli.

March 6. The moment the military and naval situations improve the diplomatic sky begins to darken.
Russia, despite all our representations and remon-
strances, declines absolutely to allow the Greeks to have
any part in the Dardanelles business or the subsequent
advance on Constantinople, and the French appear inclined to agree with her. On the other hand, the
Greeks are burning to be part of the force which enters
Constantinople and yet wish to avoid committing themselves to fighting against anybody but the Turks and
possibly the Bulgarians. They won't raise a finger for
Serbia, and even want all the time to keep on not unfriendly terms with Germany and Austria.

In regard to things abroad there have emerged two
most infernal problems. In the first place there are
significant indications that before very long Italy may
come in on the side of the Allies. That seems natural
enough, but what is strange is that Russia strongly objects. She thinks that as Italy kept out from the stress
of the War she will demand an exorbitant territorial
prize, and that the three Allies should continue to keep
the thing entirely in their own hands. Both we and the
French take quite a different view.

The other question is the future of Constantinople
and the Straits. It has become quite clear that Russia
means to incorporate them in her own Empire. That
is the secret of her intense and obstinate hostility to the
idea of allowing the Greeks to take any share in the

present operations. I do not know how it will be
viewed in France or in this country. It is, of course, a
complete reversal of our old traditional policy.

March 10. We had our War Council this morning,
which was attended for the first time by Landsdowne
and Bonar Law. They did not contribute very much.
The main question was what we are to demand in return for the recognition of Russia's ultimate claim to
Constantinople and the Straits. I thought that Grey
did the best, and after him A. J. B.

March 12. I have just been reading the Admiral's
report of the operations so far. They are making progress, but it is slow, and there are a number of howitzers
and concealed guns which give them a good deal of
trouble. I think the Admiral is quite right to proceed
very cautiously. Winston is rather for pushing him on.
It is characteristic of W. that he has worked out since
midnight, and now sent me, a time-table according to
which Ian Hamilton, by leaving Charing Cross at five
this afternoon, can reach the Dardanelles by Monday.

March 13. I think I have already referred to Herbert Samuel's dithyrambic memorandum, urging that
in the carving up of the Turks' Asiatic dominion we
should take Palestine, into which the scattered Jews
would in time swarm back from all the quarters of the
globe, and in due course obtain Home Rule. Curiously enough, the only other partisan of this proposal
is Lloyd George, who I need not say does not care a
damn for the Jews or their past or their future, but
thinks it will be an outrage to let the Holy Places pass
into the possession or under the protectorate of " agnostic, atheistic France."

March 18. Before lunch K. came to see me and we had an interesting talk. He is really distressed and preoccupied by the reckless way in which ammunition, particularly shells, was expended last week. It works out at two shells per square yard gained. He has just sent me a private letter from Rawlinson which confirms what we suspected, that the whole operation, successful as it was, just failed being the most brilliant success in the whole war through the mishandling at a critical moment of one division. K. also showed me a very interesting telegram from Ian Hamilton, who got to the Dardanelles on Tuesday night. The Admiralty have been over-sanguine as to what they could do by ships alone. Every night the Turks under German directions repair their fortifications, and the channel is sown with complicated and constantly renewed minefields. The French general, d'Amade, arrived at the same time as Ian Hamilton, and they are going to make a really thorough and, I hope, scientific survey of the whole situation.

K. spoke to me very confidentially about French. He says he is not a really scientific soldier; a good capable leader in the field, but without adequate equipment and expert knowledge for the huge task of commanding 450,000 men. K. is going out there at the end of the week.

Meanwhile, here at home, all sorts of things are going on, and it is quite on the cards that I may create a new office for Lloyd George — Director of War Contracts, or something of the kind — and relieve him of his present duties.

March 22. I had a long interview with Cambon,

who is rather nervous about the approaching interview between Kitchener, Joffre, and Millerand. He wanted to hurry it up as his Government are apparently afraid that K. may plan out the dispositions and theatre of operations of his New Armies without due consultation with them. K. has since seen Cambon and he will probably go to France for the interview at the end of this week. He is going to-morrow to Dover to dine with Sir John French, who is coming over for a few hours. We had our little Committee, which consisted of myself, Lloyd George, A. J. B., Winston and Montagu, to consider the much-vexed question of putting the contracts for munitions on a proper footing. The discussion was quite a good one and we came to some rational conclusions. But we may have some difficulty with K., and I am going to suggest to Lloyd George, who is to be Chairman of the new Committee, that he should take on Montagu as his curate. Winston is fairly pleased with the situation in the Dardanelles and K. appears not dissatisfied.

March 23. We had a long Cabinet this morning. The news from the Dardanelles is not very good. There are more mines and concealed guns than they ever counted upon, and the Admiral seems to be in rather a funk. Ian Hamilton has not yet sent his report, but the soldiers cannot be ready for a big concerted operation before about April 14. I agree with Winston and K. that the Navy ought to make another big push so soon as the weather clears. If they wait and wait until the Army is fully prepared they may fall into a spell of bad weather or find that submarines, Austrian or German, have arrived on the scene.

March 24. K. came to see me and gave me an account of his talk with French at Dover last night. F. strongly denied that he had let off too much ammunition from his big guns in the fighting at Neuve Chapelle. On the general position he was as optimistic as ever, but rather complained that Joffre was too apt to treat him like a corporal. K. is going over himself on Sunday to make things square with Joffre, and can be trusted not only to hold his own but to carry the war into the enemy's country. K. talked at length about the proposed new War Supplies Committee of Lloyd George, Montagu and company. He is naturally rather suspicious of its intruding into his own domain, and upsetting some of his plans and arrangements. On the whole he spoke very fairly and temperately, and tomorrow morning I hope to get a *modus vivendi* between him and L. G. Winston came to talk about the Dardanelles. The weather is infamous there and the naval experts seem to be suffering from a fit of nerves.

March 25. Massingham came here with a horrible tale which he swears can be proved to be true on the best authority. It is that Winston is intriguing hard to supplant E. Grey at the Foreign Office and to put A. J. B. in his place. There is no doubt that Winston is at the moment a complete victim to B.'s charm. Lloyd George has been here for his favourite morning indulgence, ten minutes' discursive discussion on things in general. I asked him what he thought of the Massingham story, and rather to my surprise he said he believed it was substantially true. He thinks that Winston has, for the time at any rate, allowed himself to be swallowed whole by A. J. B., on whom he, L. G., after

working with him for a week or two, is now disposed
to be rather severe. It is a pity that Winston has not
a better sense of proportion. I am really fond of him,
but I regard his future with many misgivings. I do not
think he will ever get to the top in English politics with
all his wonderful gifts. By the way, it is characteristic
of L. G.'s versatility of interest and mind that, though
he was on his way to a deputation of working men,
whom he is going to try to cajole to accept his terms,
and has to go through a similar proceeding with the
employers to-morrow, he is for the moment red-hot with
a plan, or rather an idea, for nationalizing the drink
trade. He has had a lot of brewers with him at and
after breakfast and has already made an appointment
with two skilled accountants to go into figures this
afternoon. I warned him to go warily, as a State
monopoly in drink would, I think, be a most dangerous
thing politically.

Grey and I had a really interesting conversation
about the whole international situation. Winston is
very anxious that if, when the War ends, Russia has got
Constantinople, and Italy Dalmatia, and France Syria,
we should be able to appropriate some equivalent share
of the spoils — Mesopotamia with or without Alexandretta, a sphere in Persia, and some German colonies, etc. I believe that at the moment Grey and I are
the only two men who doubt and distrust any such
settlement. We both think that in the real interests of
our own future the best thing would be if at the end of
the War we could say that we had taken and gained
nothing, and this not from a merely moral and senti-
mental point of view. Taking Mesopotamia, for in-

stance, means spending millions in irrigation and development with no immediate or early return, keeping up quite a large army in an unfamiliar country, tackling every kind of tangled administrative question, worse than any we have ever had in India, with a hornets' nest of Arab tribes, and even if that were all set right having a perpetual menace on our flank in Kurdistan. The great thing for the moment is to bring in Italy.

March 28. I have a tiresome pouch this morning from Bongie. There is a truly royal row on the stocks between Kitchener and Lloyd George in regard to the proposed Committee on Munitions. Neither is disposed to give way. K. threatens to give up his office and L. G. to wash his hands of the whole business, leaving on record all sorts of solemn protests and warnings. Montagu, who revels in gloomy situations, sends me a dirge of considerable length.

March 29. The Italians, Edward Grey tells me, are slightly contracting the orifice of their gullet, and would now be content to neutralize the Dalmatian Coast from Spalato southwards, provided they can keep and fortify the outlying islands. The Russians are still on the haggle, and it is not likely that any final agreement will be reached before Wednesday. In the circumstances I told him that I shall take on the Foreign Office work, instead of either Haldane or Crewe, for at any rate a week or ten days, while he takes a rest.

Finally I had an extraordinary and really very interesting talk with L. G. We first tried to get at a working arrangement with Kitchener about the Munitions Committee, and I think we hit upon something that ought to do. Then before he left I said I thought it right to tell him that only to-day I had heard the sinister and, as I believed, absurd interpretations which were being given to the articles in *The Times, Observer,* and *Morning Post.* I have never seen him more moved. He vehemently disclaimed having anything to do with the affair. Kitchener, he said, is the real culprit because in spite of every warning he has neglected up to the eleventh hour the proper provision of munitions, and K. being a Tory, or supposed to be one, the Tory Press, afraid to attack him, are making me the target of their criticism.

As for himself (L. G.) he declared that he owed everything to me, that I had stuck to him and protected him and defended him when every man's hand was against him, and that he would rather (1) break stones, (2) dig potatoes, (3) be hung and quartered (these were metaphors used at different stages of his broken but impassioned harangue) than do an act or say a word or harbour a thought that was disloyal to me, and he said that every one of his colleagues felt the same. His eyes were wet with tears, and I am sure that, with all his Celtic capacity for impulsive and momentary fervour, he was quite sincere. Of course I assured him that I had never for a moment doubted him, which is quite true, and he warmly wrung my hand and abruptly left the room.

March 30. L. G. and McKenna came here at 3.30 and we had an hour together. It was at moments rather exciting. L. G. began on a very stormy note, accusing McKenna of having inspired Donald to write the article in the *Chronicle* which was headed " Intrigue against the P.M." McKenna as hotly denied that he had ever said or suggested to Donald that L. G. was in the plot, while admitting that he had had a talk with him on the subject of the attacks in the Tory Press. L. G. proceeded to accuse McKenna of always seeing or imagining plots, *e.g.* in this very matter of Winston's supposed campaign against Grey, to which McKenna rejoined that the person he really suspected was A. J. B. There was a lot of hitting and counter-hitting between them, but I am glad to say that in the end I not only lowered the temperature but got them into first an accommodating and in the end an almost friendly mood. I have now to perform a similar, but I hope easier, operation between K. and L. G. in the matter of the Munitions Committee.

March 31. The most serious thing I have done to-day is to try to compose the Kitchener and Lloyd George dispute about the new Committee. I think I shall probably succeed, particularly as L. G. is now off thinking of anything but drink and K. is preoccupied with shells. No sooner had I settled the row between L. G. and McKenna and all but settled the earlier row between Lloyd George and K. than this versatile and volatile personage goes off at a tangent on the question of drink. His mind apparently oscillates from hour to hour between the two poles of absurdity, cutting off all drink from the working man — which would lead to something like a universal strike — or buying out the whole liquor trade of the country and replacing it by a huge State monopoly.

April 1. In this very room in which only two days ago L. G. and McKenna were fighting like fishwives, the same pair have just been and spent over half an hour with me cooing like sucking doves in a concerted chorus of argument and appeal to bring me round to take a favourable view of L. G.'s latest scheme for buying out the drink trade at a cost of some 250 millions. You never saw two people on such friendly and even intimate terms or any such complete and happy concord. I am bound to say they have left me entirely unconvinced, and indeed neither of them seems to have had time to think out even the elements of the problem. Upon one point we are all agreed, that it is not the least use even bringing such a proposition before the Cabinet. Lloyd George, whose sanguine temperament is never easily daunted, is accordingly going to utilize his Easter holidays in a daring attempt to reconcile all the warring interests.

I spent most of the afternoon at the Foreign Office and saw in turn the Italian, French and Russian Ambassadors. I had a stiff argument with the Italian, who was afraid to concede anything. I am disposed to think they will give way.

April 5. A lot of Foreign Office stuff came in yesterday and to-day, but nothing very encouraging. The Italians are still holding out for their one and a half pounds of flesh, but I do not mean to give them up, particularly now that it is clear that Rumania will be inclined to hang back until they definitely come in. The delay in the Dardanelles is very unfortunate. Visible progress and, still more, a theatrical coup in that quarter would have goaded all the laggard States into the arena.

April 6. I had a hopeful talk with Imperiali at the

Foreign Office this afternoon, and I am much more sanguine than I was twenty-four hours ago about Italy. It would be a great reward for a week or ten days at the Foreign Office if that could be brought off. We had rather a stormy assemblage here yesterday afternoon, K., L. G., A. J. B., Montagu and myself. To-morrow I mean to settle the thing finally one way or the other about the Munitions Committee. I gather that afterwards L. G. and Winston nearly came to blows, but Winston tells me that this morning he has had an apologetic letter.

April 8. Lloyd George has been here expounding his great scheme for buying out and nationalizing the liquor trade. He is engaged in his usual process of roping in everybody, Opposition leaders, Labour, temperance men, etc., and is persuaded that he will succeed in getting them all. Meanwhile I have appointed a Munitions Committee with the fullest possible powers.

April 14. Rodd telegraphed last night that the delay in Italy is due only to the necessity of consulting the King and that he is sanguine that it will be all right.

April 15. We had a really interesting Committee, Lloyd George, Crewe, McKenna, McKinnon Wood, Samuel, Montagu, Lord Reading and Charles Roberts on the great drink question. I only came to-day in order if possible to administer the *coup de grâce* to the nationalization proposition. L. G. did not press it against my judgment, and has produced an ingenious substitute of much more modest dimensions, which we are now discussing. The whole thing bristles with the most contentious points. The result is that L. G. is going to open a new series of *pourparlers* with brewers, teetotallers, and the whole motley crowd of interests.

April 16. I have been through a rather stormy experience. K., who is evidently a good deal perturbed, has been attacking L. G. for having disclosed to the Munitions Committee the figures which he, K., had confidentially communicated to the Cabinet. He declares that he can no longer be responsible for the War Office under such conditions. L. G. and Winston are both (the former having quite a presentable case) aggressive, and the situation is for the moment all the worse, particularly as Grey, a good deal to L. G.'s chagrin, strongly champions Kitchener. All this has come literally like a bolt out of the blue. I had not the faintest premonition of it. However, by dint of appeals and warnings and gives and takes and all sorts of devices and expedients, I have succeeded in getting us back into more or less smooth water. Still, it leaves a disagreeable taste in one's mouth, particularly as L. G. let slip in the course of the altercation some injurious and wounding innuendoes which K. will be more than human to forget.

Later. I have been talking it over with Crewe, whose judgment I rate highest of any of my colleagues. Not for years—and he agrees with me—have I been more disillusioned from the personal point of view and depressed. The man who comes out of it best is Kitchener, clumsy in expression as he often is. As Crewe says, he is one who has been all his life accustomed either to take or to give orders, and he therefore finds it difficult to accommodate himself to the give and take of Cabinet discussion and comradeship. He was really moved to-day, though I am sure he would not have persisted in his resignation, and showed in the end a largeness of mind and temper which I greatly admired.   I hate this side of politics, for it compels one to revise for the worse one's estimate of men whom one likes.

April 17.   K. referred to his talk with Sir John French.   He, K., says he is supplying not only our troops but the French with ammunition, or at any rate with explosives.

April 19.   We did a little good work at the Cabinet to-day of a destructive kind.   The Great Purchase Folly is as dead as Queen Anne, though McKenna and Runciman are still disposed to drop a perfunctory tear over its grave, not, however, for love of it, but to discredit its successor and substitute.

To-day I am glad to say we also cleared out of the way total prohibition, whether of spirits or of heavy beers.   Altogether the thing is beginning to assume some rational dimensions.

May 3.   I had rather an interesting talk with K.   He is strongly for our retaliating against the Germans with asphyxiating shells.   The news from the Dardanelles is satisfactory, and K. has no doubt that we shall break through.   The interesting place for the moment is the Flanders side of France.   Relations are very strained between Joffre and French.   K., however, for the first time takes a very optimistic view of this part of the field.   He thinks he has evidence that the Germans have resolved to fall back on a considerable scale, in fact to shorten their line and substantially reduce their numbers in the West.   It looks as if they knew by this time that Italy is coming in and are preparing to meet the new dangers in the East and South.

Next there appeared L. G., who came ostensibly to talk about to-morrow's Budget, which will be a humdrum affair. He, as usual, launched out into irrelevant topics, amongst others an interview he had to-day with Bonar Law on the subject of the drink taxes. Bonar Law seems to have told him frankly that the Tory party was so much in the hands of the Trade that they must oppose these root and branch. L. G. replied that if so he could not persist with them, and he would throw the whole responsibility for doing nothing in that direction on the Tories.

May 11. We had a Cabinet this morning of a rather straggling kind. There is no very good news from any quarter, but K. is still fairly hopeful about the Russians, who generally manage after a hard knock to swing back again. There was a lot of talk about the *Lusitania* and the United States. The one thing to fear and avoid is that they should be provoked to prohibit the export of munitions of war to us, which would be almost fatal. I do not think that in their present mood they are in the least likely to do anything of the kind, but in view of possibilities K. has conceived the grandiose idea of transplanting to Canada three or four big works which are now making guns and shells for us in the States.

CHAPTER VII

LORD KITCHENER AND MUNITIONS [1]

LORD FRENCH, in his book "1914," charged the Government of the day, and Lord Kitchener in particular, with deliberate and criminal apathy in the supply of munitions. His statement teems with unpardonable inaccuracies. Some of them, which are in flat contradiction to contemporary documents, I felt bound, as soon as they appeared, in justice to Lord Kitchener's memory, to expose.[2]

Lord Kitchener, who was assisted in this matter from the first month of the War by a strong Cabinet Committee, laboured night and day to enlarge the area of supply and to multiply the output. What had actually been achieved in the first six months was set out in detail in a speech in the House of Commons on April 21, 1915, by Mr. Lloyd George, who had become Chairman of the Munitions Committee. The armies in the field had been multiplied between four and five times; the supply of munitions nineteenfold. Between two thousand and three thousand firms, not previously so employed, had been brought into the industry. The multiplication of factories, the diversion and dilution of labour, the more extensive employment of women, had been pressed upon all the departments by Lord

---

[1] This chapter to a large extent reproduces what I wrote in my appreciation of Kitchener in *Pearson's Magazine*.

[2] In a speech delivered at the Connaught Rooms, London, June 3, 1919, and republished in a pamphlet entitled "The Great Shell Story" (Cassell, London, 1919). The real facts are fully stated there.

Kitchener in the spring of 1915 with constant and ever-increasing urgency. One of our most eminent scientific men, Lord Moulton, had, at his instance, been engaged ever since November, 1914, in the development and fabrication of high explosives. Immense orders had been placed both in America and Canada. By the end of April, 1915, we were, despite heart-rending delays in delivery by contractors, producing in three days the amount of ammunition produced before the War in a whole year. Never was there a case in which the charge of apathy or lethargy was worse founded.

The prospect, however, in the near future was a very serious one. It was not our business to encourage the enemy by revealing the nature and extent of our disquietudes, which were great and real. It was for that reason that both Mr. Lloyd George and I were careful to say, on Lord Kitchener's authority, that there was no immediate dearth at the Front. That Lord Kitchener did not give us those assurances without full inquiry is shown by the letter which he addressed to me on April 14.

Secret.

WAR OFFICE,
WHITEHALL, S.W.

MY DEAR PRIME MINISTER, —

I have had a talk with French. He told me I could let you know that with the present supply of ammunition he will have as much as his troops will be able to use on the next forward movement.

I think the next move will be much better than the last, with co-operation from the French forces, which failed last time.

Yours very truly,
KITCHENER.

LORD KITCHENER

We now know that a fortnight later — on May 2 — a week before the battle of Festubert, Sir J. French concluded a letter to Lord Kitchener with the words, "The ammunition will be all right."[1]

But, subject to that condition, it was of the utmost importance to arouse public opinion at home to the gravity of the need. Accordingly, on March 15, Lord Kitchener made one of his rare appearances in the House of Lords. It was just after the battle of Neuve Chapelle, where nearly as much artillery ammunition was spent as was spent by our army during the whole two and three-quarter years of the Boer War. He delivered a solemn and reasoned appeal to employers and workmen. I myself in the following month (April 20) went to Newcastle to urge that, in view of these new exigencies, wholly unforeseen by any of the combatants, and the consequent prospect of a serious shortage, the provision of munitions had become even more vitally important than the progress of recruiting.

The task had become too great for an already over-burdened department, and Lord Kitchener completely approved of the creation of the Ministry of Munitions, which afterwards did such admirable work. But it is bare justice to him to put it on record that, throughout the serious fighting in the autumn and winter, 1914–15, there was never any lack of ammunition, and that until the late spring of 1915 the armies in the field were entirely supplied by War Office deliveries. A singularly competent historian, Professor A. F. Pollard,[2] thus describes the situation on the Western Front in the early autumn of 1915:

[1] Arthur's "Life of Lord Kitchener," Vol. III, p. 236.
[2] "Short History of the Great War," p. 164.

The Entente advantage in bayonets on the Western Front was between three and four to two, and it had also the ampler reserves. Sir John French commanded nearly a million of men, and General Joffre more than double that number, while our advantage in guns and machines was not less marked; an almost unlimited supply of shells had been accumulated during the summer.

Meanwhile, there was set on foot a violent newspaper campaign, directed mainly against Lord Kitchener, and engineered, as we know from Lord French's avowals, by the Commander-in-Chief in France himself, behind the backs of his official chief and the Prime Minister.[1] It is quite possible, and certainly not unnatural, that Lord Kitchener should at, or about this time, have said or written: "I am deadly sick of this system of intrigue." But he never allowed it to ruffle or rattle him. He treated with what Matthew Arnold calls a quiet deep disdain the clamorous cat-calls of a section of the Press. He showed both equanimity and magnanimity. "I am out," he said, "to fight the Germans, and not to fight Sir John French."

I confess I never knew until I read Lord French's statement that it was to him we owed the Coalition Government. Whether Lord Kitchener or I was the chief villain of the piece, we both retained our old offices; and while I should be the last, and will always be the last, to belittle the splendid work which was subsequently done by the Ministry of Munitions, to the formation of which I was a principal party, and which, in the early days of its life when there was a good deal

---

[1] He "furnished evidence" to *The Times* correspondent, Colonel Repington; and he sent over here his A.D.C. Captain Guest, to lay this "evidence" before leading statesmen of the Opposition.

of friction with the War Office, I strongly backed with all the authority that I possessed — yet Lord French appeared to have forgotten that during the whole of the time that he remained in command in France, and for months afterwards, the British Army in France and in Flanders lived and fought with great determination and with many successes on the ammunition ordered by the old regime, before the Ministry of Munitions came into existence.

Lord French's suggestion that his action in the matter had something to do with his subsequent removal from the command is hardly worthy of serious notice. He remained in full command for more than six months, and though I heard strange rumours I never took the pains to inquire what part he had played, or whether he had played any part, in the newspaper campaign he claims to have inspired.

When his retirement came I took myself, as will presently appear, the full and sole responsibility for it. It was for reasons which had no more to do with the supply of shells than with the next eclipse of the moon.

His whole case was that he was obliged to do what he did because in the highest interests of the Empire it was essential to get rid of an apathetic Government, negligent of its first duty to the Army and presided over by a supine and lethargic head. But I have a letter in his own writing, addressed to me from Headquarters of the British Armies in France, and dated May 20, 1915, three days after I had taken steps to form the Coalition Ministry, for which Lord French claims a sort of parental responsibility. It is a private letter to which I should not have referred had not Lord

French, who himself made the freest use of secret and confidential documents, compelled me, by his statements, to do so.

HEAD-QUARTERS, BRITISH ARMY,
May 20, 1915.

MY DEAR PRIME MINISTER, —

For two days I have been hesitating to add one iota to the troubles and anxieties which must weigh upon you just now. You have, however, shown me so much true, generous kindness throughout this trying campaign that I venture at this critical juncture to convey to you what is in my inmost thoughts. I am sure in the whole history of war no General in the field has ever been helped in a difficult task by the head of his Government as I have been supported and strengthened by your unfailing sympathy and encouragement.

My own acquaintance with Lord Kitchener before August, 1914, was very slight. His visits to England were rare and irregular. Whenever he came it was my practice to invite him to attend the meetings of the Committee of Imperial Defence, where more than once we profited by his special knowledge. On one of my official visits to the Mediterranean, he came over from Egypt to Malta (strangely enough in the same cruiser, the *Hampshire,* in which years later he met his fate) to confer with Mr. Churchill and myself on the naval and military situation in that part of the world. It was impossible not to be impressed with his striking and formidable personality, and his actual achievements in the East and in South Africa had shown a resourcefulness and versatility which are not always at the command of even the most accomplished soldier.

At the beginning of August, 1914, I was still combining the two offices of Prime Minister and Secretary of State for War, and it was plain that I must hand over the second of those posts to another. Lord Kitchener's appointment was "represented," to use my own words, nearly three years later (March 20, 1917) in the House of Commons, "as having been forced upon a reluctant Cabinet by the overwhelming pressure of our intelligent and prescient Press." The truth was, that the only person whom I ever thought of as my successor was Lord Kitchener, who happened by a stroke of good fortune to be at that moment in this country on the point of returning to Egypt. Lord Haldane, who had re-created our army, warmly approved of my choice.

From that day, for nearly two years, Lord Kitchener and I were in the closest and most intimate contact. Except during his few and brief absences in France and the Dardanelles, he came to see me every day, generally more than once, often three and four times. With the single exception of the devoted Fitzgerald, who perished with him, there was, I believe, no one to whom he opened his mind and heart more fully and with less reserve.

Kitchener was a great man with certain obvious limitations: some of them congenital, others the natural, perhaps the necessary, results of the environment of his past career. He was disposed to be secretive, and did not find it easy to throw his knowledge and judgment into the common stock. It is, however, an absurd travesty of the facts to say that at the War Office he "neither asked nor took the advice of any man." He was to my knowledge, from the day when he took over the post, in constant communication and consultation with that great soldier, the lamented Sir John Cowans, the Quartermaster-General, whose department with a stupendous and ever-growing burden of responsibility during the whole course of the War not only never broke down, but exhibited no sign of strain or stress.

Lord Kitchener had perforce in the first months to be in effect his own Chief of the Staff. All the men qualified by special knowledge for the post were on active service at the Front. But he attached, as I did, the greatest importance to bringing into the staff at the War Office officers who had had actual daily experience of the new methods of warfare in France and elsewhere. It was for this, among other reasons, that first Sir Archibald Murray, and after him Sir William Robertson, were given the post of Chief of the General Staff. Robertson, before he would accept the office (in December, 1915), wisely, in my opinion, insisted upon certain conditions which would define its functions and safeguard its independent authority. Lord Kitchener reluctantly and somewhat grudgingly acquiesced, but, having accepted them, he loyally submitted to them, and from that time until his death there was between him and the Chief of the Staff complete and cordial co-operation.

"As to the alleged habit of over-centralization," Robertson says in his autobiography, "From Private to Field-Marshal," "it was never displayed during the six months that I had the privilege of working with him, and he was as ready to listen to the advice of his departmental heads as were any of the other seven Secretaries of State under whom I have worked. . . . He was a kind and delightful chief to serve, once his ways were understood " (pp. 287–8).[1]

Kitchener was entirely without the drawback of personal vanity or self-consciousness. He did not pose for posterity; he never laid himself out either for contemporary or posthumous applause. I was once urging upon him the importance of ignoring the rules of seniority and promoting young officers of promise. He replied that he had been himself twelve years, I think, a subaltern in the Royal Engineers. Two years later he had become a major or lieutenant-colonel in the Egyptian cavalry. Every man, he said, gets his chance.

He was, perhaps, a little lacking in the corrective sense of humour, which is a rare and invaluable asset. But he was quite aware of his own foibles, such as they were, and did not in the least mind being rallied about them.

It is well known that he was, if not a connoisseur, a diligent and assiduous collector of objects of art. There were all sorts of legends, more or less authentic, of the methods by which in every variety of climate and environment, he was supposed to have pursued one of the capital designs of life — the adorning and enriching of his Kentish home. I will give an illustration which I can personally attest.

On one of my visits to the Front in the first year of the War — I think it must have been in June or July, 1915 — I accompanied Lord Kitchener from our headquarters at St. Omer to Ypres. It was a stormy day; the German guns had for a few hours relaxed their

[1] See also his testimony in "Soldiers and Statesmen" (1926).

150700

activity; and the gutted houses were swaying like fabrics of cardboard in the wind. We found ourselves, with a retinue of generals and staff officers, in the Grande Place, confronting the magnificent ruin of the famous Cloth Hall. Large parts of the fine arcades of statues were still intact, and I observed that Kitchener was scanning them with an expert's gaze. A young staff officer came up to me, and nudging my elbow, said: "Do you see that? Those statues have been bombarded by the Germans for a hundred days, but they have never been in such danger as they are at this moment."

"Do you mean," I replied, "that we may some day hope to see one or more of them at Broome Park?"

The audacious youth nodded, and disappeared quickly into space, nor, to my regret, was I ever able to establish his identity.

As we drove back I related the conversation to Kitchener, who — far from showing any sign of resentment — was genuinely and immensely amused.

The last week of his life was a busy one, and, to him, the happiest he had spent since the first day of the War. It began with the auspicious news of the great sea battle of Jutland. A day or two later his salary came on for discussion in the House of Commons, and after his critics had said their worst, a vote of confidence in him was carried by an imposing majority. On June 2, 1916, at his own suggestion, he attended a large private meeting of members of Parliament, addressed to them a memorable speech in vindication of his administration, and submitted himself to cross-examination. He completely carried his audience with him, and the

meeting ended with a unanimous resolution of gratitude and admiration.

On the evening of the same day he came to see me to
say good-bye. He was in the highest spirits, and described with gusto and humour some of his friendly
passages of arms with his hecklers at the House. He
left the room gay, alert, elastic, sanguine.

I never saw him again.

Kitchener's destination was Petrograd on a mission
to the Russian Government, and I have always thought,
and still think, that his arrival there might have de-
flected the subsequent course of history. The diplomatist, whom Grey and I had selected to be, on the
political side of his task, his chief adviser, was Hugh
O'Beirne, who had not only in the course of his career
been, before the War, for something like ten years a
member of our Embassy at St. Petersburg, but had also,
from the various posts which he had held, an almost
unique knowledge of the tangled relationships of the
Balkan States. He came from an Irish Roman Catholic family, and had gone with me on my visit to Rome
in May, 1916. He was present at my interview with
Pope Benedict XV, and was in attendance when, for
two days, I had the honour of accompanying King Victor Emmanuel in a tour which embraced both the
Julian and the Isonzo fronts. I had formed a high
opinion of his capacity, and, like all who knew him
well, a strong personal affection for himself.

It was part of the arranged programme that he was
to go by the same train as Kitchener to Sir John Jellicoe's fleet, where the cruiser *Hampshire* was to take the
whole mission through the Baltic to Petrograd. By

some mistake O'Beirne was driven to Charing Cross instead of King's Cross station, and missed the train to the North. He chartered a special train, and by a melancholy mischance arrived just in time to join his Chief, and to share his tragic fate.

The Russian situation at the moment was, both on the financial and the military side, precarious, but it was not an unreasonable hope that it might be reinstated and stabilized by the powerful personality of Lord Kitchener, whose prestige both with the Allies and their enemies was at its highest point. It must be remembered that, even six months later, when Lord Milner's mission had been dispatched on a similar errand, the most experienced and clear-sighted observers had no prevision of the Revolution which had then become imminent, and which not only swept aside the Tsardom, but in time submerged in its own swelling torrent the Miliukovs and the Kerenskys, and, when the waters subsided, presented the world with the spectacle of a Bolshevik Russia with Lenin as its autocrat.

If the *Hampshire* had not been struck and sunk by a hidden mine, there would have been a problem the less for the writers of hypothetical history.

CHAPTER VIII

THE DARDANELLES: LORD FISHER'S RESIGNATION

THE Government were ill-advised enough, yielding to parliamentary pressure, to consent in the second year of the War to the appointment of two Royal Commissions, to inquire respectively into the campaigns in the Dardanelles and Mesopotamia. The one was presided over by Lord Cromer, and the other by Lord George Hamilton. It was a mistaken procedure, as the reports were presented to Parliament without the evidence upon which they purported to be founded, the reason alleged being that, as hostilities were still going on, it was impossible to run the risk of disclosing matters which might be useful to the enemy and embarrassing to the Allies. This might have been a good ground for deferring publication till the close of the War, but as the reports were studded with references to the evidence that was for the time withheld, the persons affected by the conclusions—politicians, diplomatists, sailors, soldiers—were obviously placed in an unfair and embarrassing position.

The reports, however, produced very little effect. The earliest and most important of them—the first report of the Dardanelles Commission—did not survive four hours' debate in the House of Commons, in the course of which it was riddled by the criticisms of Mr. Churchill and myself.

The commissioners had gone out of their way to express the opinion that for the first four months of the War our machinery was both "clumsy and inefficient." This, as I pointed out in my speech, was a mere *obiter dictum,* but it gave me the opportunity to describe, as clearly as I could, the organization which during those early months was actually at work. It consisted of the Cabinet, the War Council (corresponding to the Committee of Imperial Defence in pre-War times) and the heads of the executive departments with their staffs and expert advisers.

The mode of procedure was as follows:

The daily conduct of the operations of the War was in the hands of the Ministers responsible for the Army and Navy in constant consultation with the Prime Minister. When serious questions involving new departures in policy or joint strategic operations arose, the War Council with the expert advisers of Army, Navy, and sometimes Foreign Office, was summoned. The proceedings of the War Council were exactly similar to that which had prevailed at the Committee of Imperial Defence. When a conclusion was reached, it was formulated in writing, and read out either at once or at the end of the meeting by the chairman, as had always been the case at the Committee. The only change which I made was that, for greater certainty and security, the conclusions were immediately after the meeting circulated in writing to the departments concerned: in cases of urgency, on the same day. There was never any excuse for want of precision or for delay.

As to the position of the experts, it was precisely the same as it had always been at the Committee of Imperial Defence. They were there — it was the reason for

their being there — to give the lay members the benefit
of their opinion and advice. During ten years' experience of the Committee of Imperial Defence I have
never know them to show the least reluctance to do so,
invited or uninvited, and that was the view taken by
all my ministerial colleagues on the War Council.

In regard to the Cabinet, it never abdicated its ultimate authority, though it, very properly as I think,
was content normally to delegate the active conduct of
the War to the Ministers concerned and the War Council. All important steps were reported to it, and there
were times when it took an active part and asserted its
overruling authority.

I am not going over the ground — much travelled,
and already covered with the dust of controversy — of
the merits or demerits of the Dardanelles Expedition,
or of its chequered fortunes, naval and military, which
were one of the many subjects of our constant solicitude
throughout the year 1915. But I must in justice both to
Lord Fisher and my colleagues in the Government say
a few words as to its inception and its earliest stages.

Early in January, 1915, the Grand Duke Nicholas,
Commander-in-Chief of the Russian armies, made a
strong appeal to the Allies to combine in striking a serious and, if possible, decisive blow in the Eastern theatre
of the War. The consequences — political, diplomatic,
economic, strategic — of a successful operation of the
kind were almost incalculable. The continued concentration at that moment of all effort and resources on the
West — the leaving of the East, so far as England and
France were concerned, practically derelict — might
have been fatal to the general cause of the Allies. That

was, I believe, the opinion of every member, with a single exception, of the War Council at that time.

After careful consideration of other alternatives, an expedition to the Dardanelles, with Constantinople as its objective, was resolved upon as the most likely to attain the desired result. But the only practicable way under the then existing conditions was not—as every one would have preferred—a joint naval and military expedition, but a naval expedition alone. Why? Because Lord Kitchener, who strongly favoured the project, declared that he had not available a sufficient number of troops for the purpose.

So far from the War Council (as the report of the commissioners suggests) taking no steps to satisfy themselves as to the correctness of Lord Kitchener's calculation, they spent the best part of three whole days— January 7, 8, and 13—in surveying in the most comprehensive manner, and in the greatest detail, all our available resources in men and the calls which could be made upon them. Sir John French was sent for from France on purpose to assist in this investigation. We satisfied ourselves that Lord Kitchener was right, and accordingly on January 13 the Admiralty were ordered to prepare plans for an expedition, mainly naval in character, in February.

The final decision was postponed for a fortnight, and meanwhile the French Admiralty was consulted, expressed its approval, and promised its co-operation.

Then came, on January 28, the critical meeting of the War Council at which the final decision was taken. I assert unhesitatingly that at this time the whole of our expert naval opinion was in favour of a naval operation. It is true that Lord Fisher disliked it. But his opinion, as he told me the same morning, was not based upon the technical or strategic demerits of a Dardanelles operation, but upon the fact that he preferred another and totally different objective in the Baltic. In that opinion, as Lord Kitchener appears to have pointed out to him, he was on the War Council in a minority of one. It was no doubt for that reason that he did not press his view. At the evening meeting the same day, in Lord Fisher's presence and with his consent, it was announced that he had decided to undertake the operation.

A fortnight later (February 16) there was an important new development. The 29th Division — a fine Regular division — which had previously been earmarked for other purposes, was believed to be now at liberty, and the repulse of the Turkish attack on the Suez Canal at the beginning of February had set free also a substantial part of the Egyptian garrison. The War Council ordered the division and a contingent of troops from Egypt to go to the Dardanelles to the support of the fleet.

Lord Kitchener was urgently pressed by both the British and French commanders in France not to divert the 29th Division from their theatre, and for the moment yielded to their appeals. With much reluctance his civilian colleagues deferred to his decision, and it was not until March 10 that he raised his embargo, and consented to the dispatch of the division to the East. There is no doubt that this delay of three weeks gave the Turks time to improve their defences. The first naval attack — March 19 — failed in its purpose; the admiral on the spot deemed it unwise to renew it; and the actual landing did not take place until April 25.

Personally I was anxious, as I believe was Mr. Churchill, that the naval attack should be pushed. I thought at the time, and am still disposed to think, that it offered the best prospect for the prompt success of the expedition. But naval and military opinion was on the whole decidedly adverse to taking such a risk.

Apart from its later strategic developments, the early course of the Dardanelles operation had important political consequences at home. It led to the resignation of Lord Fisher.

On May 12 I received a letter from him of which the material part is as follows:

It will be in your recollection that you saw me and the First Lord of the Admiralty in your private room prior to a meeting of the War Council to consider my protest against the Dardanelles undertaking when it was first mooted. With extreme reluctance and largely due to earnest words spoken to me by Kitchener I by not resigning (*as I see now I should have done*) remained a most unwilling beholder (and indeed a participator) of the gradual draining of our naval resources from the decisive theatre of the War.

Enclosed was a memorandum for the War Council (dated May 11) in which he announced that he could not be a party to any order to Admiral de Robeck to make an attempt to pass the Dardanelles "until the shores have been effectively occupied."

This was followed almost immediately by a letter (undated) in the following terms:

My dear Prime Minister,—

As I find it increasingly difficult to adjust myself to the increasing policy of the First Lord in regard to the Dardanelles I have been reluctantly compelled to inform him this day that I am unable to remain as his colleague — and I am leaving at once for Scotland so as not to be embarrassed or embarrass you by any explanations with anyone.

Your admiring Master of Balliol said *"Never explain"* — but I am sure you will understand my position.

Yours truly,

FISHER.

I enclose a copy of my letter of resignation to the First Lord.

In the letter of resignation to the First Lord, dated May 15, Lord Fisher says, "I find it increasingly difficult to adjust myself to the increasing daily requirements of the Dardanelles to meet your views — as you truly said yesterday, I am in the position of continually vetoing your proposals. This is not fair to you, besides being extremely distasteful to me. I am off to Scotland at once to avoid all questionings."

When I received this letter I at once sent to the Admiralty to ascertain Lord Fisher's whereabouts. I was told that he had disappeared without leaving any address. I accordingly wrote him a peremptory letter ordering him in the King's name to return at once to his post, which I entrusted to Mr. Masterton Smith, the First Lord's private secretary, with instructions that it should reach Lord Fisher, if he could be found, without delay. The German fleet, it was believed, had actually put to sea, and a decisive battle might well have been fought with no First Sea Lord functioning: an intolerable position. Mr. Masterton Smith succeeded in getting my message into Lord Fisher's hands and he returned to the Admiralty.

The three junior Sea Lords thereupon addressed to the First Lord and the First Sea Lord the following Minute, which is initialled by them all with the date (May 16).

FIRST LORD.
FIRST SEA LORD.

The First Sea Lord has caused us to be informed of his resignation and to be shown a copy of certain minutes which have passed from the First Lord to him and vice versa.

It appears from these documents that Lord Fisher's resignation is due to two causes.

(1) Disagreement with First Lord as to the conduct of the naval operations in the Dardanelles. And

(2) Dissatisfaction with the procedure adopted for the executive control of the movements of the Fleet.

With regard to (1) we stated in a minute to the First Sea Lord, dated April 8, that we have not sufficient acquaintance with the political situation to enable us to form an opinion as to the correctness of the policy, and this holds good as to the conduct of the operations: but as we said then, and now repeat, we hold that these operations most certainly jeopardize the crushing superiority of the Grand Fleet which is essential to the successful prosecution of the War.[1]

With regard to (2) we associate ourselves with Lord Fisher, and are of opinion that the present method of directing the distribution of the Fleet, and the conduct of the War by which the orders for controlling movements and supplies appear to be largely taken out of the hands of the First Sea Lord is open to very grave objection.

However dissatisfied we may feel with the present procedure we recognize that we are faced with a national crisis of the first magnitude, and that the disastrous consequences which must inevitably follow on Lord Fisher's resignation must be averted.

---

[1] It is to be noted that all the battleships (with a single exception) sent to the Dardanelles were of an obsolescent type, and, though well fitted for hammering the Turkish forts, would have been of little, if any, value in a naval action.

Whatever differences of opinion or defects in procedure may have arisen or become apparent should be capable of adjustment by mutual discussion and concession, and we therefore venture to urge you both to consider whether the national interests do not demand that you should follow the advice we have tendered.

Mr. Churchill informs me that he replied to the three admirals that no order had ever been sent to the fleet except upon the written authority of the First Sea Lord.

All attempts to induce Lord Fisher to reconsider his determination to resign having proved ineffectual I wrote to him (on May 22): "I am commanded by the King to accept your tendered resignation of the office of First Sea Lord of the Admiralty."

In going through the papers quite recently I found the following singular document, of which I at once sent a copy (September, 1927) to Mr. Churchill. He replied:

The document is new to me, and certainly has never been made public. I knew of course that Fisher had demanded powers similar to Kitchener's, but am surprised — and now I think I may say amused — at the categorical manner in which his requirements were explained. The submarine campaign to which he referred was of course the first submarine campaign. It was already thoroughly defeated, and did not appear again as a danger for more than eighteen months, and then in entirely different circumstances. The document seems to show that Fisher used the uncertain course of events at the Dardanelles as a means of making a bid for the supreme naval power.

The document, dated May 19, is in these terms:

Preamble

If the following six conditions are agreed to I can guarantee the successful termination of the War and the total abolition of the submarine menace. I also desire to add that since Lord Ripon wished in 1885 to make me a Lord of the Admiralty, but at my request made me Director of Naval Ordnance and Torpedoes instead, I have served under nine First Lords and seventeen years at the Admiralty, so I ought to know something about it:

1. That Mr. Winston Churchill is not in the Cabinet to be always circumventing me, nor will I serve under Mr. Balfour.

2. That Sir A. K. Wilson leaves the Admiralty and the Committee of Imperial Defence and the War Council, as my time otherwise will be occupied in resisting the bombardment of Heligoland and other such wild projects, also his policy is totally opposed to mine and he has accepted position of First Sea Lord in succession to me, and thereby adopting a policy diametrically opposed to my views.

3. That there shall be an entire new Board of Admiralty, as regards the Sea Lords and the Financial Secretary (who is utterly useless). *New measures demand New Men!*

4. That I shall have complete professional charge of the War at sea, together with the absolute sole disposition of the Fleet, and the appointments of all officers of all rank whatsoever, and absolutely untrammelled sole command of all the sea forces whatsoever.

5. That the First Lord of the Admiralty should be absolutely restricted to policy and parliamentary procedure and should occupy the same position towards me as Mr. Tennant, M.P., does to Lord Kitchener (and very well he does it).

6. That I should have the sole absolute authority for all new construction and all dockyard work of whatever sort whatsoever, and complete control of the whole of the Civil establishments of the Navy.

The 60 per cent of my time and energy which I have exhausted on nine First Lords in the past I wish in the future to devote to the successful prosecution of the War. That is my sole reason for the six conditions. These six conditions must be published verbatim so that the Fleet may know my position.

Lord Fisher was undoubtedly a man with streaks of genius, but he was afflicted with fits of megalomania, in one of which this extraordinary ultimatum must have been composed. I always remained on the best of personal terms with him, but the whole of his conduct at this critical time convinced me that it had become impossible that he should remain responsible for the Admiralty.

CHAPTER IX

THE FIRST COALITION

ON May 17, 1915, I addressed the following two letters to my colleagues in the Cabinet:

Secret.

10 DOWNING STREET,
WHITEHALL, S.W.

For the Cabinet.

I have come to the conclusion that, for the successful prosecution of the War, it is essential that the Government should be reconstructed on a broad and non-party basis.

I, therefore, with sincere reluctance and regret, ask my colleagues to put the resignation of their several offices in my hands.

H. H. A.

May 17, 1915.

10 DOWNING STREET,
WHITEHALL, S.W.

I wish to put on record exactly what has happened, and what has led me to resolve on an entirely new departure.

I have for some time past come, with increasing conviction, to the conclusion that the continued prosecution of the War requires what is called a "broad based" Government. Under existing conditions, criticism, inspired by party motives and interests, has full rein, and is an asset of much value to the enemy.

The resignation of Lord Fisher, which I have done my best to avert, and the more than plausible parliamentary case in regard to the alleged deficiency of high-explosive shells, would, if duly exploited (as they would have been) in the House of Commons at this moment, have had the most disastrous effect on the general political and strategic situation: in particular, such a discussion might have had the result of determining adversely to the Allies the attitude of Italy.

Upon a full review of all the circumstances, I have come to the conclusion that, in the best interests of the country, the reconstruction of the Government can no longer be deferred.

Neither I nor any of my colleagues have anything to regret or to be ashamed of in the steps, legislative and administrative, which we have taken, in the face of unexampled difficulties, since the War began. I am proud to think that we have a record which, when it is impartially appraised by history, will stand the most exacting scrutiny, and be always gratefully and approvingly remembered.

I tender to them, one and all, my warmest and most heartfelt thanks for the inestimable service which they have rendered to the country, and for their unwavering loyalty to myself.

There is not one of them from whom it is not a real pain to me, even temporarily, to part; and no one among them would more readily step aside than I.

But, in the time in which we live, all personal ties and associations must be disregarded, at whatever cost, in the general interest.

And it is for that purpose and in that spirit that, with infinite reluctance, I ask them to help me in the discharge of a most repugnant but most imperative duty.

May 17, 1915.   H. H. A.

I had received earlier on the same day a communication from Mr. Bonar Law which ran as follows:

LANSDOWNE HOUSE,
    BERKELEY SQUARE, W.
        May 17, 1915.

DEAR MR. ASQUITH, —

Lord Lansdowne and I have learnt with dismay that Lord Fisher has resigned, and we have come to the conclusion that we cannot allow the House to adjourn until this fact has been made known and discussed.

We think that the time has come when we ought to have a clear statement from you as to the policy which the Government intends to pursue. In our opinion things cannot go on as they are, and some change in the constitution of the Government seems to us inevitable if it is to retain a sufficient measure of public confidence to conduct the War to a successful conclusion.

The situation in Italy makes it particularly undesirable to have anything in the nature of a controversial discussion in the House of Commons at present, and if you are prepared to take the necessary steps to secure the object which I have indicated, and if Lord Fisher's resignation is in the meantime postponed, we shall be ready to keep silence now. Otherwise I must to-day ask you whether Lord Fisher has resigned, and press for a day to discuss the situation arising out of his resignation.

Yours very truly,
A. Bonar Law.

The determination recorded in my two Cabinet letters was not the result of this communication, important as it was, nor of any representation from my own colleagues.   It had been come to by me quite independently in the exercise of my own judgment, and for the reasons set out in my second letter.   Nothing would have been more inopportune than a controversial discussion in the House of Commons, which must have had the effect of discouraging our own troops, of inspiriting the enemy, and of upsetting the arrangements which after delicate and difficult negotiations were on the point of being concluded for the accession of Italy to the cause of the Allies.

The circumstances which had led to the resignation of Lord Fisher are summarized in the preceding chapter, and are detailed in Mr. Churchill's book, " The

World Crisis." Mr. Churchill had already arranged
that he should be succeeded as First Sea Lord by our
most distinguished naval strategist and tactician, Admiral Sir Arthur Wilson. I ought to add that two days
later Admiral Wilson informed me that he was not
prepared to undertake the duties under any First Lord
other than Mr. Churchill. The place which Lord
Fisher filled in the public eye made it certain that the
transfer would provide fuel for an acrimonious and un-
seasonable debate. The alleged "shell shortage," which
was already the pretext for a violent newspaper campaign against Lord Kitchener, and, as I have stated,
connived at and indeed engineered by Sir John French,
the commander at the front, would also, if it was to be
adequately countered in the House of Commons, have
necessitated disclosures which, upon military grounds,
it would have been highly inexpedient to make. In
the compulsory absence for a short time of Sir Edward
Grey, I had been myself in charge of the negotiations
with Italy, and I knew better than anybody the danger
to the Allied interests, frankly indicated by Mr. Bonar
Law in his letter, of a controversial parliamentary discussion.

But it was not merely a question of the particular
situation with which we were at the moment con-
fronted. That situation, in one form or other, under
the existing conditions, was certain of recurrence, and
I had come to the conclusion that the best chance of an
effective prosecution of the War was at once to admit
leading men of all parties in the State to a share in the
counsels and responsibilities of Government. I accordingly wrote to Mr. Bonar Law the following letter:

10 DOWNING STREET,
WHITEHALL, S.W.
May 18, 1915.

DEAR MR. BONAR LAW, —

After long and careful consideration, I have come definitely to the conclusion that the conduct of the War to a successful and decisive issue cannot be effectively carried on except by a Cabinet which represents all parties in the State.

I need not enter into the reasons (sufficiently obvious) which point to this as the best solution, in the interest of the country, of the problems which the War now presents. Nor does the recognition of its necessity involve any disparagement on my part of the splendid service which, in their several spheres, my colleagues have rendered to the Empire in this great and trying emergency.

My colleagues have placed their resignations in my hands, and I am therefore in a position to invite you, and those who associate with you, to join forces with us in a combined administration, in which I should also ask the leaders of the Irish and Labour parties to participate, whose common action (without prejudice to the future prosecution of our various and divergent political purposes) should be exclusively directed to the issues of the War.

Yours very faithfully,

H. H. ASQUITH.

The Rt. Hon. A. Bonar Law, M.P.

Mr. Bonar Law's reply was as follows:

HOUSE OF COMMONS,
May 19, 1915.

DEAR MR. ASQUITH, —

The considerations to which you refer have for some time been present to the mind of Lord Lansdowne and myself. We have now communicated your views and your invitation to our colleagues, and we shall be glad to co-operate with you in your endeavour to form a National Government.

Yours faithfully,

A. BONAR LAW.

19 May 1915

Dear Mr Asquith

The considerations
to which you refer have
for some time been
present to the mind
of Lord Lansdowne & myself.
We have now communicated
your views & your invitation
to our colleagues & me

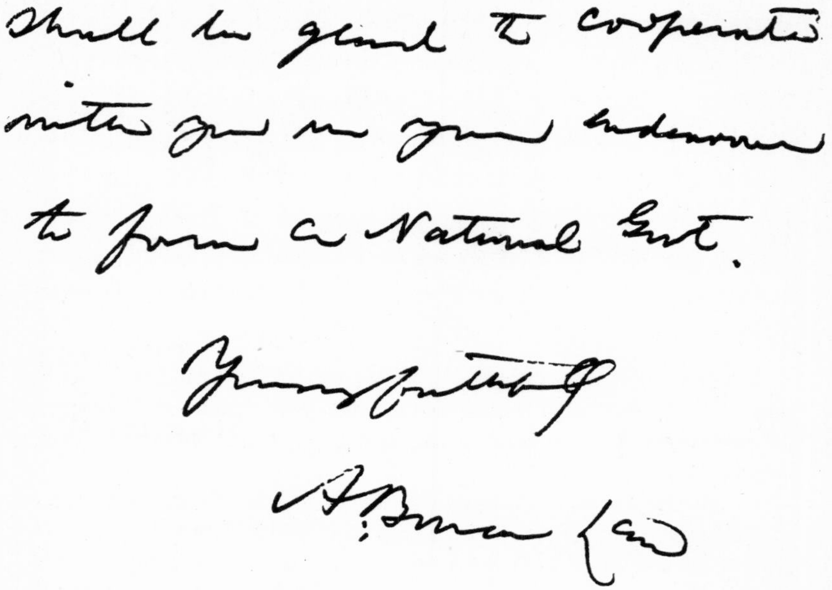
shall be glad to co-operate with you in your endeavour to form a National Govt.

Yours faithfully

A. Bonar Law

This was, therefore, the task to which I immediately set my hand, my colleagues having one and all unselfishly and patriotically put their offices at my disposal. It was the most uncongenial job that it has ever been my lot to carry through. I let it be publicly understood from the first—lest there should be any suspicion that there was to be a new departure in policy—that three of the principal offices would remain unchanged: those of Prime Minister, of Foreign Secretary, and of Secretary of State for War. But it was sorely against the grain to find myself obliged to cut the tie which bound me to old and valued friends and fellow-workers and to put in their places men with whom I had been almost daily exchanging blows during the greater part of a political lifetime.

One great disappointment befell me on the threshold of my undertaking. Mr. Arthur Henderson consented to join the new combination as the representative of Labour. But Mr. John Redmond, the Nationalist leader, upon whom, remembering his fine speech in the House of Commons on the first day of the War, and his subsequent services in the promotion of Irish recruiting, I had counted with some confidence, felt obliged to refuse. His first message was in the following terms:

PRIME MINISTER, —

Your telegram received. While thanking you I feel sure you will understand when I say the principles and history of the party I represent make the acceptance of your offer impossible.

From the commencement of the War, the Irish party and myself have been anxious to do, and have done, all in our power to aid your Government in the successful prosecution of the War, and in the future you can fully rely on us for all the help in our power to give, but even if I was free to accept your offer I am convinced my doing so would not increase my power to be of service.

REDMOND.

Through Mr. Birrell, the Chief Secretary, I tried to press him to reconsider his decision, but unavailingly, as appears from his second message:

IRISH OFFICE,
OLD QUEEN STREET, S.W.
3.9 P.M., *May* 21, 1915.

My objections are not in the least personal and apply with full force to anyone representing the Irish National party. By adhering to the principles on which our party was founded our power to help any Government which may be formed will be much greater than it would be if we joined.

At proper time I shall be quite ready to make plain to the public the grounds on which I have refused to join, and that the Irish party are prepared to give most cordial support to any Government that may be formed under your presidency to carry on the War.

REDMOND.

It is right to add that in a subsequent message Mr. Redmond deprecated the inclusion of Sir Edward Carson, which, he said, "would make our efforts to help far more difficult."

There were two concessions of a personal kind which were insisted on by Mr. Bonar Law and his friends, and which I made with the greatest reluctance. One was the substitution of another Lord Chancellor for Lord Haldane, against whom, on the strength of his having once referred to Germany as his "spiritual home," there had been started one of those fanatical and malignant outcries which from time to time disgrace our national character. The other was the transfer of Mr. Churchill from the Admiralty, where he was to be succeeded by Mr. Balfour, to an inferior office in the Cabinet.

Lord Grey of Fallodon has described in his book[1] his indignation at the supersession of Lord Haldane, and I insert here the letter which he wrote to me on the subject at the time:

FOREIGN OFFICE,
May 21, 1915.

MY DEAR ASQUITH, —

I think Bonar Law should be told that it is at least doubtful whether I shall stay if Haldane goes; that the injustice of the mad and malicious attacks upon Haldane in the *National Review* and Harmsworth Press have caused more resentment to Haldane's friends and those who know

---

[1] "Twenty-five Years," Vol. II, pp. 237–9.

VISCOUNT HALDANE

the truth about him than any political question has ever aroused; and that now when these attacks have come to a head in this way, it is impossible not to show how one resents them.

If Bonar Law is really pressing the point, I think I had better see him and any of his friends who share his view, and tell them what I think, and how the matter stands.

If you don't object, I will write to Bonar Law and save you further trouble on this point.

Yours sincerely,
E. GREY.

The process of reconstruction under such conditions involved many nice and some invidious personal questions. At a very early stage, Mr. Bonar Law wrote to me: "Lord Lansdowne is willing to join in view of the strong desire not only of his old colleagues but of yourself as expressed to me yesterday." He became a member of the Cabinet without portfolio. The most generally interesting of the changes were the appointment of Lord Buckmaster to the Woolsack, and of Mr. Balfour to the Admiralty, the substitution at the Exchequer of Mr. McKenna for Mr. Lloyd George, who undertook the newly created office of Minister of Munitions, and the admission to the Cabinet as Attorney-General of Sir Edward Carson.

I have now before me the final list of the new Cabinet as initialled by the King. An asterisk is prefixed to the names of those who belonged to the previous administration.

Prime Minister ⎰ . *Mr. Asquith.
First Lord of Treasury ⎱
Without portfolio . . . Lord Lansdowne.

Lord Chancellor	*Sir S. Buckmaster.
Lord President of the Council	*Lord Crewe.
Lord Privy Seal . . .	Lord Curzon.
Chancellor of the Exchequer	*Mr. McKenna.
Secretaries of State:	
Home	*Sir J. Simon.
Foreign	*Sir E. Grey.
War	*Lord Kitchener.
Colonies	Mr. Bonar Law.
India	Mr. A. Chamberlain.
Minister of Munitions . .	*Mr. Lloyd George.
First Lord of the Admiralty .	Mr. Balfour.
President of the Board of	
Trade	*Mr. Runciman.
President of the Local Gov-	
ernment Board . . .	Mr. Long.
Chancellor of Duchy . .	*Mr. Churchill.
Chief Secretary for Ireland .	*Mr. Birrell.
Secretary for Scotland . .	*Mr. McKinnon Wood.
Attorney-General . . .	Sir E. Carson
Board of Agriculture . .	Lord Selborne.
Office of Works	*Mr. Harcourt.
Board of Education . . .	Mr. Henderson.

The official communication contained also the following statements:

A place in the Cabinet was offered to Mr. John Redmond, but he did not see his way to accept it.

The Prime Minister has decided that a new Department shall be created, to be called the Ministry of Munitions, charged with organizing the supply of munitions of war. Mr. Lloyd George has undertaken the formation and temporary direction of this department, and during his tenure of office as Minister of Munitions, will vacate the Office of Chancellor of the Exchequer.

It is understood that Mr. Henderson will assist the Government in relation to Labour questions arising out of the War.

The King has been pleased to confer upon Viscount Haldane of Cloan the Order of Merit.

The formation of the Coalition Government was to the knowledge of all concerned a hazardous experiment. But a sense of patriotic duty made them feel that they must face its risks, on the express understanding that participation in it involved no sacrifice or compromise in any quarter of settled convictions and principles.

Mr. Churchill, though he had always inclined, as he says, to some such fusion for the purposes of the War, expresses the opinion that it was brought about at the wrong moment and in the wrong way. He thinks it ought at any rate to have been preceded by a Secret Session, in which both Lord Kitchener's administration and his own would have been vindicated. "Moreover," he adds, "on May 23, towering over domestic matters, came the Italian declaration of war against Austria. The Prime Minister's share in this event was a tremendous fact." I could then have challenged a vote of confidence: "had he fought he would have won . . . and he could then have invited the Opposition to come not to his rescue but to his aid."[1] Hypothetical solutions and retrospective short cuts always have their attractions, but in this case I am unable to concur in Mr. Churchill's reasoning. A Secret Session is at all times a questionable expedient—for one reason (amongst many), that it is under modern conditions impossible to make it effectively secret. We tried the experiment once at a later stage of the War, and no one—so far as I know—ever proposed to repeat it. Nor does it seem

[1] "The World Crisis, 1915," p. 373.

probable that the temper and atmosphere needed for the formation of a genuine Coalition would have been more easily attained if it had been preceded by a contentious debate, in which the leaders of the Opposition could hardly have avoided appearing and acting as the challenging parties.

CHAPTER X

CONTEMPORARY NOTES: 1915

THE year which followed the installation of the Coalition Ministry in May, 1915, was marked by a succession of dramatic events both in the political and the strategic field. I will not go over them here, as they are already, for the most part, the property of the historian. One of my most valued and intimate correspondents at this time was Mrs. Henley.[1] With her permission I have extracted from my letters to her some passages which, along with other contemporary notes, throw light upon matters which engaged the attention of diplomatists and soldiers in these critical months.

Conference with the French. July 6, 1915. I left London with my comrades, civil and military, last night at eight, and crossed in a Scout to Calais, where we spent the night. The French arrived in the early morning, and we began our conference at ten; it lasted till one, when we had lunch and dispersed. You may like to see how we sat at our conference (plan on next page).

I opened the proceedings with a carefully typewritten harangue in French, and then we proceeded to a full and free discussion of all sorts of important things, which lasted for three hours by the clock. I

[1] Sylvia, daughter of Lord Sheffield, and wife of Brigadier-General the Hon. Anthony Henley, who was my Military Private Secretary during my short tenure of the War Office. He fought with distinction throughout the War, and died suddenly and prematurely at Bucharest in 1925.

H. H. A.

K.		Viviani
A. J. B.		Millerand
Crewe		Augagneur
Delcassé		Sir J. French
Joffre		Aide de Camp

have never heard so much bad French spoken in my life (I think——deserved the prize). On the whole the man who came best, not only linguistically, but altogether, out of the whole thing was K. Not one of the French could speak a word of English. Viviani is the cleverest, though he looks sleepy and rather commonplace.

Visit to Ypres. July, 1915. We descended from the motors and took a long walk through the trenches and dugouts, and finally through the principal streets of the town: "We" being K. and myself, Plumer, and a bevy of Second Army generals and officers, including Allenby, whom I found the most intelligent of the lot. There was some little risk of shells (as it was the favourite German hour for that pastime) and still more from falling houses: they literally shake and totter in the wind; but no evil befell us.

It is one of the most wonderful and tragic sights in the world, or I should think in history: not a single house has escaped, and there is not an inhabitant left. The famous Cloth Hall is, as it stands just now, a most beautiful and picturesque ruin: some of the pinnacles quite untouched, and the tracery is still in a lot of the windows, and the statues in their niches.   Some good artist ought to make a picture of it at once: in another month it may all be gone.   It is a hellish business, for Ypres is not of the slightest strategical value, either to the Germans or us, and in my opinion ought long ago to have been abandoned — or indeed never attempted to be held.   It must have cost us already the best part of 50,000 casualties and the Germans probably many more, and nothing can ever repair the damage.   Unfortunately it has now become almost a point of honour with both sides.   Great progress has been made since I was there a month ago in making trenches and dugouts: mainly owing to the cavalry, who are the best "diggers" in the Army.

I saw the 5th Dragoon Guards and Queen's Bays hard at work (officers included) with their spades. Thence we proceeded to the Belgians, had a brief interview with the King, and went to see the celebrated "inundations" which safeguard most of their lines.

I was walking, either on this or a later visit to Ypres, through our dugouts when I came to a compartment in which was a fine piece of old French furniture.   I remarked to the Tommies who were in possession: "You seem to be doing yourselves pretty well here." They explained that it had been left behind in the general exodus, and they had thought that it would come in useful.   It was a couch covered with red damask on which a tired man could recline at full length.

July, 1915. I motored after lunch to Munstead to talk to McKenna about two or three things: notably the scope and composition of his proposed Committee on Economy in the State. He does not see his way to carry on the War at the rate of three millions a day, *plus* financing France, Russia and Italy, beyond next spring. I think we shall have very soon to fix the maximum number of men we can put in the field, after allowing for all we need, not only to make munitions, but to work the land, and carry on the various manufactures upon which our export trade depends—all of them very heavy requirements. The Allies cannot reasonably complain of such a limitation of the number of our fighting men: for we are discharging the whole burden of keeping the seas open, and of financing them. They ought to be ready to disgorge a lot more of the gold of which France, and Russia particularly, have an enormous hoard. The French dare not either put on taxes or try to float a big loan; they are simply living from hand to mouth on short borrowings.

August, 1915. Runciman, who has been in close touch with all the Trade Union leaders, says that, with a single exception, they are hotly against compulsion in any form and will use the whole force of their organizations to fight it inch by inch.

There are two vital matters, from a practical point of view, which it seems to me the compulsionists have never thought out, viz.: (1) How you are going to run financially and in the way of discipline a mixed army of volunteers and conscripts, and (2) Where are you going to draw the line of exemption? When you have made adequate provision for the various economic needs of a country like ours in time of war, you may find that you have left for compulsion only a small residuum of the dregs of the nation: and you will have set aflame a blazing controversy—for nothing!

I went to see the King and was joined at the Palace by Kitchener, Balfour, and E. Grey. We four sat in conclave with the Sovereign on the subject of compulsion for nearly two hours: a very unusual proceeding. What, of course, affects him the most is, not the abstract merits of the question, but the growing division of opinion, and the prospect of a possible political row.

August 26. I dined with Baker. The other guests, all males, were McKenna, Runciman, and Eric Drummond. The talk, I need not say, was mainly of conscription, of which McKenna and Runciman are among the most stalwart and even passionate opponents. Gulland,[1] whom I saw this morning for the first time for weeks, tells me that he gets letters from Liberal chairmen, etc., all over the country denouncing as a lost soul, and some of them predicting that conscription would bring us to the verge, or over the verge, of revolution. I have had several interviews with colleagues—Harcourt, Simon, etc.,—all strong in the same sense.

* * * * *

In November, 1915, Kitchener at the request of his colleagues went to make a personal inspection of the situations at the Dardanelles and at Salonika. He was away for a month, during which time I discharged his duties at the War Office.

November 22. After I had put in a short time at the

[1] The Chief Government Whip.

House, I went to the War Office, where I had a succession of rather interesting (and exacting) interviews: (1) with Sir Douglas Haig, who was as usual somewhat tongue-tied, but sooner or later got to the point; (2) with Sir H. Smith-Dorrien, who is disposed to be obsessed with his grievance against Sir J. French. We have given him (S.-D.) the East African Command, with Tighe and Bridges as his major-generals, and he is so happy not to be *désœuvré* that I think he will take on the new job *con amore*. (3) With Von Donop, to whom I had to make the revelation that two or three of the remaining leaves of his attenuated artichoke are to be snapped off by Lloyd George. I handled him as well as I could, and I hope broke his fall.

November 27. As K. threatens to return on Tuesday morning, I seem to be drawing to an end of my double life — for the present at any rate. Redmond came to the War Office to see me, to recount his experiences at the Front, and his hopes and fears. He is rather strongly pro-French,[1] and anti-Haig: full also of the super-eminent virtues and claims of Sir William Robertson.

December 5. We (*i.e.* self, A. J. B., and K., with a whole retinue of generals and experts) left Charing Cross about 10.30 in the morning and crossed from Dover in the destroyer *Zulu* under fair weather conditions to Calais, where we arrived about one, and were greeted by the French — Briand, Joffre, Galliéni, etc., etc. We lunched together in more or less gloomy silence, and then proceeded to our conference. I was

[1] *I.e.* Sir John French.

asked by Briand to preside, and without much pre-
amble called upon K. to expound our view of the military situation at Salonika, and the need of prompt
evacuation. Briand at once replied, in one of the ablest
and most brilliant speeches I have ever heard, dwell-
ing on the political and diplomatic troubles incident to
such a course. A. J. B. made a very clever reply, in
moderate but intelligible French. Remaining silent
myself, but watching the situation narrowly (while
Galliéni and Joffre made their contributions), I soon
came to the conclusion that if we stuck to our guns we
should not only hold our own, but the French would on
the whole feel relieved. So I turned on K. again, who
played his part of the sullen, morose, rather suspicious,
but wholly determined man, with good effect. Then I
asked the French to retire for a few minutes and we
drew up, in such French as we could command, our
conclusions. They acquiesced with some show of reluctance and regret, and we parted ostensibly — and I
think really — on excellent terms.

Soon after six we started back home on our destroyer
on one of the foulest nights I have ever seen. We took
two and a half hours to cross the Channel — with a head
wind, dirty and continuous rain, and pitch-black darkness. Everybody except K. and myself was sick and
miserable — in particular A. J. B. I said to him when
at last we reached Dover, "Well, at any rate we have
not been mined or torpedoed." To which he replied,
"I wished to God we had!"

December 6, 1915. The French are once more in
full cry for the retention of Salonika.

December 22. I knew that you would sympathize

with me in the intense relief of knowing the almost incredible, and indeed miraculous, methods and results of the evacuation at Suvla and Anzac. It has been for the last two weeks a veritable nightmare. And, as you say, what a commentary on expert advice! Even K., who discounted the extreme view of our potential loss —not less than 30, and probably more than 50 per cent —was very pessimistic.[1] Not a single life lost, only six guns left behind and all those destroyed, with a few hospital tents and the remnants of stores, which were shelled and burnt by the Navy at daylight. It is the most wonderful retirement in war history, far surpassing even Sir John Moore's at Corunna.

Monro[2] is now pressing for the evacuation of Helles also, before the middle of January, when the weather for two months becomes increasingly bad. Personally, of course, I should be more than delighted.

As an illustration of the hazards of war, we had this morning a telegram from the Admiral (Wemyss), who has done extraordinarily well, to report that the wind had suddenly changed and was blowing a S.W. gale. If this had happened twentyfour hours sooner, the whole thing might have been frustrated, and perhaps turned into a gigantic disaster. It is, I think, almost the first blow which Providence has struck in our favour since the War began.

December 22. The moment that one emerges from one crisis one is engulfed in another. The Cabinet met

[1] Lord Curzon circulated a Memorandum, of which I cannot find a copy, which drew a lurid prophetic picture founded on the 6th and 7th Books of Thucydides.

[2] General Sir C. Monro, who had been sent from France to the Dardanelles to report on the situation there. His advice was acted on — with the best results.

to consider for the first time the Derby Report. The impression left upon me is profoundly disquieting.

The discussion unhappily followed party lines (Lloyd George and Henderson were away), and to judge from to-day's experience, we seem to be on the brink of a precipice. The practical question is — Shall I be able during the next ten days to devise and build a bridge?

Another good story from the Front which I heard was of some English Tommies, foraging in France, who had succeeded in getting two or three *lapins*.

The peasant asked them what they were going to do with their spoil.

Answer (from a Berlitz-instructed Tommy) : " Pour faire la *messe*."

Peasant: " Quelle drôle de religion! "

CHAPTER XI

RECALL OF SIR JOHN FRENCH

DURING Lord Kitchener's absence from England in November, 1915, I took over his duties at the War Office, where, notwithstanding the changes in its personnel since I left it fifteen months before, I soon felt at home. I decided without any hesitation or delay one or two outstanding questions which had been hanging fire for some time between that Office and the Ministry of Munitions. But the most serious matter that occupied my attention was the bringing about of a change in the Commander-in-Chief in the field. I had for some time past felt fears and growing doubts as to Sir John French's capacity to stand the strain of his task with its ever-increasing and unforeseeable responsibilities.

I had many conversations on the subject with Lord Kitchener, who shared my misgivings, but was indisposed himself to make any change. I had no doubt that among the generals available Sir John's fittest successor would be Sir Douglas Haig, and I found that His Majesty the King was of the same opinion. The form and manner of the communication to be made to the Commander-in-Chief was obviously a very delicate matter, calling for the exercise of no common degree of tact. I accordingly entrusted the duty to Lord Esher, then on service in Paris, whom I knew to be an old and attached friend of Sir John French. He was good enough to undertake it, and went to the Field-

Marshal's Head-quarters, whence he reported to me on November 26, 1915:

I saw Sir John directly after my arrival. I told him that you had wired to me asking me to return from Paris, and had entrusted to me, as an old and most attached friend of his, the duty of conveying to him your views and *decision* that, owing to the strain of the past fifteen months, he was no longer able to conduct the campaign.

I told him that you had spoken in warm terms of his person and achievements, terms of appreciation and affection.

Your intentions in regard to the future I repeated in your own words: that you would recommend him at once to the King for the honour of a peerage; that you would, in due course, ask Parliament for a grant, according to precedent; and that you would ask him to assume the duties and position of Commander-in-Chief of the Home forces, with a view to their higher training, which in his hands would be assured, and to their effective use should occasion require.

Sir John, who has seen this letter, has written to you himself a letter which I am certain you will consider as only one more proof of that modest, warm-hearted and honourable nature which has endeared him ever to his friends, and above all to the officers and men of the Army he has loved so well and so gallantly commanded.

Sir John came forthwith to London, and he wrote me the following letter (dated November 29):

My dear Prime Minister,—

I have seen Esher, who has conveyed to me your kind message. For this and for all your personal kindness to me since I was called upon to command the Army in France I desire to thank you most warmly.

As regards the main subject of our conversation no one knows better than you how grave and important are the issues at stake. My sole desire is to serve my country and the Army to the best of my ability in whatever capacity you and the Government choose to employ me. The strain of the last fifteen months has been a very heavy one, and although I am happy to say I am not conscious that it has had any serious effect upon my mental or physical powers, others may take a different view, and in these circumstances I need not assure you that I shall accept their decision without question.

As I felt able to get away for two or three days I have come over to ask you to be good enough to see me as soon as you conveniently can in order to discuss the whole question, as I think this method is infinitely preferable, in the first instance, to doing so by letter.

Yours sincerely,
JOHN FRENCH.

We accordingly met, and after some friendly conversations, I authorized the issue of an official announcement from the War Office, which was published on December 16, 1915, in the following terms:

General Sir Douglas Haig has been appointed to succeed Field-Marshal Sir John French in command of the Army in France and Flanders.

Since the commencement of the War, during over sixteen months of severe and incessant strain, Field-Marshal Sir John French has most ably commanded our Armies in France and Flanders, and he has now, at his own instance, relinquished that command. His Majesty's Government, with full appreciation of, and gratitude for, the conspicuous services which Sir John French has rendered to the country at the Front, have, with the King's approval, requested him to accept the appointment of Field-Marshal Commanding-in-Chief the troops stationed in the United Kingdom, and Sir John French has accepted that appointment.

His Majesty the King has been pleased to confer upon Sir John French the dignity of a Viscount of the United Kingdom.

Nov. 29. 1915.

94. Lancaster Gate.
W.

My Dear Prime Minister —

I hear Mrs Eliza who has arranged to see your kind Message... for them, and for all your personal kindness to me since I was called upon to command the Army in France I desire to thank you most warmly.

As regards the main subject of our conversation than on terms better than you have given an important are the issues at stake

My sole desire is to serve my country

and the energy to the limit of
my ability in whatever capacity you or
the Government choose to employ me.
The strain of the last 15 months has been
a very heavy one & although I am happy
to say I am not conscious that it has had
any serious effect upon my mental
or physical powers, others may take a
different view and in these circumstances
I need not assure you that I shall
accept their decision without question.
As I felt able to get away for two or
three days I have come once to ask

94. Lancaster Gate.
W.

You to be good enough to see them as
soon as you conveniently can in order
to discuss the whole question, as I
think this method is infinitely
preferable, in the first instance, to
closing it by letter.

Yours sincerely,
R. H. Brand

CHAPTER XII

MY VISIT TO ITALY

AT the end of March, 1916, I paid a visit to Italy at the invitation of the King, with whom I had had the honour of a long talk at Rome many years before when I was Chancellor of the Exchequer. I was even then much struck with his command of English, vocabulary, idiom, pronunciation, and at the end of our interview I ventured to tell him so. He laughed and said: "Well, it would be a wonder if I could n't speak English: my nurse was English, my governess was English, my tutor was English, and till I was fourteen I rarely spoke any other language."

I was accompanied on this second visit by my private secretary (Bonham Carter), Colonel Hankey, and Mr. O'Beirne of the Foreign Office, the delightful and accomplished diplomatist, who was destined later in the year to share Lord Kitchener's tragic end. I spent *en route* two days in Paris, where I see that I recorded that there was a "plentiful explosion of rhetorical gas." I took the opportunity of going over, in the company of Hankey and a French officer, the battlefield of the Marne, "the only decisive battle (up to then) of the War—September, 1914—as it just saved Paris." "Few people," I wrote, "realize that the Germans were as near the capital as Slough or even Hounslow is to London. There is a high plateau at Barcy which was swept from three miles distance by the invaders' artillery, and is now (1916) literally covered by groups of graves, both French and German."

I had a most cordial reception at Rome, where the Anglo-Italian Alliance, then just a year old, was very popular. After depositing a wreath on the tomb of King Victor Emmanuel in the Pantheon, I went to the Vatican under the escort of our Minister, Sir Henry Howard, to pay a visit to the Pope, and to Cardinal Gasparri, his Secretary of State. We went in a lift to the top of the palace, and there in a suite of unpretentious rooms, decorated with some French prints, we were received by the Pope — Benedict XV. He was a scion of an old Genoese family, had spent a large part of his life in diplomacy, as Nuncio at some of the principal European capitals, and spoke French with ease and fluency. He was not a man of imposing appearance or presence; to my eyes the most impressive thing about him was his costume. He was dressed completely in white, except for his purple shoes, with a fine diamond pectoral cross round his neck. My companions, who were for the most part pratiquant Catholics, knelt and kissed his ring, with the exception of O'Beirne (himself a devout son of the Church), who in the confusion of the moment omitted to do so — a lapse upon which he was a good deal chaffed by the rest of us when we left the room.

Our talk was naturally confined to the War and germane topics: the Pope carefully refraining from indicating any leaning of his own to either side, and I giving no encouragement to a feeler which he incidentally threw out that he might act as mediator. On my way out of the Vatican I went to Cardinal Gasparri's room, and he and I talked with more freedom. He was a man of the world and a scholar, having spent twenty years or so in Paris as head of the Italian College there. His brother, as the King afterwards told me, was still His Majesty's chief shepherd on one of his principal estates.

While I was in Rome I was most hospitably entertained at the British Embassy by Sir Rennell and Lady Rodd, and after a stay of two or three days I went to the North to the two fighting fronts — the Isonzo and the Julian Alps, where I found the King, quartered in a small farm-house in a single room which served him as bedroom and study. He was good enough during the next two days to drive me round both the areas where the conflict was going on. At that time the Italians were on the aggressive, and so far as I remember there was not an Austrian soldier on Italian soil.[1] During my two days I saw some interesting and picturesque developments of modern warfare — a spirited battle between aeroplanes on the Isonzo, and a gigantic gun being dragged with ropes by about one thousand men to the top of a seemingly inaccessible Alpine height.

My return journey was marked by an amusing incident. The train to Paris was to stop at Milan, and I received a telegram just as we started that it was hoped that during the stoppage there I would deliver a short message of farewell to our Italian Allies. Accordingly I set to work, with the aid of O'Beirne, who was a good linguist, and the chief of General Cadorna's staff, who

---

[1] It is to be remembered that technically Italy was at war with Austria, and not with Germany.

understood English, to compose in the train a brief allocution in the purest Italian our joint efforts could command. To avoid obvious errors of pronunciation I rehearsed it to the Italian general, who was pleased to express his approval. When the train drew up at Milan, I discovered to my horror that it was the English community there who had expressed a wish for the harangue. So I descended and found a small company of my fellow-countrymen in a waiting-room, whom I addressed in their own tongue. Just as the train was re-starting, a couple of the editors of two principal Italian newspapers boarded it and begged me to say a few parting words in Italian. I pulled out the MS. upon which so much pains had been apparently wasted, and made them a present of it.

CHAPTER XIII

COMPULSORY SERVICE

WHEN the War broke out our Army consisted at home of six Regular and fourteen Territorial divisions, which, with the addition of the Regular garrisons overseas, made a total of twenty-six. In less than two years the number had been increased by voluntary recruiting to forty-two Regular and twenty-eight Territorial divisions, making with the Naval division a total of seventy-one. To these had to be added the contribution of men from the other parts of the Empire (twelve more divisions), a grand total of eighty-three divisions. I was able to say with truth in the House of Commons at the beginning of May, 1916, that the "total naval and military effort of the Empire from the beginning of the War up to that moment exceeded 5,000,000 men." This was before compulsion.

Such figures speak for themselves, and are conclusive evidence of the efficacy and elasticity of the voluntary system. The military authorities, when asked how many men they wanted, replied with good sense "all the men available." It was not their business how the men were to be obtained, so long as they were obtained. As Lord Kitchener said in his last public words, at the meeting of members of the House of Commons on the eve of his departure for Russia (June, 1916) : "Why did not the War Office demand compulsory service? I think that is easily answered. The question of a social change involving the whole country and running counter to the ancient traditions of the British people is not a matter for a department to decide. So long as sufficient men came in, it was not my duty to ask for special means of obtaining them. In my opinion compulsion came at the right time and in the right way as a military necessity, and for no other reason."

I had laid it down on behalf of the Government as a whole, as far back as November, 1915, that for the purpose of the War compulsion was a pure question of practical expediency, and that from that point of view the sole limitation which I recognized was that, if compulsion were to be applied, it must be with something of the nature of general consent.

For a long time it appeared that there was no prospect of obtaining such "general consent." Voluntary recruiting had undoubtedly, as the figures quoted above sufficiently show, achieved marvellous results. As I said in introducing the Compulsory Bill in May, 1916, there was no reason to believe that by a measure of general and immediate compulsion we "should get a larger number of men, or get the number that we want in an appreciably shorter time." On the other hand, it was all important "to get rid of piecemeal treatment, and the sense of temporary injustice and inequality which that mode of treatment is apt to engender." The two main sources of difficulty were the co-ordination of the claims of military service with those of other departments of work equally necessary to the successful prosecution of the War, and the distinction as regards priority of liability between the married and the unmarried men.

We had made the most strenuous efforts to avoid recourse to compulsory service. In October, 1915, Lord Derby patriotically undertook a new national recruiting campaign, but despite the most strenuous and ingenious efforts on his part, and on the part of those associated with him, the results as reported to the Cabinet early in the following January were disappointing. Out of 900,000 men who had been accounted for, less than half were really available for military service. The matter absorbed much time and led to much controversy, both inside and outside the Government. There were distinguished Ministers — among them Sir Edward Grey, Mr. McKenna, Mr. Runciman, and Sir John Simon — who doubted the practicability or wisdom of direct and wholesale compulsion. The Labour party held a conference at Bristol in January, at which it was denounced root and branch.

My letters at the time illustrate the diversity of opinion which prevailed. I see that I wrote to a correspondent (Lady Scott) on October 30, 1915: "On the whole the sky is rather less clouded. Anyhow, three out of the four attend our meeting to-morrow morning. As to the one (your friend) whom Satan is after I am more doubtful." Even as late as April 19, 1916, I wrote: "Things look as black as Erebus this morning, and I was preparing to order my frock-coat to visit the Sovereign this afternoon. But the effect of a three hours' Cabinet was to relieve the situation, for the moment at any rate. I begin to think that we shall either discover an immediate *modus vivendi* or force a crisis, which will emerge in a broad-bottomed Government, with perhaps one or two of our lightweights left."

At Mr. Balfour's suggestion a Cabinet Committee on the economic situation, consisting of McKenna, Austen Chamberlain and myself, was appointed to examine all the aspects of the matter, with especial reference to the allocation of man-power.

At last, early in May, I was able after much negotiation to bring in on behalf of the Government a Bill the effect of which was that, as from June 24, every male British subject ordinarily resident in Great Britain and between the ages of eighteen and forty-one was to be deemed duly enlisted in the Regular Army for the duration of the War.

The Bill received a third reading by a large majority. The minority was only thirty-seven, of whom twenty-seven were Liberals, including Sir John Simon, who to my great regret could not overcome his scruples and resigned his office. The Labour members were divided, fourteen voting for the Bill and ten against: among the ten were Mr. Ramsay MacDonald, Mr. Clynes, Mr. Snowden, and Mr. J. H. Thomas.

The Bill received the Royal assent on May 25. In a message issued on that day the King expressed to his people his recognition of the patriotism and self-sacrifice which had raised already by voluntary enlistment no fewer than 5,041,000 men — "an effort far surpassing that of any other nation in similar circumstances recorded in history, and one which will be a lasting source of pride to future generations."

Mr. Buchan, in his "History of the War," declares that the Government in this matter "lagged behind their followers in nerve and seriousness." At the same time he acknowledges that such a "revolutionary change" could in all probability not have been "wrought by any sweeping or heroic measure in the early days of the War." "It needed time for opinion to ripen and the necessities of the case to force themselves upon the public mind." For myself I adhered throughout to the view that if the change was to come, it must be by "general consent," and I have never had a harder task in public life than to secure the fulfilment of that condition.[1]

The following letter from the King, which I have His Majesty's gracious permission to publish, reached me on the day on which the Cabinet arrived at an agreement:

BUCKINGHAM PALACE,
April 20, 1916.

MY DEAR PRIME MINISTER, —

It is with the greatest satisfaction that I learn from the letter to Bigge of the happy agreement arrived at by the Cabinet to-day. I do most heartily congratulate you on having by your patience and skill extricated the Country from a position the dangers of which it was impossible to over-estimate.

I do indeed trust that this solution will prove final and that your Coalition Government, once more united, will gain renewed strength and greater confidence of the Country, to enable you to prosecute with the fullest energy the continuance of the War to a victorious end. During the last six years you and I have passed through some strenuous and critical times and once again, thank God, we have "weathered the storm"! I am so glad to hear that the matter will

---

[1] It was while I was engaged in this thorny business that Sir Henry Wilson, who had just been appointed to the command of the IVth Corps at the Front, after a brief visit to London, records in his Diary (January 30, 1916): "From my visit home it is clear to me that so long as we keep Asquith as Prime Minister we shall never go to war. And this is a most dangerous thing. *He will do nothing himself and will not allow anyone else to do anything.*" (Vol. I, p. 274.)

be submitted at a secret session in each House on Tuesday next.   In expressing my relief at the termination of the crisis, I wish again to assure you of my complete confidence in my Prime Minister.

                    Believe me,
                         Very sincerely yours,
                              GEORGE R.I.

CHAPTER XIV

THE BREAK–UP OF THE FIRST COALITION

By the Marquis of Crewe, K.G.

I am indebted to Lord Crewe for permission to publish this memorandum. It was, as the date December 20, 1916, shows, written by him when all the events referred to were still fresh in his memory.

IT had for some time been becoming evident that strong currents of dissatisfaction were affecting the smooth flow of the Coalition Government, and this unrest found vent, as is usual with Cabinets, by the issue of several suggestive or warning memoranda. Possibly the veritable *causa causans* of the final break-up is to be traced to Lord Lansdowne's striking paper of November 13, 1916.[1] It has been rumoured that the present Prime Minister [Mr. Lloyd George] regarded this document as the danger-signal marking an obstruction in the road, the barrier being a supposed invitation to the "elder statesmen" or soberer spirits of the Government to anticipate an enforced conclusion of the War. Study of the memorandum does not confirm this fear. It is rather to be regarded as a plain and courageous exposition of the facts, perhaps erring somewhat in the direction of mistrust, but displaying no poverty of spirit or lack of determination. Lord Robert Cecil's paper of November 27, 1916,[1] struck a note of anxious warning; and it is certain that no member of the Gov-

[1] Both Lord Lansdowne's and Lord Robert Cecil's memoranda are printed as an Appendix to this chapter.

ernment was undisturbed by a conviction that a prompt change in methods was demanded. The recent lack of progress on the various fronts, the Rumanian disaster, and the crisis in Greece, might stand in no direct relation to such a change; but ill-success in war always encourages heart-searchings at home and the increasingly venomous assaults by part of the Press on the Government as a whole, and particularly on the Prime Minister, Lord Grey, and Mr. Balfour, made it clear that the atmosphere was becoming more and more highly charged.

Amongst ourselves there existed a general feeling that the War Committee, though much of its work had been promptly and capably carried through, had not succeeded in fulfilling the purpose of its creation — that of a quite small body of selected Ministers advised by a few picked naval and military experts and enabled by almost daily sittings to effect rapid decisions on all matters directly concerned with the War. Much of its time and energy had been consumed by discussions on subjects of domestic importance, all claiming a bearing on the conduct of the War, but demanding the presence, and the inclusion in discussion, of a number of other Ministers not themselves members of the Committee. Nor did the creation of the Man Power Board seem to afford much relief to the supreme body. Its examination of the facts was thorough and valuable, but its conclusions were *ad referendum,* and differences of opinion had to be dealt with. The general result was that the meetings of the War Committee tended to become far too large and to produce general discussions similar to those that had clogged the action of the earlier War Council; while the Cabinet remained in the background as the final court of appeal, furnished with the records of proceedings and with many of the memoranda — though not all — with which the War Committee worked, and from time to time engaging in general discussions on War policy, with which its size and its composition alike unfitted it to cope.

It was in these circumstances that a suggestion was made at the Cabinet of November 29 for the formation of a Committee to deal with the domestic aspects of war policy — labour, food supply, and the like — covering the ground administered by the Boards of Trade and Agriculture and some other departments, and advised by suitable experts, as with the War Committee. The idea was generally favoured and the principle was agreed, but it was not then attempted to enter on any details. Towards the end of the same week I wrote to the Prime Minister pressing the adoption of this suggestion, pointing out that its complete acceptance in a practical shape involved the abolition of the Cabinet as a consultative body, though with no actual change in the position of Ministers; and I believe that other of our colleagues were also engaged in working out a scheme. But either the movement came too late or it precipitated an intended crisis; for on Friday, December 1, Mr. Lloyd George wrote to the Prime Minister suggesting the formation of a new War Committee entrusted with practically absolute powers for the conduct of the War; and on Sunday the Unionist members of the Cabinet, except Lord Lansdowne, who was at Bowood, and Mr. Balfour, who was unwell, met in a conference which proved to be decisive.

I have no means of knowing the true relation of these two events; but I am clear that Mr. Bonar Law and Mr. Lloyd George were acting in close concert throughout, but that several other Unionist Ministers were not. As it happened, I was less favourably placed than usual for following the events of these memorable days, being greatly occupied by the important deputation of scientific societies, which I received on Friday, December 1, and by other public engagements. I remained in London over Sunday, the 3rd, and was surprised by receiving at luncheon on that day, from the Prime Minister, whom I believed to be at Walmer, a request to come to Downing Street at once. I found Mr. Asquith sitting on after luncheon, and with him Mr. Edwin Montagu.

For the first time I then heard of the correspondence with Mr. Lloyd George, and saw the letters that had passed up to that date. The Prime Minister pointed out that there were two quite distinct points at issue. The first was his own relation to the War Committee from which Mr. Lloyd George had suggested he should be entirely dissociated, merely retaining as Prime Minister a general power of veto, presumably in concert with the Cabinet. He did not see how he could be anything but chairman of the War Committee, even though he might not always be able to attend, and Mr. Lloyd George acted in his absence. He was confident that an arrangement could be come to on this point, and that it would work well in practice. But on the second point he was far less hopeful, that of the composition of the committee. As proposed, this included Mr. Bonar Law, Sir E. Carson, and a representative of Labour, probably Mr. Henderson. Mr. Asquith's objection to this body was its absolute inefficiency for the purpose of carrying on the War; but he questioned whether Mr. Lloyd George would agree to modify it. We entirely agreed with the Prime Minister that this would be a hopelessly bad War Committee; and that in the matter of powers he ought to retain the chairmanship, while coming to any terms he could with the Secretary of State for War on the conduct of business.

I then heard the startling news that at the Unionist meeting of that morning it was agreed that the Prime Minister ought to resign his office,[1] and that Mr. Bonar Law had just been at Downing Street with this message, it being added that in the event of a refusal the Unionist Ministers must themselves hand in their resignations. The intimation was curtly delivered, it appeared; but in further conversation it was implied that the demand was not made in Mr. Lloyd George's interests, but in order that the Government might be reconstructed. Assuming this to be the fact the action of the Unionist Ministers seemed disproportionate to the need, for reconstruction could quite well have pro-

---

[1] The Resolution referred to by Lord Crewe, which was passed by the Unionist Members on Sunday, December 3, but was not shown to me by Mr. Bonar Law, was to the following effect:

We share the view expressed to the Prime Minister by Mr. Bonar Law some time ago that the Government cannot continue as it is.

It is evident that a change must be made, and in our opinion the publicity given to the intentions of Mr. Lloyd George makes reconstruction from within no longer possible.

We therefore urge the Prime Minister to tender the resignation of the Government.

If he feels unable to take that step we authorize Mr. Bonar Law to tender our resignations.

ceeded as it did last year by the resignation of all the
Prime Minister's colleagues, he himself retaining his
place and the commission to form a new Government.
Still, whatever might be the motive, there the fact was
and it had been arranged that the Prime Minister
would again see both Messrs. Lloyd George and Bonar
Law later in the day. He would be dining at Mr.
Montagu's house, and I arranged to call there after
dinner to hear what had passed.

Accordingly I proceeded to Queen Anne's Gate at
about 10 P. M. and found the Prime Minister with Mr.
Montagu and Lord Reading. The interviews with the
two discontented colleagues had produced no positive
change in the situation, but seemed to have confirmed
Mr. Asquith in the belief that an accommodation with
Mr. Lloyd George would ultimately be achieved, without sacrifice of his own position as chief of the War
Committee; while it appeared that a large measure of
reconstruction would satisfy the Unionist Ministers.
After some conversation, in which Mr. Asquith was
strongly supported in his opinion that no compromise
of principle could be admitted regarding the War
Committee, he decided to inform the King at once that
the Government must be reconstructed; and a notice
was drafted for the Press to that effect. We separated
with the hope, though with no assurance, that the resignation of all Ministers, as in the summer of 1915, might
lead to the formation of a stable administration on a
new principle.

On Monday, December 4, appeared *The Times*
article of which the effect was explained by Mr.
Asquith at the Liberal Meeting held at the Reform

Club on December 8, when he also described the gist of his ensuing correspondence with Mr. Lloyd George; and that afternoon the Prime Minister briefly informed the House of Commons of the intended organic reconstruction of the Government, moving the adjournment till Thursday, the 7th. It was abundantly clear by this time that Mr. Lloyd George was determined to develop to the utmost the possibilities of the situation, and that the chances of continued union were fast diminishing.

At the same time it appeared to some of the Unionist Ministers that the action taken at their meeting of December 3 was open to possible misconstruction, and that it had probably been so misconstrued by the Prime Minister after Mr. Bonar Law's delivery of his message. Accordingly Lord Curzon, Lord Robert Cecil, and Mr. Chamberlain went to 10 Downing Street to explain on their own behalf and on that of Mr. Walter Long that their consent to the demand that Mr. Asquith should be asked to resign in no way indicated a wish that he should retire. On the contrary, they did not believe that anybody else could form a Government, certainly not Mr. Lloyd George; so that the result would be the return of the Prime Minister with a stronger Government and a greatly enhanced position. There can be no reason to doubt the complete sincerity of these declarations, as the situation appeared to their authors at the moment.

On the morning of Tuesday, December 5, I attended the Privy Council at Buckingham Palace and found the King anxious about the crisis, but confident that a way out would be found without a complete change of Government. I explained to His Majesty the plan for instituting two small committees, one for the actual conduct of the War, the other for business necessary to the War; but I did not touch nearly on the personal questions.

Later in the morning I received a summons to 10 Downing Street, to talk over the situation with the Prime Minister before a meeting of Liberal members of the Cabinet summoned for one o'clock. He showed me the text of Mr. Lloyd George's letter of the previous day, announcing his resignation in the absence of agreement with his War Committee proposals. It seemed as though the gravity of this step depended on the extent of support to be anticipated from the Unionist Ministers; if they refused reconstruction and insisted on Mr. Asquith's resignation, whether in order to substitute Mr. Lloyd George or not, the Government could not continue in any form. Such was also the opinion of Mr. Asquith's Liberal colleagues, who unanimously agreed that the terms imposed by the Secretary of State for War could not be accepted.

Since the Unionist Ministers for their part refused to agree to even the most drastic reconstruction without the resignation of the Prime Minister, only one course was open to him. He therefore wrote declining Mr. Lloyd George's plan, and the same evening placed his resignation in the King's hands, with the suggestion that Mr. Bonar Law should be sent for. This was done the same night, when it is understood that Mr. Bonar Law explained his inability to undertake the duty. At any rate, unless Mr. Asquith would serve under him. As it happened, we were dining at 10 Downing Street and our host was called away to see Mr. Bonar Law, who had come on from the Palace in order to inquire whether he could look for Mr. Asquith's help as a colleague if he proceeded to form an administration. The reply was altogether discouraging, if not definitely in the negative.

On the morning of Wednesday, the 6th, Mr. Lloyd George was in turn received at the Palace, and apparently declared that he also could not expect the necessary support, but I am not aware whether any stipulation regarding Mr. Asquith's support was made by him. Thus a deadlock was produced, but a suggestion was conveyed to Lord Stamfordham, at the particular instance it is believed of Lord Derby and Mr. Montagu, that it might be ended if the King would confer with the principal personages concerned, as in the attempt to settle the Irish question in 1914. This proposal naturally appealed to His Majesty; and Mr. Asquith, Mr. Bonar Law, Mr. Lloyd George, Mr. Balfour, and Mr. Henderson attended at Buckingham Palace accordingly the same afternoon.

The general course of the discussion there was described by Mr. Asquith to his late Liberal colleagues at 10 Downing Street immediately after the meeting. It appears that at the opening there was some expression of opinion by the two alternative Prime Ministers that Mr. Asquith should endeavour to continue, but both, when asked by him if he could claim their assistance in any capacity, declared that this was impossible. Mr. Lloyd George, however, urged Mr. Asquith to attempt to form a Government from among his own supporters. It was next discussed whether if Mr. Bonar Law or Mr. Lloyd George became Prime Minister Mr. Asquith would serve under either. Both Mr. Balfour and Mr. Henderson hoped that he would do so, and the King may also have favoured this course; Mr. Asquith, however, neither declined nor accepted, but decided to consult his friends before replying.

Another meeting of Liberal ex-Ministers was therefore called at Downing Street that evening, Mr. Henderson also attending. In the first place it was unanimously agreed that it was not feasible to proceed with a Government including no Unionist representation and without Mr. Lloyd George, more especially if the latter carried out the intention frankly stated in his letter of resignation, of conducting a campaign throughout the country against the methods hitherto pursued in carrying on the War. The next subject of discussion, for which the meeting was indeed principally called, was the possibility of Mr. Asquith's joining an administration formed by Mr. Bonar Law or Mr. Lloyd George. No mention was made on this occasion of any other alternative premiership, so that the issue was in some degree simplified. Mr. Henderson began by strongly urging the adhesion of Mr. Asquith, in order that a truly national Government might be formed. The only other Minister sharing his opinion was Mr. Montagu, who held that the prestige of Mr. Asquith ought not to be lost to the country. All the rest took the view that the combination would be mistaken and futile, and it was strongly expressed by Mr. McKinnon Wood, Lord Buckmaster, Mr. McKenna, Mr. Runciman, Lord Grey, and myself.

Mr. Asquith entirely concurred with our statements,

which were to the effect that no sentiments of personal dignity or of *amour propre* ought to prevent him from accepting a lower position, but that two fatal objections barred the way. The first was that, given the personalities involved, the scheme would not in fact work. Mr. Asquith had declined to become a Merovingian ruler as Prime Minister, and as a subordinate member of the new Government he would not submit to the autocracy of the War Committee, of which there was no assurance that he would even be a member. A collision was therefore probable, perhaps before very long; and it was felt that while the present break-up might be a national misfortune, it would amount to a serious disaster if later on Mr. Asquith and those Liberals who might join with him felt compelled to bring about another crisis. Mr. Lloyd George would in all probability find no difficulty in getting the requisite support; and if a new system was to be tried it had best be entrusted to colleagues of the same school of thought as the new Prime Minister.

In the second place, it was felt that Mr. Asquith's influence, though now so powerful and pervading, would melt away if he were thus to accept office. There would be no little resentment among many of his supporters both in Parliament and in the country. This was all the more significant because the advent of a new administration under a headstrong Minister mistrusted by many might of itself quicken extreme and reckless opposition, and perhaps drive not a few recruits in the direction of peacemaking. The creation therefore of a sober and responsible Opposition (if that be the proper term) steadily supporting the Government in the conduct of the War, criticizing when necessary, and in the last resort offering an alternative administration, was the best outcome of the crisis in the national interest. Mr. Asquith therefore stood out, and the present Ministry was formed by Mr. Lloyd George.

It should be observed that concurrently with this gathering at Downing Street the Unionist members of the late Government were meeting in Mr. Bonar Law's room at the Colonial Office, whence Lord Curzon came over to "Number Ten" to hear the result of our conference, and was told of Mr. Asquith's refusal.

A survey of these quickly succeeding events compels the conclusion that the issue depended more upon a clash of personalities than upon any basic contradiction of principles. Victory was the goal of both; but Mr. Lloyd George undoubtedly held that Mr. Asquith was unfitted to achieve it, from temperament not less than through the strain imposed by a long term of office, and by advancing years. He was confident, on the other hand, that his own activity and resource could inspire the country and hasten a glorious end to the War. At the same time he was by no means blind to Mr. Asquith's unrivalled parliamentary capacity or to his hold over the solid forces of Liberalism. He, therefore, it may be asserted, contemplated two distinct policies, by either of which his purpose might be attained. Mr. Asquith might continue as Prime Minister, leaving the conduct of the War to Mr. Lloyd George and two or three weaker lieutenants; the veto of whatever Cabinet was left would not be seriously hampering, because it could not in fact be exercised against a War Committee with all the knowledge, and with their resignations in their pockets. In some respects this would be the preferable system, because the Prime Minister's mastery of the House of Commons would be at the service of the practically independent War Committee. Mr. Lloyd George therefore pressed for this solution, and induced others to do the same. If it was declined, as in fact it was, Mr. Asquith must be forced to resign. In the words of Gambetta — of whom Mr. Lloyd George may regard himself as in some respects the reincarnation — *"il faut se soumettre ou se démettre."*

For this purpose the aid of Mr. Bonar Law was indispensable and it was no doubt easily secured. To prevent any rift in the Unionist party was the first object of its leader; and he perceived that a concentration under a new chief whose watchword was " action " was more likely to secure this than any possible reconstruction of the old Government. He doubtless foresaw that some of his Unionist colleagues who had small taste for a Lloyd George administration, and who disliked the methods by which Mr. Asquith was forced to resign, could be shepherded into the new Government by appeals to their public spirit. After this had occurred Lord Curzon explained to me the reasons which actuated himself and others of the same way of thinking; and I was able to tell him that in my judgment, having regard to the action of others for which they were in no way responsible, he and his friends had taken the correct course.

December 20, 1916.

LORD LANSDOWNE'S MEMORANDUM OF
NOVEMBER 13, 1916

The members of the War Committee were asked by
the Prime Minister some weeks ago to express their
views as to the terms upon which peace might be concluded. I do not know whether there has been a general response to this invitation, but the only reply which
I have seen is one written last month by the First Lord
of the Admiralty, in which he deals at some length
with the problems which might have to be discussed at
any peace conference. Mr. Balfour observes truly that
these questions cannot be profitably examined except
upon an agreed hypothesis as to the military position
of the combatants at the end of the War, and he proceeds to assume, though merely for the sake of argument, that the Central Powers, either through defeat
or exhaustion, have to accept the terms imposed upon
them by the Allies.

I venture to suggest that the attention of the War
Committee might with advantage be directed to a somewhat different problem, and that they should be invited to give us their opinion as to our present prospects
of being able to " dictate " the kind of terms which we
should all like to impose upon our enemies if we were
in a position to do so.

We are agreed as to the goal, but we do not know
how far we have really travelled towards it, or how
much nearer to it we are likely to find ourselves even
if the War be prolonged for, say, another year. What
will that year have cost us? How much better will our

position be at the end of it? Shall we even then be strong enough to "dictate" terms?

It seems to me almost impossible to overrate the importance of these considerations, because it is clear that our diplomacy must be governed by an accurate appreciation of them.

We have obtained within the last few days from the different departments of the Government a good deal of information as to the situation, naval, military, and economic. It is far from reassuring.

From the President of the Board of Trade we received on October 26 a most interesting and carefully compiled memorandum tending to show the daily growing shortage of tonnage and its consequences. Mr. Runciman comes to the conclusion that our shipbuilding is not keeping pace with our losses, and that, although the number of our vessels is down, the demands on our tonnage are not diminished. We must look forward to depending more and more on neutral ships, but we can be under no illusions as to the precarious nature of that resource. I do not think I exaggerate when I describe this most important document as profoundly disquieting. But in a later memorandum, dated November 9, the President paints the picture in still gloomier colours, and anticipates, on the advice of his experts, "a complete breakdown in shipping . . . much sooner than June, 1917."

The President of the Board of Agriculture has recently presented to the Cabinet his report on Food Prospects in 1917. That report goes to show that there is a world's deficit in bread-stuffs, that the price of bread is likely to go higher, that there has been a general failure of the potato crop, that the supply of fish is expected to be 64 per cent. below the normal, that there is considerable difficulty in regard to the supply of feeding-stuffs, that the difficulties of cultivation steadily increase, that land is likely to go derelict, the yield to decline, and the number of livestock to diminish greatly.

Lord Crawford's later note, dated November 9, on Home Food Supplies, shows that these anticipations were not unduly pessimistic. The position has, he tells us, become much worse, and, owing to the inroads made upon the agricultural population by the demands of the Army, it is in some parts of the country " no longer a question of maintaining a moderate standard of cultivation, but whether cultivation will cease."

Turning to our naval and military resources, we have a report from the First Lord of the Admiralty, dated October 14, from which we learn that, in spite of the tremendous efforts which we have made, the size of our Home Fleets is still insufficient, that we have nearly reached the limit of immediate production in the matter of capital ships, that we have not got nearly enough destroyers to meet our needs for escort and anti-submarine work, that we shall certainly not have enough for our Allies, and that the position in regard to light cruisers is not much better. From the same report we may infer that the submarine difficulty is becoming acute, and that, in spite of all our efforts, it seems impossible to provide an effectual rejoinder to it. The increasing size of the enemy submarines, the strength of their construction (which will apparently oblige us to rearm our merchantmen with a heavier gun), and their activity in all parts of the world, point to the same conclusion.

The papers which we have from time to time received from the General Staff and from the War Committee prove that in the matter of man-power we are nearing the end of our tether. The last report of the Man-Power Distribution Board seems, in particular, to sound a grave note of warning. The unexhausted supply of meń is, they tell us, now very restricted, and the number available can only be added to by a still further depletion of industry. In the meanwhile Ireland still declines to add to the available supply the 150,000 men who would be obtainable from that country, and I am not aware that any serious attempt is to be made to secure them.

All these seem to me to be very serious factors in the calculation which it is our duty to make. It will be replied, and no doubt truly, that the Central Powers are feeling the pressure of the War not less acutely than we feel it, and I hope we shall also be told that our staying powers are greater than theirs; but even if this be so, it is none the less our duty to consider, after a careful review of the facts, what our plight, and the plight of the civilized world, will be after another year, or, as we are sometimes told, two or three more years of a struggle as exhausting as that in which we are engaged. No one for a moment believes that we are going to lose the War; but what is our chance of winning it in such a manner, and within such limits of time, as will enable us to beat our enemy to the ground and impose upon him the kind of terms which we so freely discuss?

I do not suppose for an instant that there is any

weakening in the spirit of the people of this country, and I should hope, although I do not feel absolute confidence on the subject, that the same might be said of our Allies; but neither in their interests nor in ours can it be desirable that the War should be prolonged, unless it can be shown that we can bring it to an effectual conclusion within a reasonable space of time.

What does the prolongation of the War mean?

Our own casualties already amount to over 1,100,000. We have had 15,000 officers killed, not including those who are missing. There is no reason to suppose that, as the force at the front in the different theatres of war increases, the casualties will increase at a slower rate. We are slowly but surely killing off the best of the male population of these islands. The figures representing the casualties of our Allies are not before me. The total must be appalling.

The financial burden which we have already accumulated is almost incalculable. We are adding to it at the rate of over £5,000,000 per day. Generations will have to come and go before the country recovers from the loss which it has sustained in human beings, and from the financial ruin and the destruction of the means of production which are taking place.

All this it is no doubt our duty to bear, but only if it can be shown that the sacrifice will have its reward. If it is to be made in vain, if the additional year, or two years, or three years, finds us still unable to dictate terms, the War with its nameless horrors will have been needlessly prolonged, and the responsibility of those who needlessly prolong such a war is not less than that of those who needlessly provoked it.

A thorough stocktaking, first by each Ally of his own resources, present and prospective, and next by the Allies, or at all events by the leading Allies, in confidential consultation, seems indispensable. Not until such a stocktaking has taken place will each Ally be able to decide which of his desiderata are indispensable, and whether he might not be prepared to accept less than 20s. in the pound in consideration of prompt payment. Not until it has taken place will the Allies as a body be able to determine the broad outline of their policy or the attitude which they ought to assume towards those who talk to them of peace.

I think Sir William Robertson must have had some such stocktaking in his mind when he wrote the remarkable paper which was circulated to the Cabinet on August 31. In that paper he expressed his belief that negotiations for peace in some form or other might arise any day, and he urged that "We need therefore to decide without loss of time what our policy is to be, then place it before the Entente Powers, and ascertain in return what are their aims, and so endeavour to arrive at a clear understanding before we meet our enemies in conference." The idea may, for all I know, have been acted upon already.

Many of us, however, must of late have asked ourselves how this war is ever to be brought to an end. If we are told that the deliberate conclusion of the Government is that it must be fought until Germany has been beaten to the ground and sues for peace on any terms which we are pleased to accord to her, my only observation would be that we ought to know something of the data upon which this conclusion has been reached. To many of us it seems as if the prospect of a "knock out" was, to say the least of it, remote. Our forces and those of France have shown a splendid gallantry on the Western Front, and have made substantial advances; but is it believed that these, any more than those made in 1915 with equally high hopes and accompanied by not less cruel losses, will really enable us to "break through"? Can we afford to go on paying the same sort of price for the same sort of gains?

Judging from the comments supplied by the General Staff I should doubt whether the Italian offensive, however successful, is likely to have a decisive effect.

At Salonika we are entangled in an extraordinary difficult enterprise, forced upon us, against our better judgment, by our Allies, and valuable only because it occupies enemy troops who would otherwise be fighting the Russians and the Rumanians. On the Russian and Rumanian frontiers we shall be fortunate if we avoid a disaster, which at one moment seemed imminent. General Brusiloff's language is inspiring, but is it really justified by the facts? The history of the Russian operations has been very chequered, and we shall never, I am afraid, be free from the danger of miscarriages owing to defective strategy, to failure of supplies, to corruption in high places, or to incidents such as the disastrous explosion which has just lost us 10,000 tons of munitions at Archangel.

Again, are we quite sure that, regarded as political rather than military assets, our Allies are entirely to be depended upon? There have been occasions upon which political complications have threatened to affect the military situation in France. I quote the following sentences from a letter written a few days ago by a very shrewd Frenchman: *"Rappelez-vous bien que la démocratic française n'est pas menée par son gouvernement; c'est elle qui le mêne: un courant d'opinion publique en faveur de la cessation de la guerre pourrait être irrésistible. . . . Au feu, le soldat français se battra toujours comme un héros: derrière, sa famille pourra bien dire: en violà assez!"* Italy is always troublesome and exacting. Sir Rennell Rodd, in a dispatch dated November 4, asks us to take note of the fact that there are already in Italy "certain symptoms of war weariness and discouragement at the protraction of the struggle. . . . Great Britain is represented as the only country anxious to prolong the struggle *à outrance* for her own ends. . . . It would be wrong to pretend that there exists here the same grim determination to carry through as prevails in France and in the British Empire." The domestic situation in Russia is far from reassuring. There have been alarming disorders both in Moscow and in Petrograd. Russia has had five Ministers of the Interior in twelve months, and the fifth is described as being by no means secure in his seat.

Our difficulties with the neutrals are, again, not likely to diminish. It is highly creditable to the Foreign Office that during the last two years we have escaped a breakdown of our blockade policy, which, in spite of continual obstruction and bad faith, has produced excellent results; but we have been within an ace of grave complications with Sweden and the United States. As time goes on the neutrals are likely to become more and more restive and intolerant of the belligerents, whose right to go on disturbing the peace of the civilized world they will refuse to admit.

I may be asked whether I have any practical suggestion to offer, and I admit the difficulty of replying. But is it not true that, unless the apprehensions which I have sketched can be shown, after such an investigation as I have suggested, to be groundless, we ought at any rate not to discourage any movement, no matter where originating, in favour of an interchange of views as to the possibility of a settlement? There are many indications that the germs of such a movement are already in existence. One cannot dismiss as unworthy of attention the well-substantiated reports which have come to us from time to time upon this subject from Belgian, Scandinavian, Japanese, and Russian sources, or such circumstantial stories as those told in Sir Esme Howard's dispatch of August 24, as to the meeting held at Prince Lichnowsky's house, and in Lord Eustace Percy's memorandum as to the intimations made by the Rector of the Berlin University. The debates in the Reichstag show that the pacificist groups are active and outspoken. From all sides come accounts of the impatience of the civil population and their passionate yearning for peace.

It seems to me quite inconceivable that during the winter we shall not be sounded by someone as to our readiness to discuss terms of peace or proposals for an armistice. Are we prepared with our reply? Lord Crawford has dealt with the question of an armistice. I am not sure that I agree with some of his suggestions, but I am sure that he is right in holding that an unconditional refusal would be inadmissible.

As to peace terms, I hope we shall adhere steadfastly to the main principle laid down by the Prime Minister in the speech which he summed up by a declaration that we could agree to no peace which did not afford adequate reparation for the past and adequate security for the future, but the outline was broadly sketched and might be filled up in many different ways. The same may be said of the not less admirable statement which he has just made at the Guildhall, and of the temperate speeches which the Secretary of State for Foreign Affairs has from time to time delivered.

But it is unfortunate that, in spite of these utterances, it should be possible to represent us and our Allies as committed to a policy partly vindictive and partly selfish, and so irreconcilably committed to that policy that we should regard as unfriendly any attempt, however sincere, to extricate us from the impasse. The interview given by the Secretary of State for War in September last to an American correspondent has produced an impression which it will not be easy to efface. There may have been circumstances of which I am unaware, connected perhaps with the Presidential election, which made it necessary to announce that at the particular moment any intervention, however well meant, would be distasteful to us or inopportune. He said, indeed, that " the world must know that there can be no outside interference at this stage"—a very momentous limitation. For surely it cannot be our intention, no matter how long the War lasts, no matter what the strain on our resources, to maintain this attitude, or to declare, as M. Briand declared about the same time, that for us too " the word peace is a sacrilege." Let our naval, military, and economic advisers tell us frankly whether they are satisfied that the knock-out blow can and will be delivered. The Secretary of State's formula holds the field, and will do so until something else is put in its place. Whether it is to hold the field, and, if not, what that something else should be, ought surely to depend upon their answer, and that again upon the result of the careful stocktaking, domestic and international, which, I hope, is already taking place.

L.

Postscript.—The above note had been written before the discussion which took place at to-day's Cabinet, from which we learned that the War Committee had already decided to take important steps in the direction which I have ventured to indicate.

L.

November 13, 1916.

LORD ROBERT CECIL'S MEMORANDUM,
NOVEMBER 27, 1916

Whether we agree with Lord Lansdowne's conclusions or not, one thing is clear. Our situation is grave. It is certain that unless the utmost national effort is made it may become desperate, particularly in the matter of shipping. The position in Allied countries is even more serious. France is within measurable distance of exhaustion. The political outlook in Italy is menacing. Her finance is tottering. In Russia there is great discouragement. She has long been on the verge of revolution.   Even her man-power seems coming near its limits.

On the other hand, our enemies, though badly injured, are not disabled. The economic position of Germany may or may not be alarming. It is certainly not yet desperate. No certain information as to her supplies is available. There is no trustworthy ground for thinking that she is starving, although she may be — very possibly she is — in want of other necessaries, such as wool, cotton, lubricating oils, rubber, which will hamper and diminish her military strength, and there is great political discontent. In Austria the position is probably worse.

Our military advisers tell us that they believe that next year we have a prospect of a great military success, and if this be so, I do not believe that the resisting power of the Central Empires would survive it.   If, therefore, we can carry on for another year we have a reasonable prospect of victory. A peace now could only be disastrous. At the best we could not hope for more than the *status quo* with a great increase in the German power in Eastern Europe.   Moreover, this peace would be known by the Germans to have been forced upon us by their submarines, and our insular position would be recognized as increasing instead of diminishing our vulnerability. No one can contemplate our future ten years after a peace on such conditions without profound misgiving.

I feel, therefore, that we are bound to continue the War.   But I also feel that to attempt to do so without drastic changes in our civil life would be to court disaster. The Germans are putting their whole civilian organization on a war footing, and we must do the same. We must unflinchingly reduce our imports, whether by rationing or other means.

Very possibly we shall have to adopt what is called industrial conscription. Quite certainly we shall have to make great innovations in our industrial organization. Besides, we have to secure a large number of additional men for the Army

To have any chance of achieving these objects we must see that the comfortable classes do not escape their share of privation. Even in their own interests this is desirable. The men who talk and write so blatantly about calling upon the people for fresh sacrifices should be made to understand something of what war means. Apart from this, we cannot expect the working class to undergo fresh burdens unless they feel that all are treated alike.

I submit, therefore, that we should be ready for such measures as taking over the industries which have made most out of the War, such as the coal mines and shipping. It may well be desirable also to take over the breweries and distilleries, in the interests both of man-power and of economy. It is a question whether rich men's clubs should be left open. Ministers may have to abandon part of their salaries.

There are no doubt many other things of the same kind which should be considered. The urgent thing is to set up machinery for the purpose. I propose, therefore, that a Cabinet Committee on civilian organization should be immediately appointed. It should not consist of more than three members, and it should be directed to make its first report within a week. As soon as that report is ready, the Cabinet should meet and deal with it.

It may be asked why this could not be left to the War Committee. The answer is that that body is already overburdened with work. But I think the two bodies should be kept in close touch with one another, and I therefore propose that one member of the War Committee should also be a member of the Civilian Organization Committee.

R. C.

November 27, 1916.

CHAPTER XV

POLICY AND STRATEGY[1]

THE remarkable book " Soldiers and Statesmen," by Sir William Robertson, is a contribution of unusual interest and significance to the history of the Great War.

I do not propose to discuss the Field-Marshal's narrative of the actual conduct of the War during the time in which he was the chief military adviser of the British Government. To those who were not behind the scenes it will throw a great deal of fresh and much-needed light both upon the statesmanship and the strategy of the years 1917 and 1918. It ought also finally to dispel the legend that the Allied situation was in a desperate case, which called for heroic remedies, in December, 1916. We have already had Ludendorff's testimony that at that date, "We [the Germans] were completely exhausted on the Western front. . . . The army had been fought to a standstill and was utterly worn out. They had to face the danger that ' Somme fighting' would soon break out at various points on our front, and that even our troops would not be able to withstand such attacks indefinitely, if the enemy gave us no time for rest and the accumulation of material": the exact policy (as Sir W. Robertson points out) which the Allied commanders had resolved upon at the Chantilly Conference of November, 1916, and

[1] The substance of this chapter has already appeared in America in *McCall's Magazine*.

which they were preparing to carry into execution at the date fixed — the middle of February — with "the full resources at their disposal." Admiral Tirpitz has also put it on record that at this time "G.H.Q. doubted seriously whether we could hold out for another year." Sir William Robertson, while naturally critical of what seemed to the soldiers' mind the slowness of the steps by which we attacked the infinitely complex problems of National Service, and of the best allocation of the man power of the country, acknowledges that "after all" it was owing to the measures taken by the Government in 1915 and 1916 that "the fighting strength of the British Armies in France was greater in the summer of 1917 than at any period of the War."

The year 1917 was indeed the worst in the whole War: its dark record is only relieved by General Maude's campaign in Mesopotamia, the plans and preparations for which had been thought out and matured at the War Office in London before I left office in December, 1916.

There is, of necessity, a good deal of controversial matter in the book. But there is abundant evidence throughout of a determination to be just, and to realize the gravity and novelty of the political, no less than of the strategical, problems of the War.

This indeed is the main question which will suggest itself to every reader of the book: What is the true relation in time of war between statesmanship and strategy? What are the respective functions of the soldier and the politician? No one will dispute the general proposition that strategy must be subordinate to policy. It is not for the General Staff of the Army or Navy, or

of both combined, to determine whether there is or is
not, in given circumstances, a *casus belli*. Moreover,
the statesmen will, if they understand the elements of
their business, keep themselves in time of peace in constant touch (as we in Great Britain endeavoured to do,
by means of the Committee of Imperial Defence in the
ten years which preceded the War) with their technical advisers, and discuss with them all reasonably
possible contingencies. The War Book, which was
drawn up under the instructions of the Committee in
1911, with its precise instructions for the steps to be
taken by every public department and all local authorities in the "precautionary" period — instructions
which proved invaluable when they were brought to
the test in 1914 — is one illustration of the importance
of such preliminary co-operation.

But when war has actually broken out, as history
abundantly proves, quite a different set of problems
arises. Napoleon, in his early campaigns in Italy,
soon freed himself from the control of the Directory in
Paris. From the time he became First Consul to the
end of his career, there could be no question of collision
of opinion between ministers and generals; for the
authority of both was concentrated in a single person.
The same was true of Gustavus Adolphus and Frederick the Great. But when, as more often happens, the
general in the field is subject to the orders of his Government at home the case is very different. Domestic
politics, and the fluctuation of party fortunes at Westminster, were constantly hampering and embarrassing
the greatest of English commanders, the Duke of Marl-
borough. The Tories were in favour of a merely de-

fensive war in the Netherlands, and only assented in a half-hearted fashion to the thanks which were voted in the House of Commons to the victor of Blenheim. The Duke of Wellington in his Peninsular campaign, whenever public opinion became critical or even hostile, always had powerful supporters in the Cabinet, though, after the fruitless victory of Talavera, the Prime Minister, Perceval, was "inclined to withdrawal from the Peninsula." In the early days of the Civil War in America, Lincoln constantly pressed upon his generals his own opinions on purely military matters. It was not until he had tried in turn McClellan, Burnside, Hooker, and Meade, that he at last found in Grant the general who won the war. Grant seems to have stipulated from the first that he was to be absolutely free from all interference; Lincoln after his appointment contented himself with an occasional suggestion; and even declared that he did not know, or wish to know, the general's plan of campaign.

The Great War of 1914–18 was upon an unprecedented scale both by land and sea. Sir William Robertson records that it became his duty, as Chief of the Imperial General Staff, at one time to exercise daily supervision over no fewer than seven distinct campaigns. It was impossible, especially in its earlier stages, to disentangle political and strategic considerations. For a long time Italy and Rumania held back; Bulgaria was still a doubtful factor; and even Greece, despite the great authority of Venizelos, could not be counted on for a steadfast policy. The soldiers on the Western front naturally grudged the diversion of men and material to a distant theatre like Gallipoli. But if the Dardanelles expedition had been pushed through and succeeded in its immediate purpose in the spring of 1915, the political and, with them, the strategic consequences, would have been of the most momentous kind. The Salonika expedition had, in my opinion, no such justification. Sir William Robertson tells us that all the leading French generals with whom he was brought into contact, including Joffre, Foch, and Pétain, showed "in manner, if not in actual words, that they intensely disliked the project," and that was also the attitude of our own General Staff. But it was persistently pressed by the French Government, and at the various conferences which were held on the subject I cannot recall any indication that they had not behind them the support of their military advisers.

Policy and strategy being, as they were, so inextricably intermingled, it would have been impossible, and indeed ridiculous, to treat them as though they could be independent of one another. But there was one rule which was both safe and simple to follow. Once the governing objectives for the time had been decided, after the fullest consultation with their expert advisers, by the ultimate authority—the responsible Ministers at home—the execution should always be left, as Lincoln discovered by experience, to the untrammelled discretion of the General Staff and the commanders on the spot. "On the whole," writes Sir W. Robertson, "it may be said that throughout 1916 the General Staff were accorded suitable freedom of action in all matters lying within their sphere, and received from the Government, as well as from individual Ministers, the guidance and assistance which the proper discharge of their duties required. To this fact, perhaps, more than to any others may be largely attributed the military achievements of the year, which left the position in all theatres of war more satisfactory and hopeful than it had been twelve months before."

If after fair and full trial of your Chief of the Staff, and of your commanders in the field, you are not satisfied of their competence for the task entrusted to them, recall and replace them. But so long as they are there give them confidence and a free hand. Sir William Robertson's narrative affords some striking illustrations, both positive and negative, of the practical importance in the conduct of war of this elementary maxim.

When I came to the War Office after the "Curragh incident" in 1914, and discovered the active part which Sir Henry Wilson (holding at the time one of the most responsible and confidential posts — that of D.M.O. — in the Service) had been playing in the inner plottings of the Ulster party, I was strongly tempted to send him for a while to cool his head and his heels

> "Where the remote Bermudas ride,
> In ocean's bosom unespied":

a disciplinary step which he well deserved. But I was anxious to promote a temper of appeasement, and I had a genuine appreciation of his military qualities. He had large and readily available stores of technical knowledge, and, as I can testify from his occasional appearances before the Committee of Imperial Defence, when provided with a pointer and a large-scale map, he was a most instructive and entertaining lecturer.   But his qualities were marred by some serious defects.   He was voluble, impetuous, and an indefatigable intriguer.[1]   As his Diaries, which the misplaced devotion of friends has disclosed to the world, abundantly show, he was endowed by Nature with a loose tongue, and was in the habit of wielding a still looser pen: and, as compared for instance with a man like Kitchener, he was singularly deficient on the professional side in prescience and sound judgment.

[1] He was at home from the Front during the first week of December, 1916, and seems to have revelled in the congenial situation. See the extracts from his Diary of that date (Vol. I, pp. 304–5), ending: *"I am confident myself that if we manage things properly, we have Asquith dead."* "We" appears from the context to be meant to include, not only Wilson himself, but Mr. Lloyd George, Mr. Bonar Law, Sir E. Carson, and Mr. Leo Maxse.

CHAPTER XVI

CONTEMPORARY NOTES — *Mainly Literary and Personal*: 1915–18

IN 1915 I formed a new friendship to which I have ever since been greatly indebted. A young couple, Roland and Hilda Harrisson, took a farm in the neighbourhood of Easton Grey in Wilts, which had long been the home of my sister-in-law, Mrs. Graham Smith. Roland Harrisson was a professional soldier — a major in the Royal Artillery — and but for the War would have gone with his battery to India. He was mobilized and sent to the Front in France, where he fought, with occasional intervals of leave, until he was killed in action in the autumn of 1917. Both he and his wife came from Liverpool, where his father was a well-known surgeon, and his wife's father a solicitor in good practice. Her maiden name was Hilda Grierson. My acquaintance with her ripened after the death of her husband when in the course of 1918–19 she came to live with her mother, Mrs. Grierson, at Boars Hill — only a few miles from Sutton Courtney: we became regular and intimate correspondents: and she has preserved a large number of my letters upon which she has allowed me to draw for the purpose of my narrative. They go back for ten years, and with the exception of what I have written to my wife they are the nearest approach to a diary of any record which I possess. In this and the following chapters I shall quote from them freely.

The first letter is dated June 13, 1915, when on a Sunday visit to my sister-in-law I first made Mrs. Harrisson's acquaintance. It runs as follows:

" I want to tell you, if I may, how much I have enjoyed your company, and I hope your friendship, and making the acquaintance of your dear little Peter. I shall not forget either you or him, and you may be sure that I share to the full the anxieties which must always be pressing upon you for your gallant husband."

A few weeks later, in acknowledging a letter, I see that I wrote: " I am glad that you read Sir Thomas Browne: no such English has been written since. ' I am in England everywhere' is very characteristic of his tolerance and insularity. . . . I have been seeking solace of an intermittent and desultory kind in turning over again Edward Fitzgerald's letters, which I expect you know. Of the unheroic dressing-gown-and-slippers kind they are quite first rate. He quotes a good thing from Bacon's essay on Friendship: 'with a Friend a man *tosseth* his thoughts.' A very good test, don't you think?"

In January, 1916, lamenting that I had been prevented from coming for Sunday to Easton Grey, I wrote that " it was very poor compensation to attend Divine Service at Westminster Abbey, and try to divert one's attention from a particularly blatant discourse by Archdeacon X. The world just now is a good deal out of joint and cannot be safely left to revolve on its own axis."

Easter Day, 1916. I escaped with a real sense of relief from London late on Thursday afternoon, having been engaged for the best part of a fortnight in a similar occupation to that of St. Paul, when "after the manner of men" he fought with beasts at Ephesus. However, they are back now in their cages—for the time being —and I am spending a more placid Easter than I could have hoped for.

July 16. I like Sir T. Browne's "villain and secretary of hell." I know about half a dozen well-qualified candidates for that post.

The problems and worries do not diminish in number or volume: as soon as one particular quarter of the sky seems clear, it breeds in the twinkling of an eye quite a good-sized tornado, and there is the devil to pay.

I am glad you are going to grapple with Boswell. I alternate between frivolities like "Lalage's Lovers" (quite readable) and rather stodgy biography. There is a lot of good stuff in Q.-C.'s "Art of Writing."

In the autumn of the same year (September, 1916) I paid a few days' visit to the Front, where amongst other things I witnessed the debut of the Tanks (which we then called "Caterpillars"). I saw my two sons— Raymond and Arthur—and was present at some of the earlier stages of the fighting on the Somme. I had barely got back home when the news came to me that Raymond had been killed in action. In acknowledging my friend's condolences, after saying that "this has been a great blow to me and I am much shaken by it," I go on, "There is or ought to be every kind of consolation, and I have numberless letters from all parts of the world, and all sorts and conditions of people. But I don't know that it all helps one very much. To-day I braced myself up to propose the Vote of Credit in the House of Commons: a trying and difficult speech, especially the last part of it. I got on better than I expected, as everyone was very kind and sympathetic."

I may supplement this by a letter which I wrote on September 20 to another friend (Lady Scott—now Lady Hilton Young): "The War has sucked up so much of what was most lovable and full of promise that I have always been haunted by a fear that a toll would be exacted from me also. But when I saw him [Raymond] last—exactly a fortnight ago to-day—he was so radiantly strong and confident that I came away from France with an easier mind. *O cæca pectora!* Whatever pride I had in the past, and whatever hope I had for the far future—by much the largest part of both was invested in him. Now all that is gone. It will take me a few days more to get back to my bearings."

November 11. I am off for Sunday to the Wharf, and early on Tuesday I shall set my face seawards. I am taking with me for light reading in my solitary motor-drive to-day A. J. B.'s reply to Curzon's attack upon the Admiralty Air Policy. I have glanced at a page or two and I can see that it is one of the raciest things of recent times; full not only of rapier pricks but of shrewd knock-out blows.

November 19. (To Mrs. Harrisson.) I see you are taking your "King Lear" in small doses. I put it very high among the plays: Lear's "Never, never," is almost the most tragic thing in Shakespeare. But one always comes back in the end to "Hamlet."

I spent the inside of last week in Paris—colloguing and arguing and give-and-taking with politicians and soldiers. It is an ill-jointed world at present: and one is sometimes tempted to think that to have been born in it in these times was a bit of "cursed spite" on the part of the Higher Powers.

In the early days of the following month (December, 1916) I resigned my office in circumstances which have already been described. "When I fully realized" (as I wrote at the time) "what a position had been created, I saw that I could not go on without dishonour or impotence, or both. And nothing could have been worse for the country and the War.

"The King offered me the Garter, which I refused.

"I am glad you are reading the book of Job. I think I must refresh my memory of it."

From among a large number of similar communications on my resignation, I may perhaps give here the text of a telegram which I received from my old friend General Botha:

Extremely concerned at manner in which you have been forced out of office. Have worked with you for a long time and appreciate highly pains you have taken and the readiness you have shown to meet me and give assistance. Union of South Africa will not forget your co-operation; and to-day you have sympathy. Calm but firm determination is only way out.

BOTHA.

To which I replied:

Deeply gratified by your very kind message. As you say, you and I have co-operated for many years both in peace and in war. My warmest wishes now and always are with the Union of South Africa, to which the Empire is under a deep debt of gratitude. We must persevere with calm and fixed resolve. Cordial personal greetings.

ASQUITH.

There is a hiatus of some months, before the correspondence with Mrs. Harrisson is resumed. "I trust that your needle is not going to dethrone your books. Why should a soldier's wife need them less than other people's wives? I remember an old judge, who apart from the Law was quite illiterate, but a great sportsman, and who used to say with much complacency: 'On the 11th August every year my boys and I start for Scotland with our guns and rods: and thank God not a bloody book among the lot of us.'"

March 21, 1917. I have at last got my books into something like decent order, but I have not yet selected which to re-read: with the exception of "Monte Cristo," which I have not read for thirty years, and of which I take a nightly dose.

I have been remaking the acquaintance of General Smuts, one of the most remarkable of our Colonial statesmen.

May 1, 1917. I am glad that you have sampled the Euripides and like the first flavour of it.

Was it the first time you had read the Acts of the Apostles? I am entertained by your citation from that once familiar work. The "image that fell down from *Jupiter*" is a mistranslation. It was supposed (like many of the more primitive statues, *e.g.* Athena Polias at Athens) to have fallen from the clear sky.

We drove over at tea-time yesterday to Windsor, where we spent the night. I had an hour's talk with the King before dinner, and another hour after. . . . They were all very nice and kind, and it is always a pleasure to explore the Castle, which is in many ways a treasure-house.

* * * * *

Towards the end of September in this year (1917) Roland Harrisson was killed in action. In my first letter to his widow I quoted the lines from "Samson Agonistes" which begin

"Nothing is here for tears, nothing to wail
    Or knock the breast,"

of which I said, "there is something simple and sublime which lifts and soothes in their very austerity. I am glad that you find comfort in my letters, but as Theseus (I think) says in the 'Midsummer Night's Dream'—'the best in this kind are but shadows'—at such a time."

October 2, 1917. I fear that your life, both in itself and its surroundings, must be a sombre tale from day to day. . . . I have read or skimmed the "Life of Dilke" —a dullish book in two huge volumes about a dullish man. Is there anything that I can send you to read? I have just been looking into Mrs. Browning: would she be of any use?

October. Pamela [my sister-in-law, now Lady Grey] sat next me at dinner and we had a "literary" conversation. She is a great Jane Austenite, and had just returned from a lecture on that immortal woman: so I was glad to be able to stump her out by asking her what was the Christian name of Mr. Darcy in "Pride and Prejudice."

October 30. We had a sort of full-dress service at the House yesterday. Ll. G. took an hour and a quarter to cover the ground. I thought the bulk of his speech what is vulgarly called "tosh," and a much-applauded passage about the "Cavalry of the Clouds"—

called (I see) by Lord Curzon the "Knight-Erranty of the Air"—brought back to my irreverent mind the remark of Lothair, as he entered a hansom in St. James's Street: "'Tis the Gondola of London."

November. It is a pity you missed the lectures on the Sublime and Beautiful. I believe that the better opinion now is that the treatise is not by Longinus, but by some other gentleman of an unknown name. I must look this up! also L.'s relation to Zenobia: it is becoming difficult to keep pace with you in your lightning marches through the Kingdom of Learning.

November 12. We had a fine and sunny Sunday at the Wharf. In the afternoon we drove to Boars Hill and called on John Masefield, the poet, whom we found in khaki, feeding his rabbits, and still struggling with his narrative of the battle of the Somme. He is a delightful man.

December 12. Yesterday we started after an early lunch for Birmingham. After a rather ceremonial early dinner, given by the Lord Mayor, we went on to the Town Hall, where I found a wonderful meeting and a noble reception. What I said was listened to in the most flattering way to a speaker—that is, not with tumults of applause, but with strained, and at times almost breathless attention—until the end. Then I had to go to an overflow meeting: and after that, supper and a toast or two, and at last to bed.

You know the lines—they go back to the reign of Henry VII:

> "For though the day be never so longe,
>   At last the belles ringeth to evensonge."

I found lying about a copy of Macaulay's "Essays"
—which I read in the train both going and returning.
I had n't taken a dose of him for years: my admiration
of his knowledge and style (with all its patent defects)
grew with each page. If only anyone could write like
that now! Read over again his essay on Ranke's History of the Popes: it is worth a Jew's ransom.

December, 1917. I have been reading Colvin's
"Life of Keats." It is what the critics call a "monu-
mental" work: nothing can ever be added to it. I like
Keats better and think more of his power after reading
it. Fanny Brawne was a bit of a minx, and he got much
more pain than pleasure out of his love for her.

December, 1917. "Oc" [my third son, Arthur] has
been rather badly wounded reconnoitring outside
Cambrai. He has a compound fracture of the left
ankle, which may lead to the amputation of the foot.
. . . It was bad luck as he had just got the command
of his Brigade and is now called General. As usual,
he was behaving with both gallantry and initiative.[1]

January 19, 1918. I am afraid that your Dominie[2]
is rather gipsy-ridden, and that before long he will be
foisting "Lavengro" upon you. There is no harm in
"The Bible in Spain," but I hope you won't join (with
Birrell and others) the sect of the Borrovians.

You want a big book? Have you read, from cover
to cover and unabridged, Lockhart's "Life of Scott"?
If not, do so at once (there are seven volumes) : and
then try to answer the question why all the best biogra-
phies are of Men of Letters and not of Men of Action.

---

[1] He received the D.S.O. with two bars.

[2] Mr. Sampson, an eminent Romany scholar, and Librarian to Liverpool
University.

February 11. So you have become a ballad-monger! I am not sure that you will carry me very far with you into that territory.

I was rather pleased yesterday, on glancing again through Trevelyan's "Life," to discover the great and impeccable Macaulay committing a "howler" of the worst kind through lapse of memory. It happens to be a rather favourite bit of mine in " All's Well that Ends Well":

> "Let me not live . . .
> After my flame lacks oil, to be the snuff
> Of younger spirits."

Macaulay (apropos of the moribund old Hallam) quotes it: "to be the *scoff* of *meaner* spirits." I wrote to Trevelyan, who is an old friend and colleague, to ask whether his attention had been called to such a unique slip: for Macaulay's memory was as a rule faultless.

March 16. We dined last night at the French Embassy to meet Clemenceau, who is here for one of the Inter-Allied pow-wows: of which I gathered he does not think much. I had a long and quite interesting talk with him: no Frenchman has a better or quicker gift of expression.

September 14. (To another correspondent.) It was more than nice of you to send me the beautiful Prayer Book, which for printing, wood-cuts and binding it would be difficult to surpass. It is a most welcome ornament to my shelves.

I looked carefully to see whether the donor had indicated, by any kind of sign-post, the particular parts of the sacred volume of which she thought that I stood in the greatest need. So far, my search has been unavailing; but as I know by experience that (like Nature) you do "nothing in vain," I feel sure that sooner or later I shall find and read (between the lines) the message that is meant for my soul's good.

November 12. (To Mrs. Harrisson). We have been this morning to a Thanksgiving Service at St. Paul's, attended by the King and Queen. I sat next Lady Lansdowne, and as one after another of our female royalties was led up the nave, I said to her, "How long do you think this will last?" "About fifty-five minutes," she replied, imagining that I was referring to the Service and not to the Institution! I see that they have got rid of eight kings in Germany in the course of the last two or three days, and there are more to follow.[1]

November 16. President Wilson is coming after all, and is expected to arrive here about our polling date, December 14. I confess he is one of the few people in the world that I want to see and talk to: not quite in the spirit of Monckton Milnes, of whom it was said that if Christ came again he would at once send him an invitation card for one of his breakfasts, but because I am really curious to judge for myself what manner of man he is. Gilbert Murray, who was here this morning and knows him, thinks that I should like him.

* * * * *

In November, 1918, Parliament was dissolved, and in the general election I took an active part.

[1] A year later the King of Spain estimated to me the number of monarchical victims as thirty-five.

Apparently I had other distractions, for I find in a letter of November 25 the statement that in the midst of my study of the works of Delafield and Winifred Boggs, I interpolated yesterday another female writer, Enid Bagnold by name: a "Diary without Dates": the experiences of a V.A.D. in a hospital at Woolwich — a most unpromising subject, but quite cleverly handled with a light delicate touch.

A foolish woman whom I met somewhere this week was once taken in to dinner by Raymond. She opened the conversation by saying: "Every young man ought to have a serious purpose in life. What is yours?" "Talking to you," was his reply, and the subject dropped.

December 8. Electioneering. I have put in here [Alderley] for a Sunday in this comfortable haven of refuge, but it is only a respite, for I go on to-morrow to Lincoln and Nottingham, and by Wednesday morning shall be back in Fife. Wherever I go, I hear the same story — confusion, apathy, bewilderment. There never was such a nightmare of an election.

President Wilson was unwise enough at this time to slip down from his oracular tripod at Washington, and to rub shoulders with European diplomacy at Paris and Versailles. I had an interesting talk with him as he passed through London: among other topics, on the difference between the position and authority of the Cabinet in the United States and here. On one rather critical occasion during the Civil War, Lincoln (he told me) summoned his Cabinet, which contained some exceptionally able and distinguished men, and asked them their opinion as to what ought to be done. They were unanimous in favour of a particular policy, and the President took the unusual course of calling for a division. When they had all voted "aye," he said curtly, "I think the noes have it."

CHAPTER XVII

THE MAURICE EPISODE: THE COUPON ELECTION

ON May 7, 1918, a letter appeared in the Press from Major-General Sir Frederick Maurice, a distinguished officer who had been throughout the War Director of Military Operations. This letter, written entirely on his own responsibility, challenged statements made by Ministers as to the strength of our Army in France. The most important of the statements so impugned was Mr. Lloyd George's in a speech in the House of Commons on April 9, that the strength of the Army in France in 1918, as compared with 1917, had been more than maintained. The facts were, as General Maurice alleged, that while it was true that the nominal strength on January 1, 1917, was 1,299,000, and on January 1, 1918, 1,570,000, the latter figure was made up by including 300,000 unarmed British labourers and Chinese coolies; that even at that date the fighting troops were 100,000 weaker than a year before; and that in the weeks which followed from January 1 to March 31 Haig had had to disband 140 battalions for lack of men to replace losses.

The matter was brought up in the House of Commons, on May 7, by myself. I asked what steps the Government proposed to take to enable the House to examine the allegations contained in the letter. Mr. Bonar Law announced that, inasmuch as General Maurice's allegations affected the honour of Ministers, the Government proposed to invite two judges to inquire into the charges and to report as quickly as possible. Sir Edward Carson asked whether the proceedings would be public, and whether Cabinet Ministers and ex-Cabinet Ministers would be examined. Mr. Bonar Law answered that the inquiry must obviously be held in private, and if the House had confidence in the impartiality of the judges, they should be the best able to decide who should be examined.

The proposed tribunal, recalling as it did the Parnell Commission, appeared to myself, and to many others on both sides of the House, not to be of a satisfactory character, and I accordingly gave notice of a motion two days later for a Select Committee " to inquire into the allegations of incorrectness in certain statements of Ministers of the Crown to this House" contained in General Maurice's letter. In supporting my motion I declared that it was not, either in intention or in effect, a vote of censure upon the Government:

I have, since I sat in this seat [*i.e.* on the front Opposition bench], now, I think, for nearly eighteen months, so far as my memory serves me, never given an adverse vote on any proposal that has proceeded from the Government. I have done all that I could — all that it was in my power to do, not only in this House but outside, without withholding what I consider to be legitimate and helpful criticism — to assist the Government in the prosecution of the War, and in particular in the definition and the propagation of the great purposes, both of war and of peace, for which we and our Allies are contending. Some of my friends I know — some of those I see around me — think that I have been in these matters unduly fainthearted and mealy-mouthed. I am quite content to submit to that criticism.

I know that there are people — not, I think, in this House,

but outside — gifted with more imagination than charity, and with more stupidity than either, who think of me as a person who is gnawed with a hungry ambition to resume the cares and responsibilities of office.   I am quite content to leave foolish imaginations of that kind to the judgment of my colleagues in this House and of my countrymen outside.   If I did feel it my duty — if I were to find it my duty to ask the House to censure the Government, I hope I should have the courage and the candour to do so in a direct and unequivocal form.   I certainly should not have selected for that purpose a motion like this, which is limited to suggesting the desirability of an inquiry which only two days ago was admitted from the Treasury bench to be appropriate and expedient, which, so far as its scope is concerned, would be confined to the examination of two or three very simple issues of fact from which the Government might, as I am sure they think they would — I do not want in any way to prejudge the matter — emerge not with diminished, but with enhanced authority and prestige.

Later on I said:

I say most emphatically that in this House we are accustomed to accept — we are bound to accept — statements made by Ministers of the Crown upon their authority as accurate and true, and unless and until the contrary is proved I hope we shall always uphold that well-founded parliamentary tradition.   It is not necessary for me to say that, so far as I am personally concerned, I hold no brief of any sort or kind for military as distinguished from civilian and what is called politicians' opinion.   Nothing of the sort, but, in view of this situation, which I have said, and the Government have themselves acknowledged, is in many ways unexampled; in view of their own deliberate statement, made only two days ago, that an inquiry was, I will not say necessary, but expedient and desirable; in view of the limitations and conditions which they themselves, of their own motion and upon their own initiative, prescribed for such an inquiry, I do suggest to the House that, in the interests of the Government, in the interests of the Army, in the interests of the State, in the interests of the Allies, in the supreme interest of all, namely, the unhampered prosecution of the War itself, it is our duty to set up a tribunal of inquiry which from its constitution and from its powers will be able to give to Parliament and to the country a prompt, a decisive, and an authoritative judgment.

I will only say one word more. I hope, I more than hope, I believe, that in regard to some of these matters there has been genuine and honest misunderstanding. It is quite possible. But the clearer the case—and I am speaking upon the assumption that it is a clear case—that His Majesty's Ministers have for asserting and reasserting, establishing and proving to demonstration the accuracy of the statements that have been impugned, the more cogent seems to me the argument that an inquiry should take place under conditions that no one can suspect of partiality or prejudice.

Mr. Lloyd George, in reply, described the demand in the motion as unprecedented, and suggested in relation to the issues raised by General Maurice that he had been treated unfairly, his most effective contention being that the statements challenged were founded on information supplied by the General's deputy. He ended with these words:

I really beg and implore, for our common country, the fate of which is in the balance now and in the next few weeks, that there should be an end of this sniping.

On a division the motion was rejected by 293 to 106, 98 Liberals voting for it and 71 against. None of the Irish Nationalists took part in the division, the members of the party being absent in Ireland. The only Ministerialist who voted in the " Aye " lobby was Mr. Aubrey Herbert.

Mr. Churchill [1] in commenting upon the debate and

[1] "The World Crisis, 1916–1918," Vol. II, pp. 421–3.

division, remarks that the "actual merits of the controversy were scarcely discussed." This was, of course, inevitable, as the object of the proposed inquiry was to ascertain the real facts. He proceeds:

The division which followed was accepted by Mr. Lloyd George as marking the cleavage between his Liberal followers and those of Mr. Asquith. When, eight months later, in the hour of victory, the general election took place, all who had voted against the Government on this occasion were opposed by the triumphant Coalition, and scarcely any escaped political exclusion.

The general election to which Mr. Churchill refers — that which will be known in history as the "Coupon" election [1] of December, 1918 — was held almost immediately after the Armistice. The Labour party had by this time resolved to sever itself from the Coalition, but the two other members of the combination — the Unionists and the Coalition Liberals — agreed to run the election together on the lines of a joint manifesto issued (November 21) by Mr. Lloyd George and Mr. Bonar Law, and summarized in Mr. Lloyd George's letter to his colleague of November 2:

If there is to be an election I think it would be right that it should be a Coalition election, that is to say, that the country should be definitely invited to return candidates who undertake to support the present Government, not only to prosecute the War to its final end and negotiate the peace, but to deal with the problems of reconstruction which must immediately arise directly an armistice is signed. In other words, the test which in future must decide whether individual candidates will be sustained at the polls by your sup-

[1] The phrase was first used by myself in a speech at Huddersfield on November 28.

porters and mine must be not, as in the past, a pledge to support the Government in the prosecution of the War, but a definite pledge to support this Government.

Under this arrangement the Coalition vote was to be withheld from all Liberals who declined to bind themselves by a blind pledge in advance, to become items in what was called a "reliable majority." The Maurice division (as Mr. Churchill says) was treated, in the slang of the day, as an "acid test." All Liberals who had voted on that occasion for an inquiry, which two days before the leader of the House, Mr. Bonar Law, had admitted to be expedient and even necessary, were marked down for slaughter. The incident was described by Mr. Lloyd George (at Wolverhampton, on November 23) as a "parliamentary conspiracy"—in which the Irish members had been asked to join—"to overthrow a Government that was in the midst of a crisis while wrestling for victory." "I cannot," he added, "trust that sort of business. If the country wants that class of men the country can choose them, but, believe me, it will be impossible to get through the great task before us."

If there was such a "conspiracy," I, of course, as I said a day or two afterwards at Huddersfield, "must have been the chief conspirator." It was true that I had expressly said in the House of Commons that my motion was in no sense intended as a vote of censure. It was true that I had also declared that "I could not be a party to any proceeding which might have the effect of preventing those who were responsible to the nation from extricating the greatest of causes from the gravest of perils." All this was represented as the canting insincerity of a man whose real purpose was to trip up the Government.

The dissolution followed rapidly. I had then represented East Fife for thirty-two years, and I confess that I felt so little apprehension for my seat that I spent most of my time during the general election in visiting and addressing other constituencies. As I drove round the voting stations in Fife on the polling day, I saw, amongst other specimens of the electioneering appeals of my Conservative opponent, huge placards with the inscription: "Asquith nearly lost you the War. Are you going to let him spoil the Peace?" I was defeated by a majority of two thousand. All my leading colleagues in the House of Commons suffered the same fate. The Liberal members of the new House were reduced to a handful of little more than thirty.

The disintegration of the Liberal party began with the Coupon election. It then received a blow from which it has never since recovered.

CHAPTER XVIII

CONTEMPORARY NOTES: 1919

AFTER the election I went for a holiday to the South of France, and I see that I wrote to Vivian Phillipps on my arrival at Biarritz:

February 17, 1919. I had a very good journey all the way: David Henderson was most serviceable in Paris. I lunched at the Embassy with the Derbys, and as usual I knocked up against (at the Ritz) some unexpected and incongruous figures: *inter alios,* Tommy Bowles (who is hanging about the purlieus of the Conference with a watching-brief for Neptune); Admiral Troubridge, who is acting Grand Master of the Danube; and Elibank, who tells me that he has informed Crewe that he can count on him as one of the non-Coalition Liberal peers.

April, 1919. (To another correspondent.) I have been skipping and skimming through Frazer's "Folk Lore in the Old Testament." I have never taken much stock in what is called Comparative Anthropology; and the multiplication of legends all over the globe about the Folk, and the Flood, and the Tower of Babel, and "Ultimogeniture" becomes rather wearisome. But he is really a learned man and an indefatigable explorer. Moreover on occasions he can write well; there is a really brilliant chapter on the Mark of Cain. I have also been browsing on the eighteenth century.

May 15. (To Mrs. Harrisson.) I went with Margot to the Cavell funeral at Westminster Abbey, where, oddly enough, there was a crowded but most undistinguished and unrepresentative congregation. The most impressive thing was the Réveillé on the drums, which gave one a quite dramatic feeling of an advancing and then retiring force.

July (*Cologne*). (I was on a visit to the British Army of Occupation.) There are of course no military movements going on. Heaven knows what would have happened if the Germans had refused to sign, and this army (numerically some 400,000), consisting mainly of boys, with a small sprinkling of " Derby" men, keen to get back home, had been ordered to advance. There is not a trace in the whole of this district of the "ravages" of war: the Allies never got farther than to drop one or two ineffectual bombs on Cologne.

Here is a little story from Cologne.

Our men in khaki are allowed to ride free in the trams and make abundant use of the privilege. In the early days of the occupation, they used to go in threes and fours, and when women got in and the Boche men refused to give up their seats, the Tommies would take the male Boches by the ear and compel them to stand. They claim by now to have effected a distinct improvement in travelling manners.

Last night after dinner I went with the general a half-hour's drive to a "torchlight" military ride given by the cavalry. Their head-quarters are an old castle, surrounded by a moat which broadens out into a small lake, on the banks of which the soldier spectators were packed. We sat on a balcony overlooking the water, which was lit up by thousands of coloured globe lamps, while the sky was covered with searchlight beams in the pattern of a Union Jack. It was a pitch-dark night with no wind. I have never seen lighting so well managed in any theatre. There were three regimental bands which came on in turn, and the cavalry themselves on horseback, with their swords drawn, went through a set of manœuvres in a blaze of light, which was suddenly extinguished, and they rode slowly round in total darkness, each man carrying a small lamp over his horse's head. Then a gondola made a circuit of the lake lit up with Chinese lanterns, having on board a fine operatic tenor in the person of a padre, who sang a rather florid and amorous solo, which was much appreciated by the gallery of soldiers. After some evolutions of the horsemen, and music from the massed bands, by way of finale, a large choir came on the scene and sang to the playing of the bands two verses of "Abide with me." It was extraordinarily impressive, with the cavalry motionless on their horses all round, and except for the light concentrated on them and the musicians, complete blackness everywhere. I have never seen a more beautiful spectacle from first to last, and it was certainly a unique performance in the very heart of Germany.

July. I have read three Scotts—"Anne of Geierstein," "The Fortunes of Nigel," and "Rob Roy." I shall take a holiday now from "the Wizard," who with all his powers was the sloppiest and most slipshod of writers. His daughter Sophia had never read "The Lay of the Last Minstrel": "Papa," she exclaimed, "says it is a bad thing for young people to read bad poetry."

Elizabeth quotes a good saying of President Wilson's about some American politician: "He has no top story to his head: he is only a bungalow."

July. Before dinner I went to see Diana Manners (that was), and found her wonderfully installed in the Holden drawing-room, surrounded by flowers enough to fill two or three ordinary hot-houses. The surgeon — Arbuthnot Lane, and his assistant — came during my visit and undid her bandages,[1] and showed me the extraordinary network of weights and pulleys and cords by which the overlapping bones are being gradually drawn apart. It will be a great thing to heal a case like this without touching the leg with knife or rivet or any surgical tool.

July. Talking of mammoths, did I tell you that I fell quite in love with the iguanodons in the museum at Brussels, which I visited in the company of Herbert Samuel? They are 23 feet high, and proportionately long, and used to waddle like ducks in the primeval slime, and fight each other with their tails for the possession of the favourite female. They lived on a vegetarian diet, and are about 15 million years old.

July. General Botha came in to-day to say farewell. He is returning to South Africa, thoroughly disillusioned with Wilson and Co., and determined never again to put his fingers in the European pie.

August. The Government asked me to preside over the Oxford and Cambridge Commission, and after consulting Gilbert Murray and others, I consented. As I wrote to Vivian Phillipps: "I shall find the work in-

[1] She had broken her leg.

teresting, and it will not in any way interfere with politics."

September (*Venice*). The Italian order of hatred among their late Allies is: (1) French: indescribable; (2) American: intense and always growing; (3) English: moderate but real.

October. I have begun Festing Jones's "Memoir of Samuel Butler." It is the kind of biography I like: very detailed and written in the true canine Boswell spirit. He (S. B.) was an interesting freak, with all sorts of more or less developed talents and interests: he loathed all the Victorian heroes — political, literary, or social. But the really attractive figure in the book is the little lame lady, who was rather in love with him — Miss Savage: she is worth a hundred Butlers. She was a virulent anti-Gladstonian, and relates with a mixture of glee and disappointment how she saw the Great Man narrowly escape being run over one morning in Portland Place. You should read it, though there is much that is skip-worthy.

November 30. I finished "Redgauntlet" last night: I now put it among Scott's best. Hardly one of the characters is either under- or over-drawn.

December 20. I got an unexpected letter this morning from Winston, announcing that the King, as a special favour, proposed to confer on me and Ll. G. the three War Medals, as having been Prime Ministers during the War. No other civilian gets them.

December 22. I made the most of my Sunday opportunities, going to a Dissenting chapel in the morning and to St. Paul's in the afternoon. The former was the more interesting, as I heard for the first time Dr.

Orchard, who is now one of the fashionable preachers of London. He is well worth hearing, as he knows what argument means and talks excellent English. But his sermon would have shocked my Puritan forbears: as someone once said of a discourse of Mayer's, "There was not" (from their point of view) "enough Gospel in it to save a tomtit."

We had some people to dinner, including young Lady Hartington. She is the Salisburys' youngest daughter. I told her I had not expected to live to see the day when the best safeguard for true Liberalism would be found in an unreformed House of Lords and the Cecil family.

I have nearly finished "Guy Mannering": it is quite readable, though rather complicated: my seventh Waverley this year.

CHAPTER XIX

ELECTION FOR PAISLEY

I WAS out of the House of Commons during the whole of the year 1919, and took advantage of my leisure to visit Spain, Italy, and our own Army of Occupation—then over 400,000 strong—on the Rhine, where I was the guest at Cologne of its commander, Field-Marshal Sir William Robertson. In January, 1920, a seat became vacant at Paisley through the death of the sitting Liberal member, Sir John McCallum. Though the prospect of occupying a seat in such a House of Commons as that which was the offspring of the "Coupon" election of December, 1918, had few attractions for me, I thought it my duty to accept the invitation of the local Liberals to become their candidate at the by-election. I thus for the second time sought the suffrages of a Scottish electorate, and it was my fortune during nearly forty years of parliamentary life never to sit, or stand, for any constituency in my native land.

There is a wider difference than most Englishmen suspect between the east and the west of Scotland. No contrast could be more striking than that between East Fife with its large area of small scattered communities, and Paisley, a compact industrial centre of nearly 90,000 inhabitants, with its huge and highly organized factories in which the bulk of the electorate were employed. The great firms, which have given its products a world-wide market, have not only been assiduous in

An Open-air Meeting

Lady Violet   Mr. Asquith   Mrs. Asquith   T. Dun Macnair
Bonham Carter   Edward Cochran   Sir John Simon

THE PAISLEY ELECTION CAMPAIGN

watching over and providing for the welfare of their workpeople, but have shown exemplary public spirit and munificence to the town and its institutions. As compared with East Fife, electioneering was a far less exacting task, and I was again fortunate in having an election agent of the highest capacity and judgment— Mr. T. Dun Macnair.

My first contest, in February, 1920, which excited a good deal of outside interest, was a triangular fight between a Liberal, a Conservative, and a Labour man. My Conservative opponent, who in the end was easily at the bottom of the poll, received a warm commendatory letter from Mr. Bonar Law, one of the joint leaders of the Coalition Government. I took the opportunity in my speeches to go over the whole political ground, foreign and domestic. They were subsequently published in a small volume—"The Paisley Policy."[1] I was returned with a majority of nearly three thousand.

I had what I suppose must be a unique electoral experience. I was member for Paisley for four years (1920–24), and during that time I fought four elections— 1920, 1922, 1923, 1924: a "narrow squeak" in 1922, a comfortable majority (1,700) in 1923, and a crushing defeat (2,000) in 1924. Out of these four contests, two, 1922 and 1924, were "straight" fights between a Liberal and a Socialist; and while my own figure was substantially the same (15,000) in both years, the Socialist vote rose from 14,700 to 17,000.

Paisley is geographically in the Clyde-side area, and though it has always shown in politics a sturdy individuality of its own, yet it had undoubtedly been influenced

[1] Cassell & Company.

by the strenuous and skilful propaganda which had now been carried on for years by the active and well-organized Socialist party in the industrial areas of the west of Scotland. I left behind me there with infinite regret a splendid body of highly trained political friends, who worked for me, and the principles which they knew I could be trusted to represent, with unfailing fidelity and devotion during my four years of service. I consider, after a long and varied experience of public meetings, that the audience which throngs their splendid Clark Hall is the most intelligent and responsive of any in Great Britain.

A new, and to me a most welcome, feature in these Paisley elections was the intervention and invaluable help of my elder daughter, Violet Bonham Carter. It was on the Paisley platform that she displayed and developed her powers of public speech, in which, in my judgment, she can hold her own against any competitors of either sex. She started with great natural gifts of voice, expression and gesture, which when matured by practice made her a real artist. The Paisley electors expect the bulk of the speaking at election times to be done by the candidate, and we resorted very sparingly to outside aid, though I always had the benefit of one, and sometimes more than one, supporting speech from my two old friends and colleagues, Lord Buckmaster and Sir John Simon, who are both of them past masters in the art. An exceptional case was the general election of 1923 — the year of Liberal *rapprochement* — when Mr. Lloyd George was good enough to pay us a visit. It was a delicate occasion which called for tactful handling, and after he and I had spoken there were insistent calls for my daughter. She was more than equal to the situation. She said that the meeting of Mr. Lloyd George and myself on the same platform had been compared by Tory and Labour critics to the lion lying down with the lamb. Which of us was most fitted for the respective parts she would not speculate. "But," she added, "I can only say, for myself, that I have never seen Mr. Lloyd George look less voracious or my father more uneatable."

I will go back to my first experience of Paisley — the by-election of 1920. After our triumphant return, my daughter was invited to a luncheon in London at the National Liberal Club, where she delivered a speech, afterwards published under the title of "The Message of Paisley," from which I will cite a few sentences.

It was (she said) a very gallant adventure. It was an enterprise undertaken at the eleventh hour in unknown territory, in a constituency which was held by a bare hundred at the last general election, in response to an invitation secured by a narrow majority of twenty-five in a divided association — half of which were, or thought they were, Coalition Liberals. Within a week of my father's arrival there wasn't a Coalition Liberal left in Paisley.

We were fighting on two fronts. We had on our left a strong Labour candidate, who knew every crease in the ground, for he had been over the course a year ago. He was backed by various manifestos and demonstrations from outside. There was one manifesto signed by certain members of this club. It didn't do us any harm; on the contrary, I think it drove some birds over our guns. There were demonstrations in the distance from Comrade Haldane and Comrade Warwick. We poor Liberals had nothing as gaudy to show as their red flags and blue blood, but there again we noticed no ugly rush, no stampede to the standard of Revolution.

On our right we had a particularly crude manifestation of Coalition Toryism, armed with half a coupon, and a few handfuls of mud. Was the other half of that coupon with-held from a genuine desire for our success? Or was it with-held because the Prime Minister [Mr. Lloyd George] is no willing godfather to forlorn hopes? He is rarely to be found on

> " the burning deck,
> Whence all but he had fled."

The part of Casabianca — that noble but ungrateful rôle — was left on this occasion, as it had been on others, to Mr. Bonar Law.

As you may have heard, at one moment there was a desperate attempt to make my father's ties the real issue of the election. This caused me great alarm, because he wore during the contest a series of ties that would easily have lost him the safest seat in Scotland; and I had to explain that he never used his ties as vehicles of his political opinions — having, thank Heaven for it, other ways of expressing himself.

Then there was my " German husband."

I was amazed to read in Mr. Bonar Law's recent speech at Glasgow that " he had followed the contest closely, and that as far as he could see, Mr. McKean had put up a plucky fight for which he deserved the congratulations of all Conservatives."

He goes on to say that there is no doubt that in the end Mr. Asquith was returned by Conservative votes. So, it appears, the Conservatives who voted for my father are to congratulate Mr. McKean! What a typical piece of Coali-tion psychology! What about the Government of which Mr. Bonar Law is one of the two accredited leaders? What does it now pretend to represent? Not Labour, and not Liberalism — that we know. Apparently not even Toryism — if the Tory vote has just returned to power its most avowed, its most determined, and its most formidable op-ponent. No, the totally unrepresentative character of the present Coalition — the fact that it expresses neither the principles of any party nor the will of the nation, that it expresses nothing but the passionate instinct for self-preservation of its own authors, is one of the plainest messages of the Paisley result.

" How did your father get the women's vote?" is a question I am asked over and over again, and I think there is no doubt whatever that we did get it. Our opponents would be the first to admit that. I think my father got the women's vote largely by treating the women voters with intellectual respect. I was amused to see some of the London papers holding up to derision what they described as his " Treasury-bench manner with the mill girls." It is the greatest mistake to imagine that the best way of reaching women is by bad sentiment and worse jokes. How often have I seen them approached on these lines, poor things! It is called the " human touch."

As one of our Paisley women said, in recommending my father to her fellow-electors, "We women have been at this business of sizing up men for many thousands of years, and is it likely that now we won't know the right one out of three?"

May I add one personal word, and that is I feel that Paisley has righted a great wrong. I was with my father in December, 1918, when he saw the party, to whose service he had given his life, shattered before his eyes, not by a frontal attack from without—that it could never have been —but by a betrayal from within. He saw himself deserted by men who owed him their political existence, by men whom he had never failed, by men whom he had led from victory to victory. He saw—and this was the hardest thing of all for him to bear—he saw those who stood by him go under.

One last scene—the closing scene of the drama of Paisley. Let us remember it together, for you have shared it with me—the sight of those great cheering crowds that thronged Whitehall and Parliament Square the day that he took his seat. When I went in out of the noise, into the silence of the House—the House in which I had seen him lead great armies to great triumphs; when I saw that little gallant handful of men which is all his following now, and heard their thin cheer raised, for a moment I felt—Is this all, are these all he has behind him? But then I remembered the great voice of the crowd—it rang in my ears; and I knew that this, *this* was the voice of England—not the drilled cheers of those conscript ranks on the Coalition benches.   And I knew that our small force that day was like that little gallant garrison of a beleaguered city that hears for the first time the great shout of the relieving forces— "Hold on, hold out; we are coming." *And they are.*

I received a shoal of congratulatory messages, from which I select the following:

Queen Alexandra.

Perfectly delighted at your Grand Success, which I never doubted for a moment.   How my beloved husband would have rejoiced with the whole Country at your splendid achievement!

ALEXANDRA.

John Masefield.

Perhaps you will be nearly smothered under telegrams and letters of congratulation, but we cannot let to-day pass without writing to say how very glad we are at your triumph.   It has been an intense delight to us to read of your success in what has been the most important political contest of modern times.   I will say nothing of the importance of the contest to Liberalism and the immediate future.   At present our delight is centred on your own personal success, and on the thought that the nation is turning back to what is sane and fine in it, after the fever —the trickery of the last years.   You have stood for what is fine in the soul of this country in the greatest months of her history, and my wife and I send you our heartiest and most thankful congratulations that you are now to bring back fineness and sanity to the councils of this heaving time.

Count Romanones (ex-Prime Minister and Liberal leader in Spain).

Congratulations on your triumph to yourself, Mrs Asquith, and your daughter.

Wilfrid Burt (son of Thomas Burt).

My father wishes to send you his hearty congratulations on your re-election to the House of Commons. Mother and he — and all of us — followed your election campaign with deep interest, and are delighted to know that you will now lead the Opposition.

Mackenzie King.

Canadian Liberals send hearty congratulation.

Henry Ainley.

This letter needs no acknowledgment please; it is merely a thanksgiving of congratulation from one Morley man to another; "the Lord hath wrought great glory."

Lord Bryce.

Besides the pleasure which your victory gives to your old friends, and the gain to the country from having you in Parliament to help to arrest the pernicious courses followed there, our thanks are justly due to you for this also, that you have given the best proof since the G.O.M. took up Home Rule in 1886 that courage has not vanished from political life. You did a very bold thing in standing at Paisley, and it is a good thing that courage should have been crowned with success, a much needed lesson in these demoralized and demoralizing days. Long experience has convinced me that far more is lost in politics by timidity than by overboldness, at least where the cause is a good one and the virtue a high one — as was yours. This is a great, and much needed, service that you have rendered.

Thomas Case (President of Corpus Christi College and a veteran leader of Toryism in Oxford University).

I beg to offer you many congratulations on your election at Paisley: it will make an immense difference. I feel sure that I am one of many who sympathized with you when you were tricked out of your office of Prime Minister, and now hope that you will restore liberty without licence.

CHAPTER XX

CONTEMPORARY NOTES: 1920–21

THE next series of letters begins with 1920.

January 1. We saw the old year out in the conventional fashion. The new one cannot have a worse record of wasted opportunities and mischievous performances.

I finished the autobiography of Lilly, the astrologer in the time of Charles I and Cromwell — a plausible impostor if there was one. He tells of a clergyman of those days who was hauled up on various charges of impiety and loose living. One of the allegations was that he had baptized a cock and called it Peter.

The Honours List is uninteresting, though I am glad that St. John Brodrick[1] gets a step in the peerage.

January 20. The Prince of Wales came to lunch. We provided him as fellow-guests with the two Bibesci, Soveral, Birrell, the McLeans, and my niece, Kathleen Granby, who was in wonderful looks. The Prince talked well and amusingly of his experiences in America: both Soveral and Birrell were in excellent form.

January. I have just been looking over the latest "Anthology of Prose" by one Pearsall Smith. There are not more than 200 pages, and of these 22 are taken from the Bible, 21 from Charles Lamb, 19 from Donne, 2 from Swift, and one from Burke. What an order of merit and quotability!

[1] Lord Midleton.

February 26. The count at Paisley to-day. My majority nearly 3,000.

March 2, 1920. I took my seat. We had a tumultuous but most enthusiastic procession from Cavendish Square to the House. I haven't seen such a crowd in London for years. The medical students enjoyed themselves thoroughly, at the expense of the car and of my new top hat, which they annexed as a trophy, and, as their ringleader writes to me this morning, as a "memento of your triumphal venture!"

It was a wonderful sight when we got to Westminster. In the House the Coalition Liberals distinguished themselves by maintaining a stony silence when I took my seat. We were entertained there later at a very gay little dinner given by our own small lot.

Like you, I am in the middle of a Trollope: "Framley Parsonage."

March 14. In a casual moment I took up a volume of sonnets, and came haphazard on Shakespeare's "No longer mourn for me when I am dead." There are only two trisyllables in the whole sonnet, and by far the largest number of words are monosyllables: and what a wonderful effect!

March. I went to dine with Antoine and Elizabeth in her bedroom, as she is not yet well enough to get up. In the midst of our repast we were invaded by Mrs. Leyel, accompanied by W. Tyrrell. She delivered a large envelope to Antoine, saying, "Here is £171,000; keep it for me." I have never seen so much money in one room. It was the proceeds of what is called the "Golden Ballot"—a charitable lottery for the Red Cross over which Mrs. L. has been presiding, and for which she is now being prosecuted by the Government under the Lottery Acts. She brought the money to Antoine under the impression that as he enjoys diplomatic immunity his house cannot be searched.

March 31. Our last night at 20 Cavendish Square (where we have lived for the best part of twenty-five years).

April 29. I went last night to Lincoln's Inn to receive in my capacity of Treasurer the new men being called to the Bar. I dined afterwards in Hall with my brother Benchers—mostly judges and ex-judges and hoary K.C.s, whose conversation is as "shoppy" in its way as that of a table full of golfers or hunting-men.

I have just finished the second of Lady Murray's Harrison Ainsworth's "Windsor Castle," all about Henry VIII and Anne Boleyn and Herne the Hunter. It is a wild travesty of history, and written in a bad early Victorian dialect, but it is quite readable.

May 3. I hope you found what you wanted in Matthew Arnold: in some moods there is no one more rest-giving or patience-inspiring.

Violet has chosen as her topic for her second article "Cant." I told her to trace the three stages: *Pose* (the new attitude), *Culte* (the group of new sectaries), and *Cant* (the dialect or jargon in which they formulate and interchange their ideas).

May 4. We had at lunch, at Cambridge, where we had a meeting of the Commission, Mr. Head, who is tutor and chaplain of Emmanuel College. During the War he was one of the chaplains of the Guards Division and attached to Raymond's battalion. He met R.

as they brought him in fatally wounded and stayed with him till he died, and buried him.

June. Colonel House came to lunch: he has a gentle voice and quiet insinuating manner. He is quite convinced that if the President could have dissolved Congress immediately after his return from Paris, he could have got a thumping majority in favour of the Treaty.

June 28 (from Mentmore). This is a wonderful Rothschild palace, which Lord Rosebery inherited from his wife: a regular museum of every kind of work of art and antiquity. Hardly less remarkable is the host; his brain is as acute and individual as it was twenty-five years ago when I served under him as Prime Minister. No one ever had the same advantages: a most definite and inimitable personality; extraordinary gifts of speech; a fine wit, both mordant and lambent; rank, wealth, cultivation: in fact, everything both to allure and compel.

We dined *à deux*—an excellent and not over-sumptuous meal, mingled with much good talk about the past. Then, while it was light, an old-fashioned phaeton was brought to the door, with a postilion mounted on one of the two horses, and another servant in the "boot" behind. We drove for over an hour in the park and woods, talking all the time, and have just come back.

July 29. The most interesting thing in the paper to-day is the discovery that the famous lines which Scott put at the head of a chapter of "Old Mortality" ("One crowded hour of glorious life," etc.) are not by Scott himself, but by an obscure Major—Mordaunt by name—published as far back as 1791 in a newspaper.

The rest of the fourteen stanzas is as poor and pointless as anything that was ever thrown into a waste-paper basket.

July. Colonel House, who came in for a few minutes, told us a good story about a negro who was being tried for theft and was too poor to pay for a lawyer.

THE JUDGE: Well, Sam, I will provide you with Counsel. There's Mr. Smith (you see) and Mr. Jones (you see) and downstairs there's Mr. Johnson.

NIGGER (looking at Smith and Jones) : Well, Judge, I'll take Mr. Johnson.

September. After dinner we read the two volumes of Repington's "Memoirs": a curious *mélange* of trivial gossip and wise and penetrating military criticism. He quotes an apt *mot* of my son-in-law, Antoine, some time in the early part of 1918: "The Germans have been trying for four years to win the War and have failed: the Allies for four years have been trying to lose it and have failed equally: who can say how it will end!"

October. I have been busy all morning with my speech on Ireland. I can see from a letter I have got from Donald Maclean that the timid spirits of the party are anxious about the strategic side of Dominion Home Rule, and inclined to think that I have gone "too far." Of course I shall stick to my guns. [This was apropos of a speech which I was going to make at Ayr.]

I may, perhaps, here recall that under the provisions of the Parliament Act the third Home Rule Bill, though its operation was suspended, was in 1914 placed on the Statute Book, with the promise of an Amending Bill, to meet all the fair scruples and objections of the Ulster Minority. The abortive Sinn Fein rising at Easter, 1916, was followed by a sincere but unsuccessful effort on my part and that of my colleagues in the Government to arrive at a settlement of the Ulster difficulty. Then followed the assembly of a National Irish Convention which sat for some months at the end of 1917 and the beginning of 1918. Owing to the conciliatory and statesmanlike attitude of Mr. Redmond on the one side, and of Unionist leaders like Lord Midleton on the other, the Convention had advanced (as appears from its Report in the spring of 1918), though not the whole distance, yet a long way on the road to agreement.

The Coalition Government, which then still contained a number of Labour members, chose this singularly inopportune moment to introduce a Military Service Bill, which could be extended to Ireland — a step which I and my Unionist colleagues in the first Coalition Government had deliberately and unanimously refused to take. They promised to introduce without delay a Self-Government Bill, and to do their best to carry it through simultaneously with the application of Compulsory Service. The whole of 1918 was allowed to pass; the whole of 1919 was allowed to pass, until we came to December. For twenty months after Compulsory Service had been upon the Statute Book (although never put in operation), the promise remained unfulfilled. The result was that Sinn Fein, which was on the downgrade, which was losing election after election, raised its head, and a disappointed and, as they said, a befooled Irish people deserted the Constitutional party at the general election of December, 1918, and rallied round the flag of the Revolutionary party.

There was all the difference in the world between the atmosphere of Ireland in 1918 and its atmosphere when the Government tried to redeem their promise. The opinion and the sympathy of law-abiding people, as I pointed out at Paisley, was not now with those who were trying to carry out and execute the law, but was very largely, tacitly at any rate, with those who violated it.

Nevertheless, I urged that we must persevere without delay in that which was the only effectual means of getting at the root of all this trouble, in completing and setting on its legs a generous system of Irish self-government.

The session of 1920 — my first as member for Paisley — was largely taken up by a Government Bill, which, as I said at the time, was passed for the purpose of giving to a section of Ulster a Parliament which it did not want, and to the remaining three-quarters of Ireland a Parliament which it would not have. I put forward as the alternative my Paisley plan of full Dominion Self-Government, repeating my adherence in regard to Ulster to the principle of county option. The Prime Minister scoffed and declared that my plan was one which no party or section of a party in Ireland countenanced, and that the Government scheme "held the field": a hackneyed but dangerous metaphor.

The argument that I had used at Paisley I developed at Ayr in October, 1920, and in a letter to *The Times*,

on the 4th of that month. In the course of the letter
I wrote:

SIR, —

In the early weeks of this year, when I was a candidate
for Paisley, I expressed the opinion that, at the stage which
we had then reached, there was no practicable solution of
the Irish problem which fell short of Dominion Home Rule.

The experience of the last nine months — perhaps the
most deplorable and scandalous chapter even in the annals
of Irish Government — has accentuated with tragic emphasis the urgency of the situation.

What have been the measures taken by the Executive of
the Crown? On the legislative side they have put forward
a paltering compromise, which is repudiated by every section of Irish opinion, though it may for the moment be
favoured with the contemptuous and cynical patronage of
Sir Edward Carson, who thinks he sees in what is proposed
the prospect of an insurmountable block to the attainment
of Irish unity. On the administrative side we have seen the
supersession of the organized machinery of law and justice
by a superior power, which derives its authority not so much
from sporadic terrorism as from the support, through all
the degrees of enthusiastic co-operation, of passive conniv-
ance, and of sympathetic acquiescence, of the great bulk of
the Irish people. The King's Executive is at once impotent
and aggressive, and its policy, or want of policy, has reached
a fitting climax in the unexampled campaign, for which the
Government must bear the responsibility, of military and
police reprisals.

*   *   *   *   *   *

There are, as it seems to me, two conditions which govern
and limit any conceivable solution.

The first is that the Irish people should be made to believe that, so far as Great Britain is concerned, what is offered comes from an honest, and also from a responsible
source. The second is that, after making all necessary al-
lowance for the provisional abstention, not of an artificial,

but of a genuine local minority, it should meet and satisfy Irish aspirations.

Nothing, I am certain, can now fulfil the second of these conditions but the bestowal upon Ireland of the status of an autonomous Dominion in the fullest and widest sense.

What does that mean?

None of our Dominions claims the right to a separate Foreign Policy of its own. On the other hand, they all show an increasing and perfectly legitimate desire for fuller confidence and freer consultation in the whole domain of our external relations, and, in particular, for a voice in the making and revision of treaties. The Dominion of Ireland should in these matters be on a level footing with the rest.

In regard to naval and military forces, I do not share the apprehensions of those who think it necessary to impose on an Irish Dominion limitations and fetters which are not to be found elsewhere in our self-governing Empire. No Irish Government would be so insane as to mortgage its scanty margin of resources for such a fruitless and costly enterprise as the creation of an Irish Navy. Nor is it readily conceivable that it would seek to deny — what it could never effectively prevent — the free access to Irish ports and harbours of the vessels of the Imperial Navy. Further, no grant of autonomy could be regarded as complete which did not include the right to raise and maintain, for the purpose of local defence, an adequate military force.

Fiscal independence is a necessary incident of Dominion status. I cannot think that it is worth while, in view of the colossal figures of our national finance, to haggle over the "nicely calculated less or more" of Irish indebtedness.

To those who are disposed to think such a policy humiliating in what it surrenders, and hazardous in its possibilities of future danger, I would put this question — What is your alternative?

Can anything be more humiliating, or more pregnant with incalculable peril, than the spectacle which has now been unfolding itself for months, before our eyes and those of the world, a spectacle in which tragedy and farce are inextricably intermixed? Its only logical sequence is to take seriously in hand the task of reconquering Ireland, and holding her by force — a task which, though not, perhaps, beyond the powers, will never be sanctioned by the will or the conscience of the British people.

I am not alarmed by the spectre of an Irish Republic. Men do not in the long run fight for phrases, but for realities.

I resume the quotations from my letters:

October 15, 1920. We had a wonderful series of meetings at Ayr, in the course of which I made no fewer than three speeches, the last at 9.30 P.M. Much the best and most important was the second one. I think it presents the Dominion solution in an intelligible and rational form. Now that Ll. G. calls me a lunatic and Carson calls me a traitor I begin to feel sure that I must be on the right lines.[1]

October 24. Life is very difficult just now. We are under a Government of reckless gamblers, and we drift on from one folly and wickedness to another. All warnings and protests are just as unheeded as Cassandra's; it would seem that people have been so perverted and brutalized by the War that they have lost all power of response to any appeal to their better and older instincts. And if one tries to strike a bold true note, half one's friends shiver and cower, and implore one not " to get in front of the band ": in other words, to renounce both the duties and the risks of leadership.

October 25. After listening to Bonar Law and others I have just made a speech [in the House of Com-

[1] On December 6, 1921, a "Treaty between Great Britain and Ireland" was signed, which gave the Irish Free State the constitutional status of a Dominion, while Northern Ireland was to remain under the provisions of the Act of 1920. The signatories to this historic instrument included Mr. Lloyd George, Sir Austen Chamberlain, Lord Birkenhead, Mr. Arthur Griffiths, and Mr. Michael Collins.

mons], which I think carried some weight even in this Toryfied and ossified House, to induce the Government to give up the most inopportune and provocative Emergency measure which they have had the folly to introduce in the very midst of the negotiations for the settlement of the miners' Strike. One good effect of it was that it was warmly cheered by J. H. Thomas and all the reasonable and responsible Labour leaders. I don't know whether the Government will give way, but I think we have scored a point.

October 28. As there was nothing of importance going on in the House, I made my way in a taxi to Euston Station, and asked my old friend the station-master to find me a good " coign of vantage " from which to view the procession [The Mayor of Cork's funeral]. In the end I was conducted to the topmost tiles of the building — a dizzy eminence from which you get a good bird's-eye view of London. I saw excellently all that was to be seen — a long procession of Irish men and women, walking in fours, a few carriages, two hearses covered with wreaths, and one or two bands playing funeral marches. It was not strikingly impressive and so far as I could judge the huge crowds in the streets, though quiet and well-behaved, were not sympathetic. The most remarkable feature was the London police, mounted and on foot, in large numbers, escorting and shepherding the processionists, the bulk of whom were probably actual or potential rebels: some of them carrying Sinn Fein flags. I was glad to have seen it, as it is quite a unique event in London.

I found Miss Titheradge at the Wharf. She is a very nice creature, and gave us a lurid picture of the six months she passed at Los Angeles posing for the films. She once spent six or eight hours in evening dress in a lifeboat in the open sea with the waves raging, and the boat refusing to sink, so as to permit her rescue by her adventurous lover.

February 17. I have just been for an hour in the House, listening to Ll. G. — a very characteristic performance, teeming with fustian, and cheered to the echo by his servile satellites. What a place it is!

February 23, 1921. The dinner to Edward Grey at the National Liberal Club last night was a very successful function. He made quite a good point of the difference between "avoiding" war (in the sense of keeping out of it yourself) and "preventing" it, which is what the League of Nations is intended to do.

Dicta of Mrs. B. at the Wharf: she is by no means wholly a fool:

(1) Rare brains — those Greeks!

(2) The Irish are all mad.

(3) God bless us. Religion does do some queer things!

(4) She's got a bit of vision, don't you know? and that sort of thing.

(5) Oh! with him the engine is too big for the chassis!

March 17. I have been making a speech on the Naval Estimates. Carson followed: I thought, not for the first time, what an asset he has in his brogue!

We were all astonished by the announcement that Bonar Law is disabled by a complete breakdown. It is very tragic: for with all his limitations he is a general favourite. He never got over the death of his son three years ago, and has had to do all Ll. G.'s unpleasant work in the House.

Cervantes — in the dedication of his last book " Persiles and Sigismunda," dated four days before his own death — writes: "There is an old couplet which was famous in its day that began: 'With one foot in the stirrup already . . .' Yesterday I received extreme unction, and to-day I write this. Time is short, fears increase, hopes grow less." He died April 23, 1616, within a few days of the death of Shakespeare.

The Bishop of —— seems determined to keep up his reputation as the most fatuous of the many donkeys who bray from the pulpit. Don't you like the saying of the old lady which I once quoted to you? — "This World; and the Next; and then all our troubles will be over."

April. I used to know North Wales very well: it was in old days a favourite holiday haunt of ours. What Dr. Johnson said in his old age of mankind in general is particularly true of the Welsh: "The more I see of them the less I expect from them."

I see that Jack Cowans is to be buried on Monday. I wonder what made him become a Catholic in his last moments? It used to be said of old Hawkins the judge, who was also a late convert, that he avowed that in the course of a busy life he had never had time to examine the different religions, but that he had now come to the conclusion that the Roman Catholic Church "offered the best terms!" Cowans was not the least like that, and I should not have thought that such peccadilloes as he had lay heavy on his conscience. I shall always remember him as one of the most staunch and devoted of friends, and among the real heroes of the War.

Later — after the funeral. My neighbour lent me a missal to follow the service in Latin. There is no doubt that the Catholics understand better than anybody what I once called — I think to you — the "apparatus of illusion."

April 23. Did you see the specimen of bad English in one of the papers to-day? "When John meets his uncle he always lifts his hat": a simple enough sentence to look at, but grammatically capable of four different interpretations. The sloppy use of "he" and "his" is peculiar to English: it could not happen in Greek or Latin.

May. I hope you read in *The Times* of the entertainment given by Northcliffe to his staff of 7,000 odd at Olympia to celebrate the twenty-fifth birthday of the *Daily Mail.* The "prayer" was offered up, in order that it might be heard by the vast horde of guests (and presumably by the Almighty), through a " radio microphone."

June. I was reading yesterday about Lope de Vega, the Spanish dramatist who was a contemporary of Shakespeare. He produced 2,000 plays with no less than 21 million verses, and was called by Cervantes, "Nature's prodigy." I doubt whether he is read now by anybody — even in Spain.

Jack Tennant tells me that the two alternative subjects set for the English Essay in the Eton scholarship exam. just over were (1) impressions of an onlooker when Julius Cæsar landed in England; (2) the advertisement (not to exceed sixteen lines) of a Girls' School. Not bad, I think.

The Canadian Prime Minister and his wife — Mr. and Mrs. Meighen — came to lunch: very nice people. He told us not a bad story of a Canadian golfer who when he came in from his round declared: "I did the first three holes in thirty-three, and after that I went to Hell."

June 21 (Alderley). This is a place of which I am particularly fond, and still more so of my dear friends the host and hostess, Lord and Lady Sheffield. He is 82, and she I suppose in the region of 70, both in miraculous preservation, and she still good-looking. Two of his daughters, Venetia and Sylvia, have been among my best and dearest companions. His eldest brother became a Mohammedan, and the youngest a Roman Catholic bishop, he himself being a militant agnostic. His mines of knowledge are inexhaustible. For fun I asked him at dinner: "What is the origin of the word 'Acrostic'?" He replied like lightning: "Why, ἀκροσ-τίχιον, of course." I said I didn't believe it occurred in classical Greek, which turns out to be the fact. But he knew (what I didn't) that the word and thing were invented by one Epicharmus in Sicily about 400 B.C.

June 29. Poor Lady Randolph Churchill succumbed this morning. I have written a letter to Winston, who was the best and most devoted of sons. She was verging on 70, and had lived every inch of her life up to the edge. An amazing reservoir of vitality, and gay, unflinching courage. I call her the last of the Victorians.

I love a phrase of Dizzy's in one of his later letters to Lady Bradford, whom he reproaches for her addic-

tion to what we now call week-end visits to country
houses: "the monotony of organized platitude."

July. I sat next an American millionairess widow,
whose "man of business"—she told me—came from
a "College called Eton." She herself, being a Vir-
ginian and born in the same "city" as Lady Astor,
was "sweet on the memory of Robert E. Lee."

August 4. Elizabeth told us of an American girl,
who spoke scoffingly of the Ten Commandments:
"They don't tell you what you ought to do, and only
put ideas into your head."

August. I had a good reading in the First Book of
Kings—mostly about Solomon, who had 700 wives and
300 concubines (I wonder what was the distinction),
and as they were mostly heathen foreigners, he built
altars for them in Jerusalem, so that they could continue to worship their native gods. And yet with such
superabundant facilities he seems to have produced
only one son—Rehoboam, who lost the kingdom.
What a waste!

A famous admiral told Orpen, to whom he was sitting for his portrait, that he (O.) was the only painter
who had succeeded in bringing out the strength of
character in his face. O. told this to an equally famous
general (who was also sitting to him) and heard him
mutter to himself, "I always thought the fellow was a
damned fool."

December. As we got no telegram last night about
the Balliol Scholarship I was a little afraid that all had
not gone well, and was the more delighted when I saw

the good news in this morning's *Times*. It will relieve
poor darling Puffin[1] of a load of anxiety, as he was
afraid that the family tradition would fail in his hands.
It is the fourth time that we have won it.

Northcliffe, who is somewhere in the Pacific, is said
to have telegraphed to the King that he was about to
join the Roman Catholic Church. The King's alleged
reply was, I thought, excellent: "Well, well—I can't
help it."

[1] My son, Anthony.

CHAPTER XXI

CONTEMPORARY NOTES: 1922–23

JANUARY, 1922. I looked in for half an hour before lunch at the Winter Exhibition of the Royal Academy — about 300 "works of recently deceased members" — splendid material for the Roger Frys and Clive Bells to wield their bowie-knives and tomahawks upon. A last legacy of the expired Victorian Old Guard — Poynter, Herkomer, Richmond, Riviere — all represented by an average of twenty works a head: and last, but not least, Sant, who died during the War at the age of 96. Far the most interesting thing there is his "Soul's Awakening," which has, I suppose, had a larger circulation than any picture in the world except the Sistine Madonna. . . . It is all very well to make fun of them, but they knew their job.

January 27. I have just been with Violet to the Memorial Service in Westminster Abbey for Bryce; it was very simple and nicely done. I enclose you the "programme" for the sake of the sixteenth-century prayer on the last page, which seems to me much more beautiful and appropriate than anything in the Funeral Service of the Prayer Book. It must surely be by Cranmer.

March 14. I went over to the House of Lords to hear Curzon's reply to Montagu.[1] When the matter

---

[1] Montagu was attacked for authorizing the publication of the Indian Government's Manifesto on the terms of peace with Turkey.

comes up here to-morrow night, I hope to be able to make the real point—that there is not, and never has been, any Cabinet responsibility since Ll. G. became Prime Minister.

March 15. We have had a dull debate on the Army, of which the only interesting feature was the maiden speech of Field-Marshal Wilson, who got into Ll. G.'s good graces in 1917, and ultimately intrigued Robertson out of the place of Chief of the Staff. Wilson, a bitter Ulsterman, has now been booted and is determined to have his revenge. He spoke very well, and *shortly,* which is a real merit, but he is not a man whom I would trust.

Easter. We had a little scrap at the House this morning on the motion for the Easter adjournment on the "Safeguarding" Bill. I treated it in a light contemptuous vein, and the House enjoyed the fun. Stanley Baldwin (the nicest fellow in the Government) made quite an amusing reply.

June. We climbed the Hampstead Hill to see Mrs. Pat Campbell in "Hedda Gabler." She did not come up to my memories of Elizabeth Robins, nearly thirty years ago. Some of the parts were quite well acted, and the Ibsen stage-craft and crisp short-winded dialogue is a refreshing contrast to Shaw with his straw-splitting, interminable dialectics.

Did you see the will of Miss Rothschild in the papers to-day? She has left Waddesdon and its marvellous contents to our friends Jimmy and Dolly. When one stayed there (as I have done more than once in old days) a servant used to appear in your bedroom between seven and nine in the morning. The dialogue (or ritual) was described by Raymond as follows: "Which will you have, sir — tea, coffee, or chocolate?" "Tea." "What kind of tea, sir — China, India, or Ceylon?" "India." "What will you take with it, sir — cream, milk, or lemon?" "Milk." "What kind of milk, sir — Jersey, Guernsey, or Alderney?" I confess I should have been tempted to reply "Sark." But it is a wonderful series of triplets, isn't it? Such is (or was) *"le monde ou l'on s'ennuie."*

June 14. After dinner at "The Club" last night, I read quite a lot of "Antigone" before I went to bed. The House is a desert of dullness to-night. Do you like Cobbett's description of Mr. Pitt as an orator, "a loud snorting bawler"?

July. I dined last night at the Garrick as the guest of Lutyens, the architect. Conversationally the situation was saved by Munnings, the artist, who recited to us two ballads on hunting and steeple-chasing. I thought they were unpublished works of our Jan,[1] but it turned out that Munnings himself was the author. He delivered them with marvellous *brio.*

August. The latest form of political propaganda is the "Summer School." We are holding one now at Oxford, which is a great success. It finished by quite a good burlesque written and acted by N. A. Beechman, Cope Morgan and Basil Herbert with a parody of "Three Little Maids from School."

"Sir D.: 'I am a House of Commons star.'

Sir J.: 'And I am a leading light of the Bar.'

[1] John Masefield.

Mr. R.: 'And I'm for the Bar where no drinks are.'"

Gilbert Murray gave me a touching account of the last days of his beautiful and charming daughter, Agnes, who died on her way home from League of Nations work, after a fortnight's illness, in Auvergne. Her parents went to see and nurse her, and summoned a London surgeon, who operated, but too late. Her last words to her father, when he went out of the room for something, were, "Daddles, come back." She was one of the salt of the earth, and it stuns one that she should have been cut down like this, when we see all these flimsy girls leading their rotten and fruitless lives.

Cara[1] brought her Italian general — Garibaldi — to see me. He is less like a conventional Italian (let alone the son of a hero) than anything you have ever seen: quite a nice fellow, speaking fairly good English, solid, prosaic, fair in colouring, and gestureless. His main interest seems to be in a new process to produce "hard steel," which he explained to me in much detail. His political ideas were of the crudest anti-Bolshevik kind. He advocated the dispatch from this country of fifteen Army Corps to Russia to establish a "rational Government" there. I told him that he would not be able to get together a single battalion for any such purpose, unless it was recruited from the Diehards, whom we could easily spare.

A rather good compositor's error, which comes from America, may amuse you. It ends a description of a revivalist meeting. "The meeting then broke up, but

[1] Our cousin, Cara Copland.

a large crow (? crowd) remained on the platform and sang lustily 'Rock of Ages' for two hours."

Did you know that in Egypt, and probably also in Greece, the women sometimes had inscriptions on the soles of their shoes, which made their footsteps leave an imprint in the dust? One that has been discovered bore the word ἀκαλουθεῖ. What did that mean?

September. Vivian Phillipps has been spending a fortnight with his family in Rhineland. They were a party of five, and with the mark at 7,000 they lived in the best hotels with bathroom, sitting-rooms, etc., at an average of 5s. per day per head.

I have now read the whole of the Kaiser's book except two or three chapters. He was a dabbler and a smatterer, and a super-dilettante in almost every department.

Talking of commemorations, I see that the City of Strasburg is about to put up a bronze statue in honour of the inventor of *pâté de fois gras* — one Close who flourished about 1765.

September 5. Lord Kilbracken has just arrived for lunch. He is, I suppose, about 77, but with few, if any, signs of age. He was the most distinguished Balliol man of his time, and then after serving as Mr. Gladstone's private secretary, he went to the India Office as permanent Under-Secretary and was the real Governor of India under a succession of viceroys and secretaries for the best part of thirty years. He is a highly cultivated man, with a vast knowledge of literature, but with all the characteristic limitations of the Civil Servant type, amongst which is excessive caution and non-committal-ness. It used to be said of one of the most distinguished of them, Sir Alfred Lyall, who was a poet to boot, that even on such a topic as the weather he would not go farther than: " I am inclined to guess that there is a touch of east in the wind; but of course you mustn't give me away."

Colonel House told us an American story (which used to be applied to President Roosevelt) of a small boy saying to his mother: " Mother, I am the best boy in the school." "Who told you so?" "I found it out for myself."

I am now studying the Kaiser, not as he sees himself (like the small boy), but as others see or saw him, Tirpitz, Bethmann, Ballin, etc.

September 11. To-morrow is my birthday. Somehow that anniversary — formidable as it looks on paper — does not depress or alarm me. I recall the well-worn French adage: *"L'homme a l'age des sentiments qu'il ressent, et la femme des sentiments qu'elle inspire";* very grateful to Mme Récamier, who, at or about the age of 70, had at least four men in love with her. Anyhow, it is not the calendar that counts.

September. I sent John Morley one of our favourite epigrams from the Anthology.

J. M. replies: "Just a word of very sincere thanks for your kindest of letters. Please tell me on the enclosed card who is your Greek?[1] I resist πάντα τὸ μηδέν — as long as I last — Ever yours, J. M."

[1] Anth. Pal., XII, 33. "All is laughter, and all is dust, and all is nothing; for out of unreason is all that is." The author is said to be Glycon, who belonged to the Byzantine age, and of whose work this fragment appears to be the solitary remnant.

Gosse has sent me a list of no fewer than *thirty-one* poets born in London. He has omitted to include in it Byron. His best additions to my collection are Ben Jonson, Churchill, Praed, Swinburne, and W. S. Gilbert.

November. You have a Coleridge, haven't you? Look at the "Ode to Tranquillity": the last four lines are as fine in their way as anything can be:

> Aloof with hermit-eye I scan
> The present works of present man—
> A wild and dream-like trade of blood and guile,
> Too foolish for a tear, too wicked for a smile.

What a genius! fuddled with opium, obfuscated by bad German metaphysics, and finally squandering itself like a fountain spraying into desert sand. There is no more tragic figure in literature. A "Lone Arab" indeed![1]

The downfall of the second Coalition occurred in the autumn of 1922. Mr. Lloyd George was succeeded as Prime Minister by Mr. Bonar Law, who was already in failing health and only held office for about 200 days. He was responsible for the dissolution of 1922, which resulted in the return of 347 Conservatives, 142 Labour men, and 117 Liberals of all shades and labels.

In connection with my own part in the general election, I wrote:

November 17. I went to the counting at Paisley (November 15), and to my surprise and that of my friends the poll was very close, and it was only in the

---

[1] "Like some lone Arab, old and blind,
  The Caravan has left behind."

last quarter of an hour that we forged ahead and proceeded to win. I polled more votes than three years
ago, and the fall in the majority was entirely caused
by the enormous addition to the Labour vote: due to
the 5,000 unemployed in Paisley, of whom there were
practically none in 1920.

The general result does not greatly surprise me. The
suicide of the Coalition before the election took much
of the punch out of the fight, and left the country divided between Tranquillity and Socialism. The
corpses of the slain include: Winston, Hamar Greenwood, F. Guest, Montagu, Kellaway; on the other
hand, I have to deplore the loss of Donald Maclean and
Geoffrey Howard, both most difficult to replace. Bonar
has a very weak team except the new Attorney-General,
Douglas Hogg, who seems to be a capable man and a
good debater.

November 28. Things here (not in the House itself,
but in its purlieus) are interesting, and not without
their comic side. There was a kind of "fraternity"
gathering last night in one of the Committee rooms between the rank and file of our lot and the ex-Coalie
Liberals. The latter seem to be prepared to " reunite "
on almost any terms. Do you remember the marvellous
chapter in Carlyle's "French Revolution" on the
"Baiser de L'amourette"? It looks as if it would soon
come to that. I am all against forcing the pace and sur-
rendering any of our ground.

December 7. I finished "Babbitt" last night: a
squalid film of sordid American bourgeoisie in a petty
environment, and without any kind of "uplift." But
one feels that it is absolutely true to life, with no fakes

or illusions; almost pitiless realism, but the work of a real artist.

December. Lord and Lady Lansdowne came to see us this morning: he is the last survivor, with the possible exception of Crewe, of the type of Grand Seigneur (Lord Spencer was another) : the mould is broken and will never be recast.

February 16, 1923. I sat all the morning yesterday, and again 2½ hours to-day, in an arbitration between the British and Canadian Governments. The substance of the controversy was drab without being dull, but what gave me pleasure was that in the discussion of it I felt all the keenness of the Old Hound who has been unkennelled and finds himself once more in the hunting-field.

Frances Horner strongly recommends " Fiery Particles "— a book of short stories by C. E. Montagu, who is at his best quite a good writer. I shall get it, as I have nothing at present for bedside reading except the " Dictionary of National Biography."

February. I came across old T. P. (the Father of the House) in the Lobby the other night. He was, as always, very friendly, and told me he had got a new slogan — " I 'm damned if I 'll be buried before I am dead." Very good.

March. Someone said to Whistler, " How you have improved: your pictures, which used to be so bizarre, are now quite life-like." " It is not I," replied he, " who have changed; it is the people who are growing more and more like what I have always seen and known them."

September. Metternich congratulated Lord Dudley

— who was for a short time Foreign Secretary — on the excellence of his French, adding that the common people in Vienna talked better French than educated Englishmen. "Your Excellency must remember," said Dudley, "that Bonaparte has not been twice in London to teach them."

November 5. I have just come from Mr. Bonar Law's funeral in the Abbey. After his painful illness his end when it came was felt to be a merciful relief. As I said in the House on his resignation of the office of Prime Minister in May, I have only the kindliest recollections of him both as an antagonist and as a colleague.

A GROUP AT THE FUNERAL OF MR. BONAR LAW

Photo: Central Press

CHAPTER XXII

CONTEMPORARY NOTES: 1923–24

THE Parliament of 1922 only lasted a year. The new Prime Minister, Mr. Baldwin, greatly daring, risked a dissolution on a frankly Protectionist issue. He sustained a heavy defeat: the composition of the new House of Commons being: Conservatives 258, Labour 191, Liberals 156.

December, 1923. I spent the night at Alderley, after speaking at Manchester. Old Lord Sheffield (aged 84) is a marvel and addresses two or three meetings every evening in support of the candidature of his son. His brother-in-law, Sir Hugh Bell, arrived after speaking at two meetings. He is a stripling of 80, and the only man in England who can talk Lord S. down. When we went to bed I left the two veterans engaged in a violent and verbose controversy as to the imports of foreign "pigs" (pig-iron) and Chinese lace. The more I see of the successive generations the more I admire the Victorians.

I have been going through the list of candidates, and I cannot for the life of me see how we are going to come back more than 200 strong.

From the electoral point of view the most remarkable feature of the contest was the reunion and consolidation of the Liberals as a fighting force. But though after the pollings, so someone said, you could travel from Land's End to Oxfordshire without setting foot in a single Tory or Labour constituency, the Liberals were still numerically the weakest of the three groups into which the new House of Commons was divided. I described the situation as it presented itself at the time in the following letter to my correspondent:

December 28. You would be amused if you saw the contents of my daily post-bag: appeals, threats, prayers from all parts, and from all sorts and conditions of men, women, and lunatics, to step in and save the country from the horrors of Socialism and Confiscation. If I were to agree at this moment to enter into a compact with the Tories, I have little doubt that I could count on a majority in the House of Commons of more than two to one.

As you may imagine, having seen so much as we have in these latter days of the poisonous effects of Coalitions, I am not at all tempted.

But one cannot help contrasting the situation with that, only exactly five years ago, in December, 1918, when I and all the faithful lost our seats, and were supposed to be sentenced to damnation for the rest of our political lives.

The City is suffering from an acute attack of nerves at the prospect of a Labour Government. One of the leading bankers came to see me this morning with a message from the City Conservatives, that if only I could set up an Asquith-Grey Government, all the *solid* people in the country would support it through thick and thin. Isn't it an amusing whirligig?

I took the earliest opportunity of offering my advice to a meeting of almost all the Liberal members of the

new House which was held on December 18, at the
National Liberal Club.   As I pointed out, it was a
novel experience for me, after being seven years the
favourite target for Tory and Coalition vituperation,
that I should now be suddenly acclaimed in the same
quarters as a potential Saviour of Society.

I was [I said] never unduly perturbed by their abuse;
nor am I unduly elated by the almost penitential exuberance
of their belated appreciation.

What had been the main plank of the Tory platform at
the election?   Protection.   What was the main plank of the
Labour platform?   The Capital Levy, with its Socialist ad-
juncts and accessories.   Both have been rejected with overwhelming emphasis by the will of the country.   If either of
them was submitted to a free vote of the new House
of Commons, it would be defeated by a majority of more
than 200.

There have been no overtures of any kind from or to
the leaders of the two other parties.   As far as we are concerned, they are free; as far as they are concerned, we are
free.   That freedom I intend to preserve uncompromised
and unfettered.

The days of the present Government are of course num-
bered.   It seems to be generally assumed that as the second
largest party in the House of Commons, the Labour Party
will be allowed to assume the responsibility of Government.
Well, this may reassure some trembling minds outside: *If a
Labour Government is ever to be tried in this country, as it
will sooner or later, it could hardly be tried under safer
conditions.*

We are not going to become a wing or adjunct of any
other party.   As the first condition of our usefulness we
shall, I hope, cherish our unfettered freedom and our unconditional independence.

This advice, in which both Mr. Lloyd George and
Sir John Simon expressed their hearty concurrence,

and which I still think was unassailably sound, was accepted by the party. Accordingly, after the formality had been gone through of defeating the Tory Government in the new House, Mr. Ramsay MacDonald and his Labour colleagues were installed in office.

Speaking a year later (November 10, 1924) at the Reform Club after the fall of the Labour Government, I said: "I do not the least regret that we allowed that experiment to be made. It has opened many eyes, and it has been put an end to (as it was certain to be) the moment it threatened danger to our national interests and our national honour."

January 23, 1924. The new Labour Government as announced to-day is indeed for the most part a beggarly array. I had a very nice and really touching letter from Haldane (the new Lord Chancellor) this morning. He says he is (as well he may be) full of "misgiving." He and the poor ex-Tory, Lord Parmoor, will have a hellish time in the House of Lords. The more I survey the situation the more satisfied I am that we have taken the right, and indeed the only sensible and sane line, over the whole business. The difficulty which I foresee will be to get our men to go into the same lobby with Labour in any case of real doubt. I wish them to have a fair run, for a few months at any rate, because there is for the moment no practicable alternative.

February 4. It was such a lovely day yesterday that I joined the golfers and went to Huntercombe, where I engaged in a foursome with Scatters Wilson as my partner, against another nephew by marriage, Lord Westmorland—commonly called "Burghy"—a long lissome young man with nice manners. Our fourth was a City gentleman, called Bendir (of the well-known sporting firm of Ladbroke), who played better than the rest of us. I was pleased with my own play—particularly my putting, which won much admiration: at the 16th and 18th holes I put the ball in at distances of from 12 to 20 feet. I wasn't the least tired and came home in quite good spirits.

February 15. "Poplar" has brought into activity a hornets' nest. I suppose we could, if we liked, force a political crisis—the last thing I want to do, as far the best policy both for us and the country is to give the Labour Government a free and full rope. Poor Ramsay—who looks every day more and more like a ghost —is suffering from neuritis, one of the most painful and disabling afflictions, and has taken on a burden far too heavy for a man, who is not composed (like me?) in equal proportions of iron and leather, to carry for long. It is a pity: for, if he has to go on to the shelf, there is none of his colleagues who could take his place.

On February 21, when the new regime was on its legs, I wrote from the House of Commons:

This would be the dullest place in Europe but for Pringle, who feeds the disgruntled and un-officed Labour members on the back benches with whole cushions of pricking pins to stick into their unhappy leaders. They are slowly learning their job. Meanwhile he is far the most resourceful Parliamentarian in the House.

One of the principal men on the permanent staff of the Foreign Office described to me with infinite gusto the delight of that department at being relieved of the incubus of the "Archduke Curzon," and at starting daily relations with the mild-mannered and so far quite rational Ramsay. What a comedy it all is!

Easter, 1924 (at Monte Carlo—with Sir John and Lady Simon). I read in my sitting-room in the morning —also at night. I have been going through the fifth and sixth volumes of Buckle's "Life of Disraeli." What a man! Mrs. Dizzy throughout their married life always cut his hair and treasured the fragments. On her death (at over 80) he took up with two sisters—Selina (Lady Bradford) aged 55, and Anne (Lady Chesterfield) aged 70, and during the last eight years of his life wrote Selina 1,000 letters. About midway in their friendship (1877) he writes to her: "Gussie has asked me to dine there on Sunday—to meet you. It is exactly four years ago that I met you dining at that very house. Four years ago! It makes one very sad. I gave you feelings you could not return. It was not your fault: my fate and my misfortune." Very pathetic! He had sound ideas about the tribe of doctors, who mismanaged him shamefully. "First of all they throw it on the weather; then there must be change of scene. Jenner, after blundering and plundering in the usual way, sent me to Bournemouth, and Gull wants to send me to Ems. I should like to send both of them to Jericho." It was only the homœopathist, Kidd, regarded as a quack by the orthodox fraternity, who in the end gave him some relief.

Photo: "Daily Record," Glasgow

MR. AND MRS. ASQUITH, 1924

I was sad at the end of our dear Corelli:[1] you and I have had such good times in her company. Duse, too! How lucky that we had a chance of seeing her last year!

May. I am glad that you liked to be reminded of the exploits of Doeg the Edomite—a man after our own heart. He "fell upon the priests" and in a single day "slew fourscore and five persons that did wear a linen ephod."[2] Almost a record bag.

July 8. Much more interesting than the House yesterday was the Dr. Clifford demonstration at Westminster Chapel: a crowd of about 3,000, for the most part Nonconformist bourgeoisie. I spoke for about a quarter of an hour, and was followed by Ll. G., who was really picturesque and interesting, without being too flamboyant—quite an artistic performance.

July 11. I went to a party last night at Wimborne House, where I must have shaken hands with some 2,000 men and women—mainly good Liberals. It is incredible that people with more or less immortal souls should find these gatherings amusing. Our hostess, Lady Wimborne, behaved like a heroine: she got up out of bed, where she had been for five days with a temperature of 103, and after a long dinner stood for an hour and a half shaking hands. She is a charming creature.

[1] Miss Marie Corelli, who had been in the habit of entertaining us at her charming house at Stratford on our periodical pilgrimages to the Shakespeare festivals.

[2] 1 Samuel xxii.

CHAPTER XXIII
DEFEAT AT PAISLEY: PEERAGE

THE Labour Government stumbled on, and came to an end in two squalid crises, each of which could have been avoided, or at least circumvented, if they had played their cards with a modicum of either luck or skill. The result was their complete defeat at the polls in the autumn of 1924.

On the day after the count at Paisley, where I was heavily beaten, I wrote to my correspondent:

October 31, 1924. We had cheering crowds at the railway stations both at Glasgow and at Euston. . . . Stamfordham came to lunch and brought me a very kind message from the King. Every one seems to agree that during these last weeks Ramsay and Co. have cut as sorry and contemptible a figure as has ever been known in British politics. We (the Liberals), though we only number about forty in the new House of Commons, seem to have polled over three million votes.

November 5. I have had a very nice letter [1] from the King, full of regrets and gratitude. He says that he feels strongly that I should not be subject to further political contests, nor the exacting, wearing life of the House of Commons. So off his own bat he offers me a peerage, in order that I may continue my parliamentary life under more peaceful conditions, adding that if he could persuade me to do this it would give him a real

[1] A facsimile of this letter, published by His Majesty's gracious permission, is given on pages 255–58.

BUCKINGHAM PALACE

Nov. 4th 1924.

My dear Mr Asquith

Nothing in connection
with the General Election
has caused me more
regret than that you should
not have been returned
to Parliament.

Your absence from
Westminster especially
in these abnormal &
anxious days, is a national
loss.   Apart from my

strong personal regard &
respect for you, & remembering
that you were my Prime
Minister (in very difficult
times) for six years & also
served my Father in that
capacity, I feel strongly
that after your long, &
eminent career, you should
not be subject to
further political contests,
with all their attendant
turmoil & unpleasantness,
nor the exacting wearing
life of the House of Commons

which is in store for the
successful. For these
reasons it would be a
matter of the greatest
satisfaction to me to
confer upon you a Peerage.

This would enable you
to continue, though under
more peaceful conditions,
your Parliamentary life,
bringing to the House of
Lords your distinguished
abilities, vast experience
& gifted speech, to the
great advantage of its
deliberations; while in
the event of your absence
from the Commons, such
an arrangement would

be welcomed by all
shades of opinion
throughout the country
If I could persuade
you to do this, it
would give _me_ _great_
pleasure.

Believe me
very sincerely yours

George R. I.

pleasure. It was very tactful and kind of him to write
in the interregnum between two Governments: so that
it would be entirely his own proposal.

I gladly assented to a suggestion of my son, Arthur,
who is a director of the Sudan Exploration Company,
that I should accompany him on a visit to Egypt and
the Sudan, neither of which countries I had ever seen.
We accordingly left London on November 11, and I
was away for a couple of months. I had before starting
obtained His Majesty's permission to defer till my return my answer to his gracious offer.

When I got to Cairo I was most hospitably received
as a guest at the Residency by Lord and Lady Allenby.
My stay was overshadowed by a tragic event — the
assassination in the streets of Sir O. Stack, Sirdar of
the Egyptian Army and Governor of the Sudan. I
transcribe from a letter which I wrote home on November 22 my impressions at the time:

" I went on Wednesday about noon with Lord
Allenby to have an interview with the King, who lives
in a gaudy French Second Empire Palace not far from
here. He is Turkish in appearance, a little over 50,
educated in Italy, knows Paris and London, and speaks
excellent French. He talked with a good deal of frank-
ness and self-commiseration about his own (truly ridiculous) position as a ' Constitutional monarch.' We had
scarcely got home and sat down to lunch when the news
came of the shooting in one of the principal streets, by
a gang of seven to ten well-organized murderers, of
Stack. He was brought into the Residency and lin-
gered on for about thirty-six hours, but his recovery

was hopeless from the first. His aide-de-camp and chauffeur were also wounded, but not mortally. Such a thing has never happened even in this country before, and Stack, though not a man of great brains, was universally liked. The wretched Egyptian Ministers, who from Zaghlul downwards have been denouncing all English officials and declaring that they must be got rid of, came cowering and huddling to the Residency where, as Allenby grimly remarked to me, they were not 'genially' received. They are completely panic-stricken, and as they are to a large extent morally responsible, they are trembling in their shoes."

There is nothing new to be said of the wonders of Egypt and Syria. But I will venture upon one or two citations from my letters:

November 26. Government House, Jerusalem. I am looking out of the window at the Dead Sea, which is only a few miles away, and am going to start very soon for a drive to Jericho. Yesterday I explored the Garden of Gethsemane, the Pool of Bethesda, Golgotha (where the Empress Helena discovered the Cross), and the supposed tomb from which the Resurrection took place. So I am saturated for the moment with Biblical lore, and shall complete the tale to-morrow when I move on to Nazareth and the Lake of Galilee.

If it were not for these historic associations no one, who could go anywhere else, would visit Palestine. It is just what I expected to find—an arid, rocky, hummocky, treeless expanse, with ranges of hills here and there rising to no great height. There are no beautiful or even interesting buildings, except the Great Mosque, which stands on the site of Solomon's Temple at Jerusalem, and the nave of the Church of the Nativity at Bethlehem.

There are less than a million people in the country, which is roughly the size of Wales—of whom about one-tenth are Jews, and the remainder Christians and Arabs, the Arabs being three-fourths of the whole. I suppose you could not find anywhere a worse representation of any one of the three religions—especially of the Christian.

The Jews are increasing (mainly from the less civilized parts of the East of Europe) as the result of the Zionist propaganda, and no doubt are much better looked after and happier here than they were in the wretched places from which they were exported. But the talk of making Palestine into a Jewish "National Home" seems to me as fantastic as it always has done.

The administration is run by the English with their usual efficiency—new roads, new drainage, new schools, new lighting, afforestation, colonization, etc. Jerusalem, which used to be one of the foulest cities in the East, is cleaner and better kept than Cairo—largely owing to the energies of the Governor, Ronald Storrs.

I am quartered with the High Commissioner, Herbert Samuel, who is the supreme dictator here. One of his edicts prevented public advertisements throughout the country—with the result that you rarely, if ever, see a poster. Government House, where he lives, is two or three miles from the city and is one of the most singular erections anywhere. It was built by the Germans at an enormous cost before the War, by order of the Kaiser, after his visit here when he preached in the Lutheran Church. It was intended to be what they call a "hospice" (for the entertainment of German pilgrims and tourists) and is upon the most grandiose scale. In the court-yard on a niche is a huge bronze statue of the Kaiser, dressed as a Crusader, and holding a shield like that carried by Richard Cœur de Lion.

The house is of course far too big to live in, and impossible to make warm or comfortable. H. S. and his wife live here a simple Jewish life, with occasional outbursts (there is going to be one to-night) of official hospitality. He has been brought under every typical English influence — Balliol, House of Commons, Cabinet — and has an excellent and very useful kind of intellect: he is rather formal, but kindly and wholly devoid of malignity: and above all things tenacious and *efficient*.

December 7. Luxor. I think when I last wrote that I left off on the threshold of Syria, which is a very superior country to the Holy Land. Damascus is delightfully situated between two ranges of mountains, in a well-rivered plain, and surrounded by gardens and orchards. When the first Moslem armies got there, straight from their sandy and waterless Arabia, they not unnaturally imagined that they had reached Paradise. . . .

The next day I drove on with my companion, Cust, to Baalbec, the most wonderful ruins in the world — not even excepting Karnak. There are the remains of two Roman temples, probably of the third century A.D.: the columns, which are still left, after centuries of battering from Arabs, Crusaders, Turks, and earthquakes, are of incredible height and bulk, and the capitals and ceilings elaborately and luxuriantly carved. They are over-ornamented as compared with the classic Greek models, and, like everything Asiatic and African, they are spoilt by a morbid passion for the colossal and gigantesque.

On my way back I stayed at Beirut—an odious and garish seaport, but beautifully situated at the foot of Lebanon. I met the French High Commissioner—General Weygand—one of the best of their generals and a most efficient administrator. He has just been recalled unceremoniously, and without any ostensible reason, except the need of finding a good place for Sarrail, the favourite soldier of the Extreme Left, who left anything but a pleasing reputation behind him at Salonika.

I found my way back to Cairo, and spent two more nights with my kind hosts the Allenbys. Everything was quiet there to all appearance, though there are all sorts of rumours of "plots" etc. My window here (Luxor) is within a stone's throw of the Nile, with a fine view of the river and the hills of the Libyan desert beyond. We are on the site of the ancient Thebes (which Homer calls "hundred-gated"). On one side of the river are the most artistic temples in Egypt (Karnak and Luxor), and on the other the famous valley where are the tombs of the Kings. It is from the sightseer's point of view the show-place of Egypt.

January 12, 1925. Paris. I left Port Said a week ago with "Oc," and we spent the time on board the *Yorkshire,* an excellent steamer of the Bibby Line. We had beautiful weather, bright sun, and calm sea, throughout the voyage and landed at Marseilles on Saturday morning.

One of the first people to turn up in Paris yesterday

was Antoine, who is just back from Rumania, and I dined with him and Marthe[1] last night. He is quite unchanged, and insisted on sending a telegram in my name to Margot to say that I find him an ideal son-in-law! I am lunching with the Crewes at the Embassy to-day, where I expect to find Winston, who is still hovering about trying to pinch *les braves Belges,* in order to provide something for our needy cousins across the Atlantic.

The weather, though considered unseasonably cold both in Egypt and the Sudan, was sunny and agreeable all through my travellings. I saw the great dam — now nearly finished — over the Blue Nile at Sennar. Otherwise the Sudan is not a place to go to for pleasure — a huge monotonous featureless plain. We travelled in great comfort; the water journey down the Nile from Halfa to Assuan is quite delightful. The two things that impressed me most in all my wanderings were the ruins of Baalbec in Syria, and the temples which lead to the Tombs of the Kings opposite Luxor.

I went alone yesterday morning to visit the Luxemburg here, which I had not seen for twenty years. As it is supposed to be confined to the works of living artists the pictures are constantly shifting. On the whole it is, to my thinking, a rather rubbishly collection, but there are some fine Degas, and one remarkable Manet.

* * * * *

During my absence I had had abundant time and opportunity for considering what reply I should make to

---

[1] Princess George Bibesco.

His Majesty's gracious offer, and in the end I came to the conclusion that I should do right to accept it.

Accordingly I wrote to the King on January 20, 1925:

SIR, —

I have ventured to take full advantage of your Majesty's kind permission that I should delay a definite reply to the gracious offer of a Peerage, conveyed to me in November last, until I should have had time for mature and deliberate consideration.

That consideration involved, as your Majesty will understand, matters both personal and political of perhaps exceptional delicacy and difficulty. As the result, I have now the honour respectfully to submit my grateful acceptance of your Majesty's proposal.

It would be impertinent in me to trouble your Majesty with any survey of doubts and hesitations (not wholly of a selfish kind) which seemed to warrant a certain suspense of judgment. Such as they were, they have now been removed. And I may be permitted to say that they were completely overcome by my deep and abiding sense of obligation and affection to the King, whom it was my privilege from the first moment of his reign to serve for so many successive years as his Chief Minister. Never was service more willingly given by a Minister or more abundantly rewarded by the constant and unfailing consideration and the unbroken confidence of the Sovereign, of which I shall always treasure this mark of your Majesty's gracious favour as the consummation and the seal.

If it should be your Majesty's pleasure, in accordance with precedent, to confer upon me the dignity of an Earl, I should propose to take the title of Oxford, which has fine traditions in our history, and which was given by Queen Anne to her Prime Minister Robert Harley.

Following my acceptance I received from His Majesty the following gracious personal letter:

YORK COTTAGE,
SANDRINGHAM,
NORFOLK,
Janry. 23rd, 1925.

MY DEAR MR. ASQUITH, —

It is with great satisfaction that I have received your letter of the 20th inst. accepting in, if I may say so, such charming terms, the offer of a Peerage, which it was my pleasure to make to you in November last, and I am touched by the kind reference which you make to our mutual relation to each other since my accession. I can quite realise and appreciate the various difficulties which required careful consideration before a decision could be arrived at. But I venture to think that, great as your wrench must be in leaving the House of Commons, where you have for long held so eminent a position, you have acted rightly. It is a gain to the public of England and the Empire that the House of Lords should have as its leaders on either side some of the foremost Statesmen of the time.

Your Peerage will of course be an Earldom, and subject to the necessary references to the College of Arms which will at once be made, I shall be very glad that the historic title of Earl of Oxford should now be restored in your favour.

I have informed the Prime Minister.

Looking forward to having the pleasure of seeing you on my return to London next month.

Believe me, my dear Mr. Asquith,
Very sincerely yours,
GEORGE R.I.

As the correspondence shows I took the title of Earl of Oxford and Asquith.

February 11, 1925. You would see in the papers today the official announcement which transforms my status, for better or for worse, but at any rate for good

Jan.ry 23rd 1925.

My dear Mr. Asquith

It is with great satisfaction that I have received your letter of the 20.o inst: accepting, in, if I may say so, such charming terms, the offer of a Peerage, which it was my pleasure to make to you in November last & I am touched by the kind reference which you make to our

mutual relation to
each other since my
accession.   I can
quite realise & appreciate
the various difficulties
which required careful
consideration before a
decision could be arrived
at.   But I venture
to think, that, great
as your wrench must
be in leaving the House
of Commons, where you
have for long held so
eminent a position,
you have acted rightly.

It is a gain to the Public of England & the Empire that the House of Lords should have as its leaders on either side some of the foremost Statesmen of the time.

Your Peerage will of course be an Earldom & subject to the necessary references to the College of Arms which will at once be made, I shall be very glad that the historic title of Earl of Oxford should now be restored in your favour.

I have informed the
Prime Minister.
Looking forward to
having the pleasure of
seeing you on my
return to London
next month.

Believe me
my dear Mr Asquith
very sincerely yours

George R.I.

and all. Clowder[1] did his best to live up to the occasion, and his first "My Lord" had an unmistakable tinge of delicate courtliness. I got the official intimation when I returned here [Bedford Square] after driving from The Wharf last night—the 10th—and then I suddenly remembered that it was my father's birthday, for he was born on February 10, 1825—exactly a hundred years ago to the day. What would the lovers of coincidence say to that?

I had sheaves of letters of congratulation—from various, and in some cases unexpected, quarters: the Bishop of Durham (Henson), J. M. Barrie, Mr. Marchant of the Goupil Gallery, Mr. Clarkson, the wigmaker, and Dame Kendal, the *doyenne* of the stage.

None gave me greater pleasure than the following from my old friend and fellow-worker—Professor Gilbert Murray—dated January 25:

MY DEAR MR. ASQUITH,

I must write to you once more under the name that I have learnt to love and honour, and which I associate with so much kindness to myself. The new title is splendid: better than one could have expected. I hardly know why the change makes one sad. Perhaps it is as if you were saying,

" . . . Si Pergama dextra
Defendi possent, etiam hac defensa fuissent."

It does seem to me that, all through the worst fortunes of Liberalism and of all the nobler causes in public life, from 1916 onwards, you have shown the right road and said the thing that ought to be said. But war conditions and post-war conditions make liberality impossible. You have at least helped the remnant of us to think rightly and to hold out.

[1] Our butler and devoted friend.

But of course it is merely silly to think of this step as a retirement. You cannot help leading us whenever you speak. And the way in which you have fought such an up-hill fight and with so few lieutenants during these last seven years is a proof that you will not cease to care and to work. I am proud to be your follower, and still more proud to have had your friendship.

Ever yours sincerely,
GILBERT MURRAY.

1925. Lindsay, the Master of Balliol, told me that when he was at the front on the Staff during the War he one day came across my second son (" Beb ") in an ammunition dump. They had been contemporaries as Balliol undergraduates. The general asked who he was, and Lindsay told him, adding that he had tutored another of my sons (Cyril).

THE GENERAL: "But I thought they were very clever fellows."

LINDSAY: " So they are."

GENERAL: " Then *you* must be a devil of a swell!"

February 4. I feel sorry that poor old John Lane[1] has dropped out of the ranks. The obituaries in the papers depict him as a mutineer and pioneer, which is exactly the impression he would most have liked to leave behind him. Yet he came of a Quaker stock and up to the last used to "go to meetings."

February 12. I spent an hour with the King this morning. Nothing could have been kinder: we chatted over old days. He told me, apropos of my double title (O. and A.) which has been criticized, that when Lord Aberdeen, on being made a Marquis, chose the style

[1] The publisher.

of "Aberdeen and Temair," Lady Aberdeen sent a friend a photograph of herself, so signed, with a Scotch terrier on her knee. The friend replied with effusive thanks, adding, "It was so nice too to see your little dog Temair."

March 9. "Zelide" turns out to be a "precious" book about a tiresome woman and a still more tiresome man—Benjamin Constant.

March 17. The great event here yesterday was the first night of Elizabeth's play—"The Painted Swan." The little Everyman Theatre was crammed with what is called "a distinguished company," including all the critics from Walkley and Desmond downwards. I was rather anxious during the prolonged verbal coruscations of the first act, but in the second we got nearer to real business, and the third was without any exaggeration fine and moving.

March 24. We had what Harcourt used to call a "full choral service" in honour of George Curzon in the House of Lords yesterday afternoon. I took some pains with the form of my little contribution, and it was well received. . . . So far I have not heard, with the exception of poor Curzon's last, even a decent speech in the Lords. It is only a fortnight since I heard him—apparently in full vigour, excellent form, and high spirits. I have known him ever since fifty years ago I examined him, then a schoolboy at Eton.

March 26. We had a rather scrambling debate in the Lords about a Second Chamber, in the course of which I gave tongue for a few minutes. The standard of speaking there is deplorably low. Men like——

and——would hardly be listened to in an average County Council. They mumble away a lot of spineless and disconcerted platitudes.

In April we went with our cousin "Nan" Tennant, and in its later stages our son Puffin, a motor tour in Provence and Touraine. The weather was very kind and we saw a number of interesting places—Carcassonne, Les Baux, etc., etc., which were new to us.

The death of Lord Curzon vacated the Chancellorship of Oxford University. I became a candidate, and it seemed at one time likely that I might be elected without a contest. Lord Birkenhead and Lord Midleton gave me generous and invaluable support. But it soon became apparent that the election would be fought on political and clerical lines, and Lord Cave was adopted as the opposing candidate. He won an easy victory.

The King was pleased about this time (June, 1925) to confer upon me the Order of the Garter, and Lady Breadalbane (an old friend) was good enough to make me a present of her husband's robes and accoutrements.

July 14. I have just come back from a rather interesting lunch given by Colonel House—all men; among them were Lords Reading and Grey, and the always delightful Paderewski. I sat between him and an eminent American Senator, Walsh by name, little known here, but a great man in his own country.

I am going to-night to preside over the dinner to Mrs. Strong, where there will be a rare collection of the highest of brows, both male and female. The proceedings ought to be conducted in Latin. She is to be presented with an address in that language from the accomplished pen of Mackail.

November 3. I read in bed some of Stevenson's "New Arabian Nights," which I had not looked at for years. They wear fairly well and he left no exact successor; but there is no doubt that one is conscious all the time of a machine very skilfully and deftly worked. The really great story-tellers are more spontaneous and less laboured.

November 8. When we came back yesterday we were met by the tragic news of the death of my niece, Frances Charteris: the eldest of Frank Tennant's three delightful daughters. She had an operation which, though serious, was not supposed to be dangerous. She never recovered consciousness, and died from failure of the heart. She was just your age, and leaves four small children.

I went in the afternoon to the heart-broken family, and was taken up to see the poor darling lying with folded hands among lilies and roses. I have never seen anything so beautiful and touching — not a trace of pain or struggle, and looking just as she used to when a young girl. I could not help crying like a child. She was full of gaiety and gentle wisdom, and was the pillar of the whole family. I thought of Ben Jonson's lines: it was not a case of falling "a log at last, dry, bald and sere"; but the cruel plucking of a "plant and flower of light." They have taken her to Scotland to be buried by the sea.

November. We have had at lunch the Dean of St. Paul's [Inge] and his wife. He is a strange isolated figure, with all the culture in the world, and a curiously developed gift of expression, but with kinks and twists both intellectual and temperamental. Still, he is one of the few ecclesiastics in these days who is really interesting.

December 11. I have just come back from a huge public luncheon to inaugurate Arbuthnot Lane's new Health Society. I delivered a brief allocution in which I had a dig or two at the doctors. Philip Snowden also spoke. The Dean of St. Paul's was of the company. Snowden told a pathetic story of a little girl at one of the London hospitals, who, being given a glass of milk, asked wistfully, " May I drink to the bottom? "

December 18. I had a terrific day yesterday and finished up with a Free Trade speech in the House of Lords — the worst audience in the world ; great politeness (except when " Chuck-it-Smith " takes the floor) but no resilience, or even response, either from friends or foes.

February, 1926. Didn't you think the old fellow [Sir R. MacLeod] a marvelous survival of Victorian vitality and *joie de vivre?* I doubt whether any of these degenerate Georgians will live to see their 79th birthday, and if they do it will only be as " lean and slippered pantaloons " . . .

Puffin writes enthusiastically from Hollywood of the good time which he and Elizabeth are having in the centre of the film world. They are guests of Douglas Fairbanks and Mary Pickford ; Charlie Chaplin drops in to lunch : Lilian Gish hovers about in the offing : and (to Puffin the climax) he has had ten minutes with Pauline Frederick. *Que voulez vous?*

Do you see the reviews of Walter Raleigh's "Letters"? There is sure to be good stuff in them. I loved him as a companion. But it must be admitted that he could both write and talk (when he was in the mood) greater nonsense than almost any really clever man I have known.

April. I have had some interesting acknowledgments of my lecture on Scaliger.[1]

Apropos of children's, and especially girls', education in Tudor times, Inge (of St. Paul's) quotes from a treatise of 1530 the author's recommendation that a child should begin Greek at seven, and "in the meantime" use Latin as a "familiar language." Aristophanes, Homer, Virgil, Ovid, Hesiod, etc., "will suffice till he pass the age of thirteen." This enables one to understand how Lady Jane Grey (at sixteen) was conversant with Hebrew, how Mary Queen of Scots wrote passable Latin verses, and how Queen Elizabeth could talk with the foreign ambassadors in at least four different languages. What a falling off we show!

[1] Delivered at Edinburgh, March, 1926.

CHAPTER XXIV

THE GENERAL STRIKE:
RESIGNATION OF LEADERSHIP

M*AY 4, 1926. General Strike.* We are plunged into the cataract of the Strike and already London presents an abnormal aspect. I cannot think that it will last long; it is very unpopular, and they are short of funds for anything like a severe struggle. Puffin, who has enlisted with his little car to help the supplies, was up practically the whole night.

I took the first opportunity of stating my own view on the Strike in a speech delivered in the House of Lords on May 4. Its salient parts were as follows:

Can there be a more lamentable fact than that, at a time when we are all in the international sphere hymning the praises and propagating the doctrine of disarmament, here at home, in the freest of all the free countries of the world, we should be witnessing a resort on an unexampled scale to one of the cruellest, because the most indiscriminating, of all forms of warfare?

For the essence of a General Strike is this — that it inflicts the maximum of loss and suffering upon the innocent mass of the common people, who are not parties to the industrial dispute, who have taken neither the one side nor the other in it, who have no interest in it whatever, except the common interest, which we all have as members of a great community of interdependent relationships in the misfortunes and embarrassments, whoever is responsible for them, of one of our greatest industries. That is the nature of the campaign, which is, I think unhappily and unadvisedly, initiated to-day.

I do not see how it was possible for any Government not to take up promptly and effectually such a challenge. They are after all the trustees of the interests of the industrial and social life of the whole community. We should be wanting in the elementary instincts, both of self-respect and of self-preservation, if we did not support heartily and unitedly all their efforts, within the bounds of reason and prudence, to assert the paramount interest — the interest of the community over all the classes of which it is composed.

I proceeded to contrast with the Government's handling of this coal dispute the Liberal Government's conduct in the Coal Strike of 1912, when the negotiations between the miners and the owners failed and the stoppage began.

Thereupon the Government took what I believe to have been the right course then, and I am not at all sure that it will not prove to be the right course now. We took the matter into our own hands. We passed through both Houses of Parliament a Bill, accepted with a great deal of reluctance on the part of the owners, and repudiated upon a ballot by the miners, to establish a minimum wage to be fixed district by district. It was not a compulsory Bill; it did not compel any mineowner to keep his mine open; it did not compel any miner to go down into a mine and work in it. What it provided was that if a mineowner opened and worked his mine, and if a miner took employment under him and went underground, it should be an implied condition of the contract of service between the two that the miner should be paid at least the minimum rate, which according to the scale prescribed, or to be prescribed in time, by arbitration in the various districts, was appropriate to the case.

What was the result? The miners, as I have told your Lordships, at first rejected the proposal by a ballot. That did not prevent us from going on with it. The Bill passed: it passed through this House, which was a remarkable achievement, because it was at a time when our relations (to put it mildly) were not of the sweetest. It passed into law. Within two weeks of its passing, the miners, after an inconclusive resolution, where the majority was not decisive, accepted it.

From that time onward, the minimum wage worked in the coal mines, up to the outbreak of war, and it would have gone on afterwards but for the abnormal conditions produced by the War, without friction or trouble of any sort or kind.

The word *reorganization,* so much used in the negotiations, means in the coal-mining industry, the abandonment of uneconomic workings. You have to face that. It is very difficult for the masters or the men to face it, but it has to be done. Reconstruction is necessary to prevent the wastage of capital and labour, to concentrate management, and to make technical improvements.

I made some practical suggestions, as to the suspension of the "lock-out" notices, and the provisional continuance of the subsidy, and urged the Government to take advantage of the prevailing good temper on both sides and to keep the door always open. As I noted at the time: "The whole thing is a piece of criminal folly which will soon break to pieces."

May 11. When I came up yesterday to our "Shadow Cabinet"[1] at Abingdon Street there was one notable absentee—Ll. G., who was in the sulks. . . . The streets to-day are full of symptoms of a return to normal life. I think we are approaching the revival of common sense.

*   *   *   *   *

The General Strike, which had no staying power behind it, came to an end on May 12.

I need not dwell on the correspondence which followed between Mr. Lloyd George and myself. I

---

[1] A body of confidential colleagues of Cabinet rank.

summed up the position, as far as I personally was concerned, in a letter dated June 1 to the Chief Liberal Whip, Sir Godfrey Collins, of which I will cite the concluding paragraph:

I see that it is insinuated that I have been the perhaps passive vessel of personal animosities. My record in those matters is well-known to my fellow-countrymen, and I can afford to disregard base imputations upon my honour. I am this month completing forty years of service to the Liberal party. For a considerable part of the time I have been its leader, and I have honestly striven during the last two years to recreate and to revive the broken fabric of Liberal unity. It has been a burdensome, and in some of its aspects, a thankless task. I will not continue to hold the leadership for a day unless I am satisfied that I retain in full measure the confidence of the party.

On the same day I received the following joint communication from twelve of my colleagues in the "Shadow Cabinet" assuring me of their support:

June 1, 1926.

DEAR LORD OXFORD, —

We cannot allow you to bear the whole brunt of the criticism which has been directed against you on the ground of your letter to Mr. Lloyd George. It is due to you that we should say unreservedly that we support the course which you, after endless patience and lifelong service to Liberalism, have felt obliged to take. Since Mr. Lloyd George broke up the first Coalition and became Prime Minister he has played many parts, and when he rejoined you at the general election of 1923 it was obvious to everybody that nothing could make this reunion effective except a willingness to forget past differences and an identity both in machinery and in single-minded devotion to the party. We have done our best to follow your lead in securing these objects, and your own forbearance and chivalry are known to every Liberal, but Mr. Lloyd George has insisted upon retaining separate head-quarters and a separate fund. He discouraged the putting forward of more than 300 Liberal candidates at the last election, and his methods have often made us suspect that he has not abandoned the idea of a new Coalition.

His action during the recent general strike has to be regarded in the light of this record. It is obvious to us that his letter to Sir Godfrey Collins was written with an eye to its possible future use if events had turned out as he anticipated in his communications to the foreign Press. When the strike was over he stated at Llandudno Junction (May 26) : "During the progress of the general strike I refrained from urging criticism as to the past. The nation had to concentrate on fighting the stranglehold." It is astonishing that Mr. Lloyd George should have persuaded himself that this version represents his attitude, for in his letter to Sir Godfrey Collins (May 10) refusing to meet you he wrote : " I cannot see my way to join in declarations which condemn the general strike while refraining from criticism of the Government, who are equally, if not more, responsible."

Practical suggestions for dealing with the coal dispute are welcomed by all of us, and have been made by none more clearly and usefully than yourself. But it seems to us to be pure opportunism to taunt the Government, as Mr. Lloyd George did nine months ago, with being "afraid of facing cold steel," to refuse to meet his colleagues at the crisis of the strike on the ground that he was opposed to the demand for unconditional withdrawal, and when that withdrawal took place to tell his constituents that he was always in favour of the policy that he refused to discuss with you.

The difficulties of co-operation in such circumstances are well known to you and to us, although they may not be always appreciated by the general public. We should, therefore, think ourselves failing in the duty which we owe to you, and to the Liberal party, to say nothing of the affection and admiration with which we regard you, if we did not make it plain where we stand. We have done our best in the interests of Liberalism to work with Mr. Lloyd George in the councils of the party, but we cannot feel surprised at your feeling that confidential relations are impossible with one whose instability destroys confidence.

Yours sincerely,

GREY OF FALLODON,	DONALD MACLEAN,
JOHN SIMON,	COWDRAY,
WALTER RUNCIMAN,	VIVIAN PHILLIPPS,
LINCOLNSHIRE,	GEOFFREY HOWARD,
BUCKMASTER,	W. M. R. PRINGLE,
BUXTON,	GODFREY P. COLLINS.

Early in June, I had a breakdown in health, and the immediate result was that I was sternly forbidden by the doctors to fulfil what had been my intention of being present at the meetings of the National Liberal Federation[1] at Weston-super-Mare on June 17 and 18, and of availing myself of this opportunity to state in clear and unequivocal language my position with regard to the General Strike. For the next three months I was disabled from active political work. The kind hospitality of my dear friends, Geoffrey and Kitty Howard, provided me with a tranquil and luxurious resting-place at Castle Howard, where I spent June and July. I took advantage of the respite to survey the whole situation, present and prospective.

In the closing weeks of September I met my colleagues for the purpose of discussing with them the

[1] The following resolution was passed by the Federation:

"This Council expresses its unabated confidence in Lord Oxford as leader of the Liberal party; places on record its deep appreciation of the service which his integrity and high character have rendered to our public life; and acknowledges with gratitude his unfailing devotion to the best interests of the nation.

"The Council expresses the hope that for many years to come these outstanding qualities will continue to inspire the Party which, in spite of recent differences, earnestly desires to retain the co-operation of all Liberals in pressing forward a rigorous and constructive policy of social and industrial reform."

general lines of the speech which I was to make to the Scottish Liberal Federation at Greenock on October 15. Early in October, I circulated to them privately the following memorandum setting forth the conclusions which I had reached upon the general situation and my decision to retire from the leadership of the party.

CONFIDENTIAL AND SECRET
MEMORANDUM

The disintegration of the Liberal Party began with the Coupon election of December, 1918. It then received a blow from which it has never since recovered. I myself was turned out of a seat which I had held against the Tories for thirty-two years. All my leading colleagues in the House of Commons suffered the same fate. The Liberal members in the new House were reduced to a handful of little more than thirty. The bulk of the old Liberal parliamentary party deserted to the Coalition.

I was much tempted to give up the formal Leadership (for it had become nothing more), but I did not think it right to leave old friends, who had remained loyal, in the lurch; and at the first available opportunity (January, 1920) I stood at a by-election for Paisley and was returned.

The Coalition House of Commons (1919–22) was the worst in which I have ever sat. The small band of Liberals whom Sir Donald Maclean had rallied were made to feel their impotence, and I myself, after I came back, was treated by the Coalition rank and file with studied contempt. I did my best with my colleagues to expose the stupidity and wickedness of Reprisals in Ireland. Outside, I urged (amidst the derision of the Coalition leaders) that Dominion Home Rule had become the only possible constructive policy. We opposed at its very outset and at every stage the legislation for the Safeguarding of Industries, supported as it was by so-called Free Traders like Sir Alfred Mond, who had become a member of the Coalition Cabinet.

Those were the darkest days for Liberalism which I have ever known. The manifest failure of the Black and Tan regime in Ireland, administered by a Liberal Coalitionist, Sir Hamar Greenwood, and strenuously defended by Mr. Lloyd George, and its growing unpopularity here, in time began to disquiet the Unionist members of the Coalition; and it was they (if we may believe Sir Austen Chamberlain) who were the first to urge its abandonment, with the substitution of the only possible alternative — Dominion Home Rule. After we had been brought to the verge of war by the adventure of Chanak, a section of the Conservatives already embittered by the "betrayal" of Unionism, became mutinous, and, under the leadership of Mr. Bonar Law and Mr. Baldwin, brought about the downfall of the Coalition, and the formation of a Bonar Law Government.

The folly of Mr. Baldwin, after Mr. Bonar Law's death, in hoisting the Protectionist flag brought about a strong movement for "Liberal Reunion." The fortunes of Free Trade were at stake, and for the purpose of the election of 1923 we joined forces with Mr. Lloyd George and the bulk of his Coalition or National Liberals. In the Parliament then elected, the "reunited" Liberals were a respectable, if not a formidable, minority.

We have now for nearly three years been trying the experiment of "Liberal Reunion." There is not one of us that does not know that in practice it has turned out to be a fiction, if not a farce. The control of the Party has throughout been divided between two separate authorities: the Liberal Central Office and Mr. Lloyd George's rival machine — the former very scantily, and the latter very richly, endowed. Things came very nearly to a crisis a year ago when the "Land Policy" as embodied in the Green Book was let loose, and followed up by an intensive and expansive propaganda. I insisted upon its being submitted to a representative Conference before it was incorporated in the Party programme. Prolonged negotiations between Sir Donald Maclean and Mr. Phillipps on the one side, and Mr. Lloyd George on the other, showed that he regarded his accumulated fund as at his own disposal, to be given to, or withheld from, the Central Office of the Party, as a dole, upon such conditions as he thought fit to impose. I was driven myself last December to the humiliating task of making a personal appeal to the better-to-do among our followers to come to the rescue and provide us with a wholly independent fund of adequate amount. Many generous contributions were made, but the fact remains that at this moment our Central Office is faced in the near future with the certainty of serious and perhaps fatal financial stress, in relief of which it is idle, in the present condition of the Party, to expect that a repetition of last year's appeal or any other expedient would meet with a substantial response.

Meanwhile, the rival organization, well supplied with material resources, is being enlarged in every direction, and has been recruited at its Head-quarters quite recently by an influx of skilled wire-pullers and propagandists.

Under such conditions, to talk of Liberal unity as a thing which either has been, or has any fair prospect of being, achieved, seems to me to be an abuse of language. If there are those who take a more sanguine view, I can only express a sincere hope that they may prove to be right.

I come now to my own personal position, which I have had to reconsider from every point of view, public and private, since the differences which arose in the early summer over the General Strike. After the fullest consideration, I find nothing to withdraw or qualify in my letter of June last to Sir Godfrey Collins. There are, it appears, not a few people in the Party who think that I acted on inadequate and even on unworthy grounds. No one has ever accused me before of being actuated in public matters by personal motives, and my career, which is sufficiently well known to my Party and the public, might, I think, have spared me any such imputation. In my judgment, then and now, grave matters of principle, vital to the Liberal Party and to its harmonious and effective working, were in peril.

I am equally resolved not to take any part, direct or indirect, in a sectional controversy in the Party, either about Leadership or funds.

I am now in my seventy-fifth year. I have been for the best part of half a century in public life. I have been Prime Minister for a longer consecutive time than anyone during the last 100 years, and for a still longer time I have been Leader of the Liberal Party. During the whole of that time I have given my time and strength without stint or reserve to the service of the Party and the State. From the principles of Liberalism, as I have always understood them, and understand them still, I have never swerved either to the right or the left, and I never shall.

I should therefore, in any case, consider that I had earned my title to release. But during the last few months I have had a serious warning, which I did not expect, but cannot ignore. My health, which has never troubled me before, gave way, and though it is now restored, I can no longer count upon it as I always have done in the past. The anxieties and responsibilities of Leadership, which do not diminish in these days, are enough to tax the strongest, and ought not to be undertaken or continued by anyone who cannot be reasonably sure that he can stand the strain.

I therefore feel it my duty to lay down the Leadership, and this decision, come to after much reflection and with many regrets, must be regarded as irrevocable.

OXFORD AND ASQUITH.

From a number of warm and affectionate messages from colleagues to whom this memorandum had been sent, the following may be selected.

Lord Buckmaster wrote:

LORD BUCKMASTER

19 Manchester Street, W.

Sunday.

My dear Lord Oxford, —

It is hard to tell all that the events of the last few days have meant to me. It is over twenty years since at Edwin Montagu's request you spoke at the Guildhall at Cambridge in support of my candidature and from that day onwards you have been my leader and so you will continue whatever the party nomenclature may declare.

Though therefore, so far as I am concerned, there is no change, yet the formal announcement of the conclusion of the leadership of the party was hard for me to hear and I know for you to utter. The dull senses and the heavy lidded eyes of the public prevent them from seeing now all you have accomplished, but history will record it and the accomplishment is vast. I doubt if even under Gladstone's prolonged power any steps were taken that will so profoundly and beneficially affect the future as those taken by you. In the long war between falsehood and truth, falsehood always wins the first battle and truth the last.

I wish so very much I could have been with you at Greenock: four times I had that honour at Paisley, and at no time would I have more eagerly come.

All the things you have been to me still and will ever remain. These only one thing can ever touch and may that be long delayed.

Yours ever,

(Sgd.) Buckmaster.

Mr. Runciman wrote:

I shall always reckon the happiest days of my official life those that I spent under you at the Treasury in 1907 and 1908. And any man might well be proud to have been eight years in your Cabinet. It has been an honour and a pleasure to have been as faithful to you in the past ten years as in those more prosperous days. Will you let me say now in plain words that my admiration and affection for you never abated? I cannot express adequately how much you have meant to me.

Sir Donald Maclean:

More than once you have been kind enough to say that I have been close to you since 1918 in many and deep waters. No one could have been as kind and considerate, helpful and magnanimous to a lieutenant, as you have been to me. You have been gentle when I erred, and over generous when I may have seemed to do well. I know that I am only one of the very many who have worked under, and with you, who can say like things, but there is none amongst them all who speaks with more deep and abiding affection, gratitude and loyalty than I do.

My resignation was publicly announced, and the reasons for it were explained, in a letter which I addressed to the heads of the English and Scottish Federations on October 14. This I amplified in my speech at Greenock.

From amongst the letters I then received I append the following from the Prime Minister, Sir Austen Chamberlain, and two other personal friends, Viscount Haldane and Sir James Barrie.

23rd October, 1926.

10 DOWNING STREET,

WHITEHALL, S.W.1.

MY DEAR OXFORD,—

I have wanted to write to you for several days, but I have been more than usually busy and it is not easy to express what I feel.

I don't think that anyone who has not been a Prime Minister can realize the essential and ultimate loneliness of that position: there is no veil between him and the human heart (or rather no veil through which he cannot see) and in his less happy moments he may feel himself to be the repository of the sins and follies of the whole world. You can understand then how my heart has often gone out to you during these last years. I have admired without reserve your courage, your dignity, your self-restraint: you have set an example in circumstances of cruel difficulty that I hope we younger men may have the strength to follow when such trials come to us.

And I shall never forget the kindly courtesy which you showed to me in the House of Commons.

The position of leader came to me when I was inexperienced, before I was really fitted for it, by a succession of curious chances that could not have been foreseen.

I had never expected it: I was in no way trained for it. You forbore to take advantage of these things and you gave me a lesson by which I hope I shall profit in the years to come.

I hope you will not feel that I have broken unduly through our English reserve in saying so much. But if I cannot speak now, the opportunity will never come, and so I have taken my courage in both hands.

Secure in the respect and affection of your friends, indeed of all Englishmen whose respect and affection are worth having, may you have as many years of peace and happy rest as you desire and not one more!

Believe me to remain,

Very sincerely yours,

STANLEY BALDWIN.

FOREIGN OFFICE,
S.W.1.

18. 10. 26.

MY DEAR OXFORD, —

Your decision to retire from the Leadership of your Party has been learned with regret far outside that Party's boundary. I don't criticize the decision—far from it in all the circumstances; but I am sorry that it should be so.

You have kept a high standard of dignity, of loyalty to colleagues and friends and of courtesy to opponents.

I have stood to you in all three relationships, and I could not let the occasion pass without thanking you for much kindness and wishing you all the happiness and success that life may still hold for you without the cares and worries of a position that I can well believe must have become almost intolerable.

Yours ever,

AUSTEN CHAMBERLAIN.

AS FROM LONDON.

18th October, 1926.

MY DEAR A.,—

A time has come in both of our lives when the bulk of work has been done. That work does not pass away. It is not by overt signs that its enduring character is to be judged. It is by the changes made in the spirit of the things into which the work has entered.

Public opinion has in these last days shown conclusively that it recognizes this and the purity and the quality of your effort through life.

I often take my walks here along the paths where I can recall our talks of over forty years since, on what could be made of the future. There have been changes in our outward relations, but none that have transformed the old inwardness. The days that were, and under other forms still are, I never forget.

And now perhaps the really best is yet to be.

Always affectionately yours,

R. B. H.

ADELPHI TERRACE HOUSE,
STRAND, W.C.2.

20th October, 1926.

DEAR LORD OXFORD, —

This is just another voice singing your praise. You have done great and splendid things for the country and I for one am mightily beholden to you therefor. May you continue to do them in the Lords.

Yours affectionately,

J. M. BARRIE.

FAREWELL SPEECH (*Greenock, October 15, 1926*)

The meeting had been organized by the Scottish Liberal Federation. Among those on the platform were Lady Oxford, Viscount Grey, Lady Violet Bonham Carter, Lady Aberdeen, Mr. J. A. Spender, Sir John Simon, Sir Donald Maclean, Mr. Walter Runciman, Sir Daniel Stevenson, Sir Robert Maule, Mr. Geoffrey Howard, Sir Archibald Sinclair, Mr. Pringle, and Mr. Vivian Phillipps.

I give the essential passages of my speech.

It is, I need not tell you, a supreme satisfaction and solace to me to-night to have around me captains of the host, lieutenants and staff officers who, whether in victory or defeat, have always helped me to uphold the Liberal flag.

The whole of my House of Commons career was passed as a Scottish member. I was for over thirty years the representative of an eastern county. When the men of the East thought fit to sever our long connection I turned to the West. I represented Paisley for the best part of five years, during which I fought no fewer than four contested elections. Scotland unlocked for me the avenue to the Leadership, and it is only fitting that it should be in Scotland that I bid the Leadership farewell.

No rational observer believes that Liberalism is or is likely to become an extinct or negligible factor in our national life. The fortunes of the Liberal Party may fluctuate. We have seen it (as in 1906) so strong as to seem able to defy any conceivable hostile combination. We have seen it (as in 1918) so battered and mutilated as to appear to be on the verge of annihilation. But there is only one way in which it can ever be killed, and that is by suicide. Because, both on its constructive and defensive side, Liberalism means two things — the preservation and extension of liberty in every sphere of our national life, and the subordination of class interests to the interests of the community. Those two ideals were and are the life-breath of

the Liberal faith. And Liberty (as I have often preached),
in our understanding of it, means Liberty in its positive as
well as in its negative sense. A man is not free unless he has
had the means and opportunities for education. A man is
not free unless he is at liberty to combine with his fellows
for any lawful purpose in which they have a common interest. Nor is there real freedom in industry if it is carried
on under conditions which are injurious to those whom a
man employs, or with whom he works, or to the health and
well-being of his neighbours. The liberty of each is cir-
cumscribed by the liberty of all.

It is in the same large sense that you must understand our
other root principle — the supremacy of the general interest
over particular interests. It matters nothing for our purpose whether the class which is seeking for a privileged or
paramount position is great or small; whether it relies upon
birth, or wealth, or numbers and organization; whether its
mouthpiece is, for the time being, the Duke of Northumber-
land or Mr. Cook. The good of all in our view is, in the
long run, the good of each; we are all members of one
another. It was for that reason that the General Strike of
last summer was a negation and a defiance of the funda-
mental articles of the Liberal creed.

The appearance of the Labour Party on the scene has
done nothing to invalidate, or to render obsolete, the mission
of Liberalism. There are, no doubt, some political and
social changes for which we could work side by side with,
at any rate, a section of Labour, just as there are some for
which we could work side by side with the more progressive
and broadminded among the Conservatives. Labour means
very different things to the different wings and platoons of
the heterogeneous army which for the moment marches
with uneven steps and discordant battle-cries under the
Labour flag. But in the two vital matters to which I have
just referred its diverse sections are one and all at issue
with Liberals. The socialization or nationalization of production and distribution and the extinction of what is called
Capitalism — by whatever name the ideal, and the process
for its attainment, is called — would starve the resources,
and, in time, drain away the life-blood of the great pro-

ductive industries which depend for their efficiency on the free play of initiative and enterprise. And Labour is becoming more and more a class organization, and expression and embodiment of what is called "class-consciousness."

That again was significantly illustrated in the General Strike, which was directed by organized Labour, and which was countenanced — it is true, in a somewhat shamefaced fashion — by the Parliamentary Labour Party leaders.

Let me point out once again that there is no analogy of any sort or kind between the General Strike and the stoppage in the coal trade. The course adopted by the miners last May, whether it was wise or unwise, was perfectly legitimate. They did not break their contracts. They simply refused to re-enter their employment on new and, as they believed, less advantageous terms; and in so doing they committed, whether individually or as a body, no offence against the rules of law or the canons of morality. Their case was mishandled throughout by blind leaders, of almost insensate folly, and they are suffering the consequences of their misplaced loyalty.

The General Strike, on the contrary, was an offence of the gravest kind against both law and morals. It was an attempt to coerce the whole community, and to substitute for the authority of Parliament that of a class dictatorship. It threatened, in the supposed interest of a particular class of workers — a class relatively high up, both as regards wages and standard of living, in the industrial scale — the interests of almost every other class, and not least the poorest and worst paid, who, but for the spontaneous uprising of the vast majority of the nation in their defence, would have been cut off from their work and robbed of their means of livelihood. It was, as it seemed to me, the first duty of Liberalism not to parley and falter, not to wait upon events, but to condemn it root and branch with promptitude and with no uncertain voice. There is a tendency, I regret to see, to look back upon the General Strike as a trivial and transient incident — a short-lived and more or less picturesque adventure. There could not be a worse example of distorted political perspective.

We hear a great deal these days about the virtues and the

necessity of unity. Unity is important, but not less — in some ways even more — important is independence. Our relations with the Irish Nationalists were never those either of coalition or dependence. We had one cause — Home Rule — put by Mr. Gladstone in the forefront of the Liberal programme twenty years before, in which we and they had a common interest. They were perfectly free to vote against us when they pleased, as they did on the second reading of the famous Budget of 1909. The Coalition which I formed in 1915, and to which I invited not only Unionists, but Nationalists and Labour men, was explicitly and avowedly for no other purpose than the effective prosecution of the War.

After the general election of 1923 we had to choose between continuing the term of office of the Protectionist Government, which had just then been heavily defeated at the polls, and allowing a Labour Government to take its place. We chose the latter course. I believe that to have been a wise and statesmanlike step; it gave the country, under safeguarding conditions, a foretaste of what Labour in office really meant, and it in no way compromised the freedom of the Liberal Party — as it would have done if, as I see is now suggested, we had as a preliminary condition entered into any bargain with them upon matters of policy.

One other illustration. A few years ago witnessed the final stage of the protracted struggle, begun exactly forty years ago this year, by Mr. Gladstone to grant self-government to Ireland. It was the Government of which I was at the head which, by means, and by means only, of the Parliament Act, was able to put Home Rule, twice approved by the electorate of the country, upon the Statute Book. And later, when we were once more in opposition, Sir Donald Maclean and I — for he was the man who rallied the Liberal Party in the worst and darkest days that in my lifetime Liberalism has ever passed through — Donald Maclean and I not only raised our voices in protest against the iniquities and stupidities of the policy of reprisals, but I remember well here in Scotland, at Paisley and elsewhere, amidst the derision of the leaders and rank and file of the Coalition, I pleaded for the grant to Ireland of what has been since conceded, the status of a Dominion. The name Unionist has been made an anachronism.

Let none of you, and especially let none of the younger among you, be content to think that the mission of Liberalism is exhausted. The new problems which confront us, and they are many and grave, are not outside the ambit of the old faith. Keep that faith; carry on the torch which we, who have done our best to keep it alight, hand over to your custody. Resist all the allurements of short cuts and compromises. Look neither to the right nor to the left, but keep straight on.

*   *   *   *   *

October 17, 1926. The meeting at Greenock on Friday night, at which I announced my resignation of the Liberal leadership, was unique in my experience: at moments thrilling in its intensity. There were a lot of my old and trusty friends from Paisley there, as well as good and true men and women from all parts of Scotland. It was sad, however necessary, to have to cause so much pain. But I have not a doubt that I have taken the only wise and honourable course.

PRAYER

(of the Fourteenth Century)

God be in my head:
And in my understanding;
God be in my eyes:
And in my looking;
God be in my mouth:
And in my speaking;
God be in my heart:
And in my thinking;
God be at mine end:
And at my departing.

But all, the world's coarse thumb
And finger failed to plumb,
So passed in making up the main account;
All instincts immature,
All purposes unsure,
That weighed not as his work, yet swelled the man's amount.

Thoughts hardly to be packed
Into a narrow act,
Fancies that broke through language and escaped;
All I could never be,
All, men ignored in me,
This, I was worth to God, whose wheel the pitcher shaped.
                "RABBI BEN EZRA."

A FINAL NOTE

By VIVIAN PHILLIPPS

I HAVE been asked to append a brief note dealing with the period between the laying down by Lord Oxford of the leadership of the Liberal party in October, 1926, and his death on February 15, 1928.

His first speech after his resignation of the leadership was made in the House of Lords on November 17, 1926, when in the course of a discussion on the League of Nations he made a strong plea that the British Government should throw its full weight on the side of international disarmament, "by a reduction upon a large and effective scale of our annual expenditure upon military and naval purposes."

On February 21, 1927, he spoke at the City Temple in support of the campaign for peace, initiated by the Metropolitan Free Church Federation.

In the course of his address he said:

Unless we can eliminate war it will be the death of civilization, and of all that makes life — individual life, communal life, international life — worth living. There can be no effective safeguard of the most treasured possessions and promises of our race, until we have wiped international warfare off the slate of possibility. That is no Utopian ideal. As difficult, if you like, as unimaginable things have been done. Slavery, private war, duelling, were all regarded in their day as natural and even necessary institutions. Why and how have they disappeared? Not by repression, not by coercion, but through the operation of moral force which sapped their vitality, which discredited their authority, and which brought them, in due time, one and all, their message of doom. So it will be when, by the same agencies, the curse of war becomes, as it will become, a memory of the past.

In the month of March, he spoke, as the chief guest, at the St. Patrick's Day dinner at the Hotel Cecil.

His last speech in Parliament was delivered during a debate in the House of Lords on March 22, 1927, upon a motion moved by Earl Beauchamp, calling attention to the need for "National Economy."

About the middle of April he was seriously disabled by an attack of neuritis which caused a complete, though happily only temporary, loss of power in the right leg. For some weeks he was unable to walk, though his general health appeared to be good, and he was able to work upon his book and to take his customary motor drives.

During the summer months he made a steady improvement, and towards the end of July, when I went down to the Wharf to spend the day with him, he had made such a good recovery that he was walking easily with the aid of a stick.

He continued to make progress and was well enough to take his holiday with Lady Oxford in September at North Berwick.

In October he went to Castle Howard to stay with Geoffrey Howard and his wife and fulfilled a long-standing engagement, to receive the freedom of the City of York.

The ceremony took place at York on October 19, and the following passages of his speech on this occasion are taken from the columns of *The Times*.

The venerable City of York, with its ancient walls and its historic Minster, is, and remains to all of us [men of Yorkshire] our Mount Zion from time immemorial. It has had what I believe to be the unique privilege among English towns of being not only a County in itself, but of possessing at one and the same time an Archbishop and a Lord Mayor. There is no other town in England of which that can be said. It is at its altar that the exiled sons of Yorkshire, of whom I am one — wherever they may reside and whatever distinctions their life may have provided — may most fittingly rekindle the torch of local patriotism which is the salt and savour of English life. And to receive its Freedom after a life largely spent, as mine has been, in the tumults and controversies of party politics, is a moving, and to me most highly prized, tribute for which it is difficult to find adequate terms to express my gratitude.

Offering to his fellow-citizens a word of counsel, founded upon an exceptionally long experience, Lord Oxford continued:

Whatever may be the state of the atmosphere and however uncertain may appear to be the prospects of the immediate future, never lose faith and hope. Never allow yourselves to be ensnared in sombre and paralysing generalities and shallow pessimism. There are moments — I am not sure this is not one of them — when the most sanguine among us are tempted to be depressed by the spectacular follies and stupidities of mankind, and as we survey this disillusioning panorama to say to ourselves, "As it was in the beginning, is now, and ever shall be, world without end." That is not a wholesome mood, nor is it, in my judgment, in the long run, justified by reason or by experience. One of the greatest theologians and thinkers of the English Church, Bishop Butler, is reported in a moment of gloom to have expressed the belief that nations, like individuals, are subject to an access of fits of madness. And he added that on no other hypothesis was it possible to explain some of the most surprising and yet most stubborn

facts of history. That may be true or it may not be true.
Whether it is true or not, it is, at any rate, the part of
wisdom not to let one's vision be obscured by the clouds of
dust which from time to time are raised in the course of its
progress by the chariot of human destiny. It is more inspiring, and in the long run, I am persuaded, a better
founded and indeed a safer faith, when men's thoughts —
and not only their thoughts in an intellectual sense, but their
ideals and their purposes — are, as one of our great Victorian poets taught us, "widened by the process of the suns."

This was his last public utterance. A few weeks
later he contracted a chill, which was followed by a
recurrence of the old trouble in the leg; but when
I visited him early in December, though confined to
bed, he was working busily on his book, and his interest
in public affairs was as keen and alert as it had ever
been. Later in the same month he enjoyed a visit from
Donald Maclean, to whom he talked interestedly about
friends and events, and about the future fortunes of the
Liberal party. It was not until about Christmas time
that there were signs of a change.

I went down to see him at the Wharf on January 21.
We had half an hour together. He seemed to have
failed a good deal since my previous visit, but he was
eager to talk, and spoke about the Simon Commission
and the new Prayer Book proposals. He was particularly pleased to hear that the Liberals of Paisley had
approached my friend, W. M. R. Pringle, with the
suggestion that he should allow his name to go forward
as that of their prospective candidate at the next election. One of the last letters which he wrote was to
Pringle expressing the hope that he would accept the
invitation.

Towards the end of our talk he turned to Lady Oxford, who was sitting with us, and said that he and she must keep in mind that when the election came he would go to Edinburgh to speak for me.

When the time came to say "good-bye" to him, he held my hand and said: "You will come and see me again — right on to the end," and then, quickly — as if he felt that he had said more than he meant to — "I mean, right on to the end of this Parliament."

It was the last time I saw him.

EXPLANATION OF DIAGRAM

This diagram is a photographic reproduction, on a greatly reduced scale, of the big situation map which was kept up to date daily for the Commander-in-Chief in France, and hung in his writing-room.

The diagram, which is dated September 25, 1918, shows the positions of the Allied and German divisions (the latter as reported to us by our own and the Allied Intelligence Departments) on the eve of three great battles. On the right, the massing of the French divisions under Gouraud and of Pershing's American divisions shows the attack mounted for the Argonne battle, opened on September 26.

On the left, or northern flank, the left wing of Plumer's Second Army and the Belgian Army, the whole under the supreme command of the King of the Belgians, are in position ready for the successful attack of September 28, which carried our line far to the East of the famous Passchendaele ridge. Three French cavalry divisions can be seen behind Horne's First Army. These were moving north to form part of Degoutte's Sixth French Army which took part in the second phase of this northern battle, opened on October 14.

In the centre, the great gathering of German divisions in line and in reserve marks in striking fashion the desperate attempts the enemy was making to stop the victorious advance of the main British attack, commenced on August 8 and persisted in without check until the Armistice of November 11. Contrast the density of German divisions on this part of the front with the scanty German forces opposed to the Allied attacks in the Argonne and Flanders. The diagram shows in unmistakable fashion where it was that the German General Staff considered that their chief danger lay.

On this front, on September 27, Byng's Third Army with the right of Horne's First Army, and on September 29, Rawlinson's Fourth Army with two American divisions, delivered the great and critical attacks which broke the defences of the Canal du Nord and the Hindenburg Line, and after more than a week of practically continuous fighting carried our troops through the enemy's defensive lines to the open country beyond. This great victory was decisive.

INDEX